How to Catch Really Big Fish

To my mother Janina
who loves me dearly
and looks after all
the fish I catch

How to Catch Really Big Fish

Tara Robinson

hancock
house

ISBN 0-88839-967-7
Copyright © 1983 Tara Robinson

Catalog in Publication Data

Robinson, Tara, 1971-
How to catch really big fish

ISBN 0-88839-967-7

1. Pacific salmon fishing — British Columbia. 2. Pacific
salmon fishing — Washington (State). I. Title.
SH686.R62   799'.1'755   C83-091207-X

Edited by Diana Ottosen
Typeset by Elizabeth Grant in Times Roman
   on an AM Varityper Comp/Edit
Production, Layout & Cover Design by Eva Raidl
Printed in Canada by Friesen Printers

Published by:

Hancock House Publishers Ltd.

19313 Zero Avenue, Surrey, B.C. V3S 5J9

Hancock House Publishers Inc.

1431 Harrison Avenue, Blaine, Washington, U.S.A. 98230

Table of Contents

Introduction

All right all you fisher-persons. I hear that most of you have read my first booklet and think that you know as much as me. But you are wrong. I have learned a lot since I did my first booklet. I've been to Seattle, Port Angeles, Neah Bay, Sekiu, Ucluelet, Tofino, Barkley Sound, Alberni, Nanaimo, Campbell River, as well as lots of little spots along the way. I even went to Fanny Bay. I am now eleven and I learned a lot in my travels. Also, my Dad invented a lot of new lures. My biggest fish last year was a 41½ pound (19 kilograms) Spring salmon.

This new book includes some of the details from my first booklet but I've added more big fish lures and stories. Besides my Dad's lures, it covers Tomic Plugs, Hot Spots, Riptide lures, Reef Raider lures and Buzz Bomb lures. I've also put in a small section on motor mooching strip and cut plug.

I hope that by reading this book you will be

Tara and her brothers with two 30 pounders, 1981

catching lots of big fish like I do. The hardest fish to catch is the salmon so most of the book will deal with salmon fishing.

Once you know all about catching salmon in salt water you can use this information to catch all types of large fish.

I have lots of fishing experience and I'm going to share a lot of my stories and secrets with you. I may also tell a couple of funny stories.

If you are reading this book in a store and are not going to buy it, put it down right now. The sales clerk is watching you.

My History

When I was two years old I started fishing (going out in the boat) with my Dad and brothers. We fish at Otter Point near Sooke, B.C. Sooke is 23 miles (37 kilometres) west of Victoria. The more I went out in the boat, the more I learned and the more interested I became. I have seen thousands of salmon caught. We kept a lot and let a lot go. We have caught large Springs, Coho, Pinks, Chums, Sockeye and Steelhead. We even caught a few sharks (Dog Fish) without really trying. I like to cut their noses off and let them go. My favourite fish is the big Spring and we always do well on them. We know exactly how to snipe them out.

Over the past four years Dad has put on a lot of fish shows and I always go. When we do a fish show we bring along a big frozen salmon and my job is fish-keeper. I have to keep it iced and make sure nobody steals it. Last year we showed a 54¼ pounder

Tara and her family with a big one.

(25 kilograms) which was caught by Mr. Carmen Angus of Sooke. He caught it at Otter Point on June 11. At these shows I meet a lot of interesting fisherpersons and many share their secrets with my Dad and I. I am always learning new fishing methods and plan to shortly put out a large book on modern salmon fishing. It will cover all the methods for catching the five Pacific salmon of North America.

Dad had my 41½ pound (19 kilogram) salmon from last year smoked and canned. I think it wasn't fair because my Dad caught a 41½ pounder in 1981 and he got his mounted. I'm going to catch a bigger one this year and show him what's what about salmon fishing. I hope it's a 60-pounder (27 kilograms).

O.K. enough history and onto the big fish and fishing.

Facts and Figures

My Dad has been fishing for over 25 years and by 1976 he pretty well mastered the lures and systems that were available. At this time he started to get serious about inventing new lures and systems. It is known that over 80% of the fish are landed by 20% of the fisherpersons. In 1978 it took us 4 hours of fishing to catch a 30-pound (14 kilogram) salmon. In 1982 it took us only 1½ hours for a 30-pound (14 kilogram) salmon. Every year we try and improve our fishing. It takes a lot of experience and knowledge to catch large salmon consistently. I hope that you learn something from my book as it took us a lot of time and many failures to come up with these conclusions. When we run experimental gear we catch skunks also. We are not experts and our ideas and methods are subject to revision and change as we see fit.

We know that when we are out fishing, our

methods and gear attract large Springs and scare off the smaller ones. This is very true for our trolling systems. Some of the drift fishing lures do catch some smaller fish. We fish from May through October in a small boat and troll two rods with natural bait. We feel June and July are the best months for big salmon at Sooke. The biggest salmon in the last few years was 60 pounds (27 kilograms). Our average catch in June 1978 was 32 pounds (15 kilograms). In 1982 we averaged 36 pounds (16 kilograms) due to all the fish being very large that year. Our testing is done at Cowichan Bay, Port Alberni, Barkley Sound, Beechy Head, Sooke and Neah Bay, Washington.

If you faithfully follow what I have written you can join the select 20% that catch most of the fish. We find it more fun to come in with 30 pounders (14 kilograms) than 6 pounders (2.7 kilograms). If we don't protect the immature salmon there is no doubt that we will not be able to catch 40 and 50 pound (18 and 23 kilogram) fish in the future. We let all Spring salmon under 10 pounds (4.5 kilograms) go free so they can grow larger.

The Area

To catch large fish you have to be in big fish waters. My Dad says that you can't catch big fish in the bathtub. Mr. Roy McGillvary caught a 51-pounder (23 kilograms) at Beechy last June and put it in the bathtub with ice. He caught it on a red True roll Spring King using anchovy as bait. It was so big he couldn't get it in the fridge. But that's the only way they get in your bathtub.

Back to fishing. You have to be in an area that big salmon frequent. If you are just starting out your best friend is the marina operator. Pick one which you have reason to believe has a good catch record and hire a top guide for a day. Let him take you to the hot areas. Ask about tides, biting patterns, hazards such as reefs, and find out about all the areas that produce big fish. Also you should have a good marine chart. You are paying so get your money's worth. Watch everything he does as he may have

43½ lb. Sooke Spring

trade secrets which he won't mention. Also ask him for tips on catching large fish. Next, head out on your own on a busy weekend and follow the group. You will observe that most boats are working a pattern. Don't try and oppose this plan but fall in with them at their average speed. Now that you are with the group be totally observant. Note where the fish are being caught and which boats are catching them. When a large fish is being landed (not played) note the approximate weight and size, the type of flasher, and the tail length. Remember, never crowd a boat which has a fish on. You can get close only when the fish is being netted.

It will take only a couple of weekends before you have a fair feeling for the area. Remember that the fisherpersons you are observing may have twenty-five years experience on the grounds. Try to develop friendships with other fisherpersons in the area. A good fishing friend can help out immensely with "hot tips," etc. Almost all the real good fisherpersons work in a "group system" where information is shared to everybody's benefit. If you don't share — you won't receive.

The C.B. Radio is a good buy — not only for

emergency use, but by making it possible for you to develop some potentially useful friendships. By listening to the airwaves you can get a very good idea how fishing is. Most of our friends have a C.B. at the house. You can get home from work and give a call and get a report right from the boats out fishing.

One other good fishing report comes from the radio stations in Victoria. CKDA 1220 has a year-round marine and fish report. Also the daily newspaper (*Times-Colonist*) has a very good fish report.

O.K. These are my favourite big salmon fishing spots. Alberni and Barkley Sound have to be No. 1. I've been going up there for three years. Fisherpersons catch so many big salmon they have to have wheel-barrows on the docks. We went up this past year and showed Mr. George Manson how to fish with anchovy. The next weekend he and three friends went out and caught 30 Springs in three days. They had over 500 pounds (227 kilograms) of salmon! There is a really big hatchery at Alberni and it produces big Springs. They have a Labour Day Derby and the biggest fish in 1982 was 61 pounds (28 kilograms) and was caught on a Tomic Plug. The best time for Alberni is August and September. The No. 2 spot goes to Beechy Head and Sooke. The big fish come in June and July. Last year the biggest was 55 pounds (25 kilograms) and was caught on an anchovy. During June and July there are many fish taken over 30 pounds (14 kilograms). Last year I believe there was over 100 salmon caught that were over 40 pounds (18 kilograms). No. 3 spot goes to Neah Bay, Washington. We always do well there. Dad takes a hundred pounds (45 kilograms) out a day when we fish there. One of the nice things about fishing Neah Bay is that they charge us Canadians the same as Americans. Their licence is only $3.50.

Getting the Boat Fishing

The boat must be considered to be a member of the fishing group. It has to be able to help in the catching of large fish. Motors, propellers and boats give vibrations which may attract or scare fish. The boat must be smoothly running with no missing, coughing or sputtering. If you use an outboard it should be mounted on rubber, such as a piece of belting. Never put a motor or downrigger directly on the boat's structure. It must be insulated from the hull or transom. Always, always have your propeller balanced. This one problem has cost sport fishermen more fish than any other. A well-balanced propeller is worth its weight in gold and the cost of balancing is very little. Our propeller has a reduced pitch, is balanced, and has two blades. A two-bladed propeller seems to work better for fishing than three.

Fiberglass boats are the best for getting good fishing results and the worst boats are those made of metal. In the latter case vibrations cause poorer results.

The rod holders and downriggers must be mounted with great care. Our rod holders are screwed to wood and the wood is then insulated from the boat with rubber. When the rod is in the holder the reel should not touch it. We try and have the reel vertical (above holder). We also put sponge-type foam rubber in our holders so that the rod will "float" in them. As well, you should mount your rod holders where the rods are easy to get at. We like the Scotty-type holders.

When the rods are fishing correctly, there should be no vibrations visible or felt at the tip of the rod. The tip may pulse due to flashers or dodger action but there should be no vibrations. If the rod tip vibrates the line "strums" in the water which is undesirable. When you look at where your line enters the water there should be V-shaped ripples, not circles.

The boat itself must have a good electrical system with no loose connections. The ground connections must be solid and the battery terminals clean.

If you are going to really get serious about big fish you should have a depth sounder, chart and a colour video output. We went down to a fish show in Seattle last December and we saw some real beauties and they were not that expensive. When we get a bigger boat I hope Dad gets one. I want a colour video output that I can hook up to play video games when there are no fish around.

Our boat does not have a down rigger as in our area the big fish are close to shore. In some areas like the Great Lakes down riggers are a must in trolling. Also, down riggers can provide fun fishing with light tackle. A down rigger is a device that takes your bait down to the fish. When the fish bites, your line is released and you battle the fish without weight and heavy line.

Well, now comes a very important point. We feel that one should prepare the fuel mix and gas up the day before you want to go fishing. When you are fishing your hands must be clean with no oil, gas or grease on them. My Dad always cleans his hands with Pepsodent toothpaste before he gets in the boat. Sometimes he uses Pearl Drops. Dad will not allow anyone who smokes to handle bait or lures in our boat.

When you come back from any fishing trip you should wash the inside of your boat with soapy water to get rid of the fish smell. Sometimes Dad uses Anise oil to keep the boat smelling nice.

The Gear

Your gear has to attract, catch and control big fussy fish. Those 50-pounders (23 kilograms) did not get that big by being dumb fish. Let's face it, when the fish are biting all over the place, they can be caught on bare hooks or a toothbrush, but when the fish are fussy, it is the equally fussy fisherperson who will still load up. We believe that there is a natural instinct that causes salmon to strike some lures. The fish may not even be feeding but they take the lure just to kill it. I'll tell more about this instinct later. Getting back to the gear — make one mistake here and you will find yourself back with the 80% group. Every year we lose fish because we get lazy or excited and don't follow the rules.

There are two really different ways of catching large fish. The most popular is trolling a lure from a boat. This can be anything from a row boat to a commercial 70-foot (21 metre) troller. The row boat may have one lure out but the commercial boat could have a couple of hundred. I feel that over 95% of the salmon landed come from trolling.

The second method is called "Drift Fishing". It has become very popular in the past ten years. Drift fishing means drifting in a boat (with no power). Most of the lures used are the metal minnow types. Lures I like are the Buzz Bomb, Reef Raider and Riptide.

Drift fishing can also be done from shore or from a dock.

The Drift fishing lures can produce big fish when there is lots of fish around. Now I bet you are confused. The reason that trollers catch so many more is that they can cover so much more ground than the drift fisherman. If there is one 50-pounder (23 kilograms) at Otter Point Dad says that in 4 hours of trolling that fish will most likely see our gear.

If you are just starting out you cannot go to the nearest sport shop and ask for a Troll-Drift fishing combo rod and reel. After you finish this book visit a good fish tackle store. Pick one that has a fishing pro. Don't go to Lucky Sam's Discount Bargain House. Perhaps you would do well to go to two or three fish tackle stores. Some big department stores have very good fishing departments. Woolco in Victoria is very good. Don't go to the store on a busy day — go on a slow day and really have a good fish-gear talk. Never economize on your equipment — you will regret it later with lost fish. Try and buy as much locally-made gear as you can because local manufacturers will be there to repair it if it breaks.

A lot of manufacturers do store promos during fishing season. I go with my Dad when he does a Spring King Show. I strongly feel you should go to all these shows and pick up new tips.

Trolling the Big Ones

This is the subject I like best as I know how to troll the big fish out. Every big fish in our boat over 30 pounds (14 kilograms) has been caught on the troll. Almost all of the trolling at Sooke is with frozen anchovy. The second most popular bait is the herring strip. Almost everyone uses either a dodger or flasher when fishing.

O.K., so you want to be a big fish troller. Here is what you need. Rods should be fiberglass and approximately 8 feet (2.4 metres) in length. The reels have to be able to carry 200 yards (183 metres) of 40-pound (18 kilogram) test and be suitable for salt water. On our boat we like medium-light trolling rods. The rod has to be able to handle a 2-pound (.9 kilogram) weight. After you get your rods and reels, purchase the largest landing net that you can find. It may look much too large, but when that 50-pounder (23 kilograms) is on your line and up by the boat the net will look pathetically small!!!

A good trolling boat looks like a duck landing on the water as in Diagram 1. Not like a duck taking OFF as in Diagram 2. If your boat looks like Diagram 2, bend those rod holders down right now. Diagram 3 shows a top view.

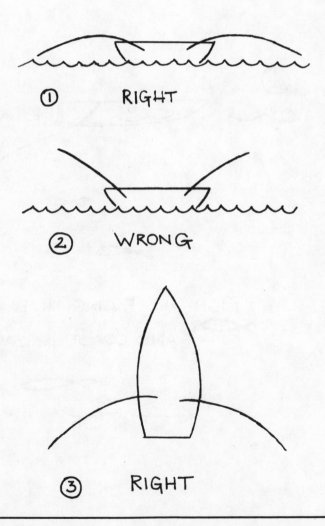

①   RIGHT

②   WRONG

③   RIGHT

We fish close to shore for large salmon. Most of the fish are caught less than 100 yards (91 metres) from shore. These fish are not down deep. We usually fish in 60 feet (18 metres) of water. Last year we went out in a boat with a graph recorder. We were surprised that most of the fish were in the top 39 feet (9 metres) of water. We fish close to the bottom. I'll explain this later. No, I better do it now. Please look at Diagram 4.

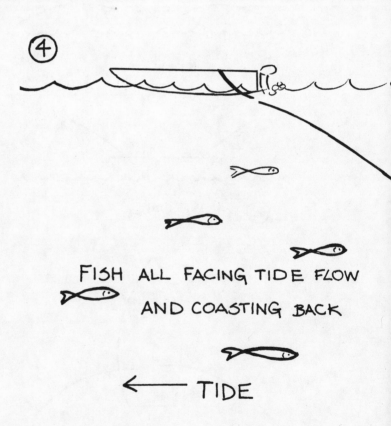

FISH ALL FACING TIDE FLOW AND COASTING BACK

← TIDE

This diagram shows the fish and our tackle. Boy, it sure looks like a good day — lots of slabs. Here's what Dad feels is happening. We are trolling very fast 3-5 knots with two pounds (9 kilogram) on the rods. We have 18 inch (46 centimetre) Dodgers on and our 40 pound (18 kilogram) line is really singing (not strumming). This is how you test your sing. You put out your line and gear and then you kiss your perlon making sure no red jellyfish are on the line where you kiss it. You can really feel it singing and so can the fish. The fish can feel the sing and it follows the line down to see what's down there — it sees the bait with that tight roll and bites it and you've got it.

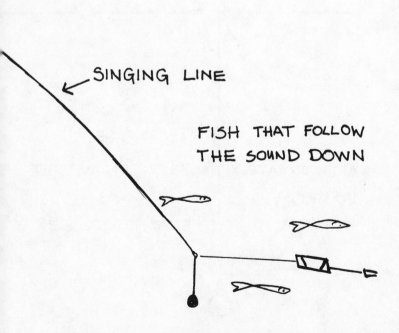

SINGING LINE

FISH THAT FOLLOW
THE SOUND DOWN

Now we get back to the 2-pound (.9 kilogram) weight. We feel that the small cannon-ball type of weights are the best. We have made a special weight hanger that slips over the bead chains. You can buy it at the store. It's called the EZon EZoff Weight Hanger. See Diagram 5. We always use 2 pounds (.9 kilograms) and only purchase weights that have a swivel on them. The swivel works better than just a wire. Flashers-dodgers and bait are a complex variable. The weights should always be kept the same distance back of the flasher or dodger. We use 30 feet (9 metres) on our boat. Jack Gaunt who invented the first plastic flasher — "The Hot Spot" — feels his works best at 15 feet (5 metres). The more variables that can be kept constant, the better you will be able to control the other variables such as

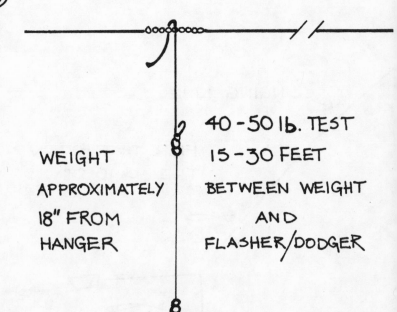

⑤

WEIGHT
APPROXIMATELY
18" FROM
HANGER

40 - 50 lb. TEST
15 - 30 FEET
BETWEEN WEIGHT
AND
FLASHER/DODGER

boat speed, tail length, dodger-flasher bends and bait action.

Now down to the natural baits. The three basic natural baits that are used for big fish are: anchovy, herring strip and whole herring. When trolling at a fast speed everybody in our area uses a plastic bait head to help secure the hook and line. In motor mooching most fisherpersons go quite slow and they use cut plug herring or herring strip. I'll tell a bit about mooching big fish later.

The anchovy is the most popular bait in Sooke and Alberni. I feel that over 80% of the big fish at Sooke take anchovy. The anchovy is like a herring but grows only to 7 or 8 inches (18 or 20 centimetres) and is round in shape. See Diagrams 6 and 7 for the difference between the anchovy and herring.

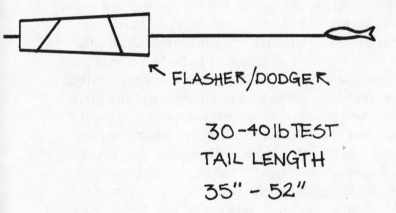

FLASHER/DODGER

30 - 40 lb TEST
TAIL LENGTH
35" - 52"

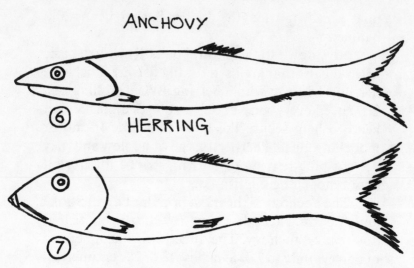

ANCHOVY

⑥

HERRING

⑦

In the cast of the anchovy the best anchovy will produce the most fish. The question is — what is the best bait? We use top quality winter-fed frozen anchovy of about 6 inches. For big Springs, anchovy is like candy to a child — they love it. We have found that even a poor anchovy will out-produce other baits and lures. Fishermen at Lake Mead near Las Vegas use anchovy for Stripped Bass and Catfish. The anchovy is also a very popular bait for fish in the Colorado River. Always, always buy the best quality bait that is available. Don't worry about the price. The best anchovy is winter-fed, ponded, bright silver and shaped like a cigar. In 1977 we had 18 pieces of perfect bait and caught 12 Springs over 30 pounds (14 kilograms) in two weeks. This bait was so good that you could troll it all day and then refreeze it for use the next day. Dad packed his own anchovy in a special way in the fall of 1981. This is one reason why we did so well in 1982. One evening in 1982 we went out fishing with 40 pieces of bait and the fish cleaned us right out. We kept 4 big Springs and 8 Sockeye and let the rest go.

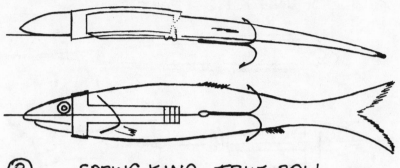

⑧ SPRING KING TRUE ROLL WITH ANCHOVY

NOTE: HOOK SET JUST BACK OF DORSAL FIN

Now on to bait heads for anchovy. In the 1960's most fisherpersons used the Les Davies-type herring aids for anchovy. They required toothpicks and did not fit the anchovy very well. My Dad invented three new bait heads for anchovy and herring. These bait heads were designed so that they positively locked the bait without toothpicks. They also kept the gills and mouth closed and allowed the eye and mouth to be exposed. We also wanted the bait heads to be streamlined and capable of a torpedo roll. It took us 20 modifications to build the perfect bait harness. We also wanted these to be capable of a reversing roll. Our harness is balanced so it will roll both ways. This bait head is called the Spring King True Roll and is shown in Diagram 8. This bait head is designed for fish in the 30 to 60 pound (14 to 27 kilogram) range. Please note that the hook is placed just back of the dorsal fin and is pulled to put a slight C curve in the bait. The Spring King Fast Flip is shown in Diagram 9. Please note that the hook is placed near the tail and the body is straight. This head is designed for fish in the 20 to 35 pound (9 to 16

SPRING KING FAST FLIP

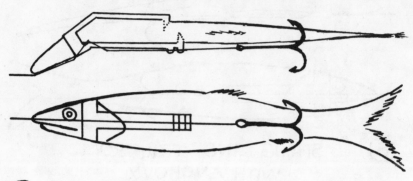

⑨ NOTE: HOOK MUST BE SET NEAR TAIL

kilogram) range. The Spring King Salmon Sity Sniper is shown in Diagram 10. It is used for 4 to 5 inch (10 to 13 centimetre) anchovy. This is the lure I used last year for my 41½ pounder (19 kilograms). It is designed for fish in the 15 to 25 pound (7 to 11 kilogram) range.

There is one other new bait head on the market. It is Jim Gilbert's Krippled Anchovy holder. It is designed for a tight roll but only rolls in one direction. I think it is best suited for a 5½ inch (14 centimetre) anchovy.

O.K. now, on to bait heads for herring strip. In the old days back in the late 1960's, herring strip was the most popular bait. In those days most fisherpersons used the toothpick-type Strip Teaser head. In the 1970's the Scotty Bait Bitters were very popular with commercial boats.

My Dad didn't like using toothpicks so he

SALMON SITY SNIPER

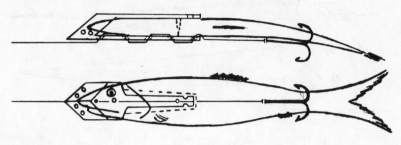

⑩

decided to invent a toothpick-less strip holder. He also wanted a tight roll with the hook at the tail. The result was the Spring King XTASEA strip holder. Dad invented three different bends, Ultra Smooth for a real fast troll, Super Slick for a mid-speed troll and Lickity Split for a slow troll. Please see Diagram 11. The exit holes on the front make it either roll left or right. The hole closest to the point is the tightest roll.

 Last year we fished the XTASEA a lot. We usually run anchovy on one side and strip on the other. Dad lost the biggest salmon he ever saw on the XTASEA last year. Dad saw it on the surface and said it was 1 foot (.3 metre) longer than my 41½ pounder (19 kilogram). We did everything right but it was better. Dad was mad. You should not get mad when you lose a whopper as we have to let some get back to spawn.

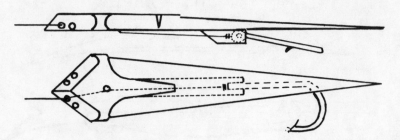

ULTRA SMOOTH
XTASEA

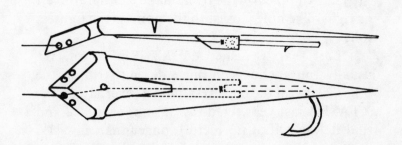

⑪ SUPER SLICK
XTASEA

The flasher-dodger does 3 things. It attracts fish by giving out both sound wave and light reflection. It also gives the lure movement and action. The speed of your boat, angles of the flasher-dodger, tail length and bait curve all determine the action or movement of the bait. The speed you troll must be as fast as possible — as long as everything is working correctly. The faster you go, the more area you pass over, hence more fish will see your gear. This sounds

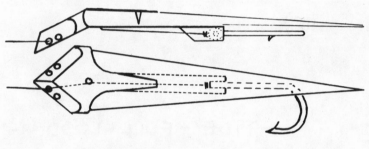

LICKITY SPLIT
XTASEA

easy, eh? Not so. The faster one goes, the more your line comes up and in Canada we can only use 2 pounds (.9 kilogram) on the rods. Also, the faster you go, the more critical will the tail length, bait curve and dodger-flasher bends become. The fast troll has two advantages. The first is you can put your gear into the exact position you want and you can block or circle zone a position. The second is that fish hit harder on a quick lure and they get stuck on your line better. See Diagram 12 for a ½-hour block and zone. Always set your trolling speed by the angle of the line entering the water.

BLOCK & ZONE

(12)

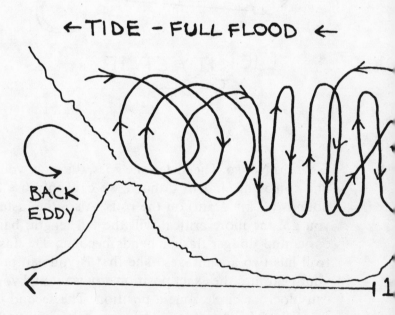

←TIDE - FULL FLOOD ←

BACK EDDY

Our tails are 30 to 40 pounds (14 to 18 kilograms) and vary between 35 and 52 inches (89 and 132 centimetres). We never go longer as it is too hard to land big fish when using long tails.

It WOULD TAKE A LOT OF TIME TO EXPLAIN EXACTLY WHAT WE ARE DOING. IF YOU GET TO ONE OF MY SHOWS, I'LL TELL YOU THEN!

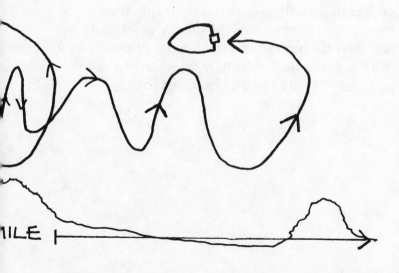

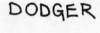

DODGER

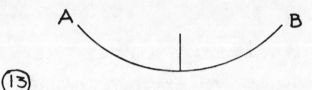

A   B

⑬

THE DODGER SWEEPS
BETWEEN POINT A & B

    We have mentioned that we use dodgers or flashers but our Spring King bait heads will fish well with just bait and weights. When using a flasher-dodger tie directly to the swivel — do not use a quick change or rubber snubber. Just a quick note on basics. A flasher can be either metal or plastic and rolls in the water. A dodger is made of the same material but only sweeps. See Diagram 13.

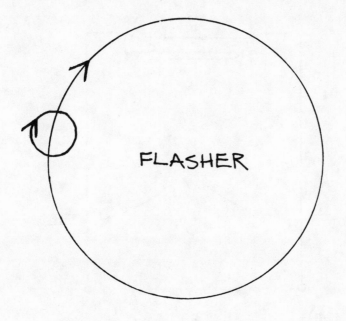

FLASHER

THE FLASHER ROTATES THROUGH
A LARGE LOOP. THE FLASHER
IS ALSO ROTATING IN A SMALL
LOOP. AT SOME SPEEDS THE
ROLL WILL REVERSE.

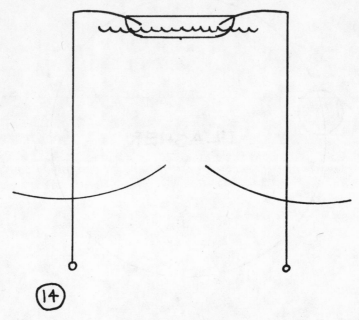

SPRING KING

SLIDER DODGER

Dad uses his own dodgers which we call "Sliders." They are made of spring brass — chrome plated and are 18 inches (46 centimetres) long. We make them in either left or right styles. One gives a clockwise sweep and the other gives a counter-clockwise sweep. We bend them so that they do not roll but rock high on one side and low on the other. See Diagram 14. As you note from the diagram, the high rock toward the boat causes the light to be reflected away from the boat. This gives a greater area from which to attract fish. We set up our tail length so the bait is 180° out of phase with the dodger. See Diagram 15.

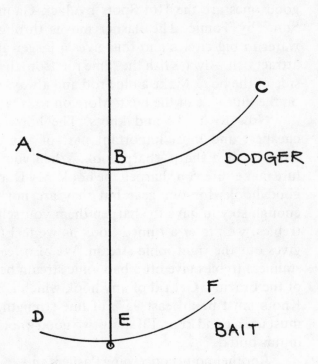

NOTE:

    1. - WHEN DODGER IS AT
        B BAIT IS AT E

    2. WHEN DODGER IS AT
        C BAIT IS AT D

    3. WHEN DODGER IS AT
        A BAIT IS AT F.

Some of our friends use another system. This is to have your rods rigged with a plastic flasher. Some good ones are the Hot Spots by Jack Gaunt and Sonic by Tomic. The flasher moves through the water in big circles and this gives a larger area to attract fish. Always fish the same rod from the same side of the boat. Make a blue rod and always put in on the blue side of the boat. More on rods later.

Now to hooks and knots. The hook is the cheapest and most important part of your gear. Always use a sharp, sharp hook. When you buy a lure make sure you sharpen the hook. My Dad buys good hooks for our gear but they are not sharp enough so you have to sharpen them yourself. For trebles, we prefer a tinned hook as we feel that it gives out the right ionic stream. We also feel that stainless trebles give off a bad ionic stream because of the brazing. Get rid of any hook which is rusty. Knots must be at least 95% of line strength. You must use a good knot. I'll show two good knots later in this book.

Another point concerning flashers and dodgers. Metal flashers have been around for years and have proven to be effective. Every fisherperson has his favourite bends and should always have a template so that he can put a bend in a new flasher-dodger easily and correctly. Plastic flashers are new and will undoubtedly take over from the metal ones because they do not lose the bend as easily and are easy on the hands and boat.

Now we are about ready to put things into the water.

Never, never, never put frozen bait into our bait heads. When you launch the boat, dip a plastic pail of salt water and place four pieces of frozen bait in it. By the time that you get to the fishing grounds it will

The Manson family with their great catch, Albernie 1982

be nicely thawed. Always have your packages of bait in your blue ice freezer chest. Now read the direction on the back of the lure card. Dad has good instructions on each of his seven bait heads. It is very important to place the hook in the bait fish as it is shown on the back of the card. If you place it elsewhere it can seriously change the balance of the bait. Now comes the most important part of this book — fine-tuning the bait.

Grab the flasher-dodger by the head and put the tail end in the water as though it were a knife. Observe the action on the bait. It must, must, must roll in a tight torpedo roll. It must look like a bullet. The head can be a little off but the tail has to roll tight. For the anchovy or herring we want it to flip approximately 1 flip per second. Our perfect action is for the bait to roll 4 times one way, then stop, then 4 times the other way. The main thing is to get it to

XTASEA   TAIL END

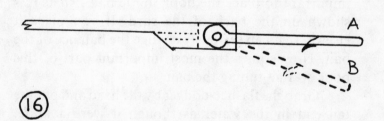

A - FAST TROLL

B - SLOW TROLL

roll tight. If it does not roll right, adjust the curve. If it still does not roll right change the position of the hook. If it takes five minutes to set it up that's O.K. because it has to roll tight. Don't look at the bait and say "I guess it's O.K.," because that's not good enough. You must say "All right, I finally got it." And mean it.

The XTASEA strip head does not reverse. It rolls either left or right depending how the line is taken out. It is still important to have the strip thawed before you put it in the holder. The speed of the roll is determined by changing the position of the hook in the tail slot. See Diagram 16. We like one flip per second for large salmon. If you flip faster you may get small salmon.

Now, it is ready to go into the water. Let the line out slowly, attach the EZon EZoff weight hanger and weight and put out 30 to 35 pulls.

Set the drag on the reel very lightly and carefully. Many big fish have been lost because the tension was too tight. Pull and check the gear constantly. We pull ours every 15 minutes or so to check the bait action.

You are now underway with the gear doing its job of attracting fish. You will get many bites but you need "salmon sense" to land the big ones.

The first rule is to let it run! Do not try to set the hook because your boat speed and flasher-dodger have done that. Most big salmon come to our boat within 10 minutes. When you use a dodger-flasher you will find the salmon fight harder but not as long. They take one long run — perhaps 100 yards (91 metres), then come back 50 yards (46 metres) and take another short run. After this they sound (head for the bottom). Remember to let the fish play as there is nothing worse than trying to land a frisky 50 pounder (23 kilograms) — it's impossible! When a fish is running always have the tip of the rod pointed at the sky — it should be at right angles to the boat. Almost all big salmon are dead by the time we land them. When they are exhausted they will roll on their sides. Go easy with the net. The net should be wet before the fish is ready to be landed. When you are ready, put the net into the water. Now tighten up the drag and pull the fish head-first over the far rim of the net. When it is mostly in, lift the net up so the rim is out of the water. Now pull the fish and net towards the side of the boat. Grab the rim and lift the net and fish into the boat. Never try to lift a 50 pounder (23 kilograms) using only the net handle.

Trolling Plugs

Now I'm going to tell you how to catch fish on plugs. My Dad caught his first salmon on a wooden plug in 1949 off Pender Island.

We are not plug experts, so we went down to see Mr. Tommy Moss, who has been making the world famous Tomic Plug for 17 years. The Tomic Plug is the favourite commercial plug on the West Coast —all the good commercial fishermen use it. The Tomic Plug comes in 3, 4, 5, 6 and 7 inches (8, 10, 13, 15 and 18 centimetres). Basically one tries to match the feed — there is over one different colour combinations.

The secret of how to sport-fish a Tomic Plug is simple. For commercial use, the Tomic comes with a tow-bar and ring. Sport fisherpersons should cut the ring off. Now comes a very important point. Most sport fisherpersons troll a lot slower than commercial boats, so to get a good sport action, tie on as

TOMIC PLUGS

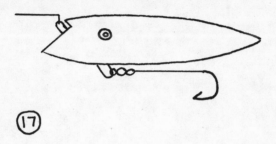

(17)

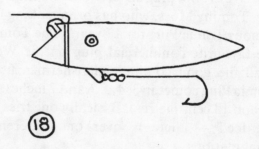

(18)

shown in Diagram 17. The knot must be tied on the top of the tow bar. Some sport fisherpersons use a rubber band as shown in Diagram 18 to get a real wiggle at slow speeds.

On a down rigger, the plug should be 30 to 60 feet (9 to 18 metres) back of the release. On a rod it should be 30 feet (9.1 metres) back of the weight. The best way of rigging the weight is with the EZon EZoff weight hanger. Never use a flasher or dodger ahead of a plug.

How do you catch salmon on plugs? It's easy. Just follow these simple rules:

Large Springs:

clear water — dark colours such as 232, 194 or 200

dark water — light colours such as 174, 118 or 50

Keep plug size to bait size.

Mr. Plug himself, Tommy Moss, gave me a lot of help, so I would like to thank him. I am not an expert, so if you find anything wrong please tell me.

Mooching the Big One

Mooching means angling for fish using light tackle and line. A great number of American fisherpersons use this method. The basic bait used are: whole herring, cut plug herring and strip herring.

I am most familiar with the way they motor-mooch at Neah Bay so I will tell you about that system.

The rods used are long and limber. The reels are the same style as trolling but lighter. At Neah Bay they use a lot of level wind-star drag reels. In Canada we use single action reels. Most moochers use 15 pound (7 kilogram) test line or lighter. For weight they use coloured banana-type weights up to 8 ounces (227 grams). Most use lighter weights. Most of the moochers at Neah Bay use cut plug herring with two solid tie bait hooks. Please see Diagram 19 for the way we were shown how to rig a cut plug. We

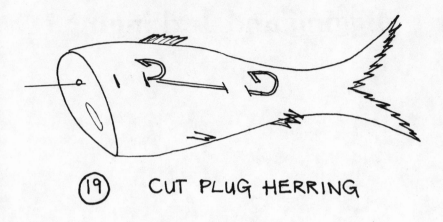

(19) CUT PLUG HERRING

use big herring — about 8 inches (20 centimetres) and bevel cut it 1/3 of the distance to the tail. Please see Diagram 20. By cutting 1/3 of the distance to the tail we do not have as much belly hole and this makes a nice face for the cut plug to roll. We use the torpedo roll with all of our mooching baits. If it does not roll tight we re-thread it. Near Vancouver they use small treble hooks in their cut baits.

You can use anchovy and strip when mooching. Set them up exactly as trolling but with lighter line.

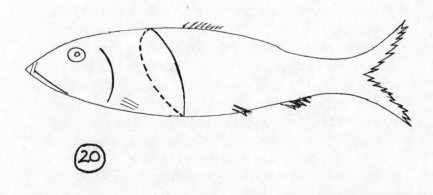

(20)

Jigging and Jerking

This is a new and popular method of catching fish. Some call it "metal minnow fishing" or "drift fishing." The Buzz Bomb was the first to really make it. With this method most allow the metal lure to float down to the fish. This is like jigging. The lures are constantly moved up and down. It seems that most fish bite when the lure is going down. The fish knows that as long as it is going up he can get it. When it goes down the fish loses sight and he thinks another fish below him might get it so he bombs down to get it before a fish he can't see gets it.

The three I like are the Buzz Bomb, Rip Tide and Bush Ape Reef Raider. Please see Diagram 21. The Buzz Bomb and Rip Tide are line minnows which means the line runs through it. The Bush Ape Reef Raider has a tie loop. Most metal minnows give off vibrations which make the fish bite.

Everyone that uses these lures should follow the

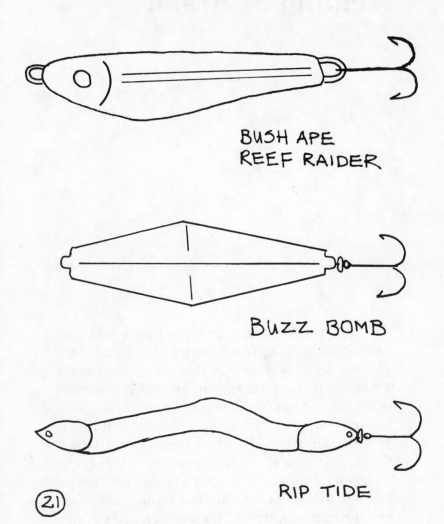

BUSH APE
REEF RAIDER

BUZZ BOMB

RIP TIDE

21

directions. Read them before you fish — not after the fishing trip.

All of these lures should be fished in bait fish. Always look for herring ball-ups, etc. In my next book, *Modern Salmon Fishing*, I'll put in a lot more on these lures.

Helping Yourself

If you will follow everything I have told you, you should catch big fish. Now it is your turn to help yourself by observing and recording information which you gather on the fishing grounds. Remember that when fish are feeding they will bite at anything — even your toothbrush! However, the best fisherpersons can catch fish when they are not biting. Know your tides and note everything, for example — 2 hours after slack tide 8 boats landed fish. Keep a logbook and enter information about tides, birds and their actions, state of the weather, and so on.

Bait means fish. If there is no bait you can be sure that the fish will not stay around very long. Diving birds and seagulls balling up indicate the presence of bait — so that means fish. Always record which rod catches which fish. After a short period of time you will note that one rod is catching more than the other. Put your "hot" rod out first and pull it in last when you are packing up. Last year my Dad got two biggies with the hot rod out as we were packing up. Try varying the "cold" rod's flasher bends or tail lengths. After some time this rod will become the "hot" one and now you can start experimenting with the former hot rod. This method provides you with constant upgrading of your fishing gear. Check the tail for nicks and kinks after having had a strike or a fish. Never put a line, leader or tail in the water which has a kink in it.

Secrets, Stories and Cartoons

I'm going to give you two cartoons so you won't find my book too boring. The first is my Dad and me out fishing for the big ones. The second is about a bunch of weird guys trying to fish. They are in the 80% group and this cartoon was done by Mrs. Pat Williams of Sooke.

Always when in rough water wear your life jacket — don't use it as a seat warmer. Make sure when you are out fishing to keep an eye open for the weather. One day we were out fishing and had a 30 pounder (14 kilograms) in the boat when we saw a big storm coming. Dad said, "Let's get out of here." So, we started to troll home. Just as we got through the rip a big slab struck. It was real big and the storm was upon us and the water was splashing into the boat. I was scared so I said to Dad, "Cut the line. It's too big." There is no use going to the bottom for a fish. Dad and my brothers had a real close call when they rescued a boat at Otter Point. Please take extreme caution when you are out in the boat.

DAD AND I FISHING

Here are Ten Secrets for You

1. Always use a good knot. See Diagram 22.
2. Never leave your line in sunlight. Sunlight destroys plastic line.
3. Never put your line in your freezer bait box.
4. Always sharpen your hook point on three sides.
5. Clean your fish as soon as possible.
6. Keep your dodgers clean with toothpaste.
7. Keep your fish nice and damp with wet cloths.
8. For big Spring try running a Sonic Flasher backwards.
9. Never use braided wire line on a rod or down rigger.
10. We support "catch and release". For real fun crimp your barbs in. Please remember, limit your kill. Don't kill your limit.

Well, now I've told you almost all my big fish secrets in this book so I'm going to close it off for now. I wish to thank my Dad and brothers for helping me. Thanks Brad, Sterling and Sean.

I hope you liked my book. I'm going to be doing two more books for Hancock House so please look for them. I may also do a video tape so you can see me catching all those slabs.

Good fishing.

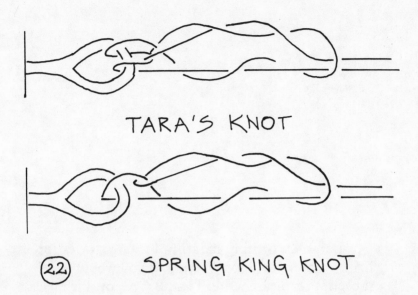

TARA'S KNOT

(22) SPRING KING KNOT

P.S. My next book will be *Modern Salmon Fishing*. Besides the Spring it will cover Coho, Chums, Sockeye and Pinks. It will tell how to use lures like the Firecracker, Disco Dancer, Best Shot, Butterfly, Trophy Hunter, Deadly Dick, Apex, Pirken, Bush Ape, Squirt, Dragonfly, Bucktails, Black Magic, Dart, Haida, Crazy Eight and many more. I hope you'll find it very interesting.

Also my Dad, brothers and I do special salmon fishing shows for non profit groups. Dad talks for three hours on salmon fishing and tells lots of secrets. We give away 5 Spring King lures. We take a percentage of the gross and the rest goes to the non profit group. If you want more details you can phone me at: 112-604-642-3608. Ask for Tara.

I am now writing monthly Fishing stories for British Columbia Sport Fishing. If you would like a subscription please write: Tara, B.C. Sport Fishing, 628 Carnavon St., New Westminster, B.C. V3M 1E3.

This just happened. Dad is going to put charter boats in Alberni. My boat is going to be called The Trophy Hunter. George Manson, "the top rod at Alberni" is looking after everything. His phone number is 604-723-6457. When you phone him tell George that I sent you.

* Remember — be observant! It's a surefire way to catch the really big fish. Note where other boats are catching the fish, and when a large fish is landed as well as the approximate weight, size, type of flasher used and tail length. Good luck!

Fisherman's Log

DATE

WEATHER
CONDITIONS

TIDE
FLOWS

LURE

FISH
RESULTS

Fisherman's Log

DATE

WEATHER
CONDITIONS

TIDE
FLOWS

LURE

FISH
RESULTS

Fisherman's Log

DATE

WEATHER
CONDITIONS

TIDE
FLOWS

LURE

FISH
RESULTS

Fisherman's Log

DATE

WEATHER
CONDITIONS

TIDE
FLOWS

LURE

FISH
RESULTS

Fisherman's Log

DATE

**WEATHER
CONDITIONS**

**TIDE
FLOWS**

LURE

**FISH
RESULTS**

Fisherman's Log

DATE

WEATHER
CONDITIONS

TIDE
FLOWS

LURE

FISH
RESULTS

Fisherman's Log

DATE

WEATHER
CONDITIONS

TIDE
FLOWS

LURE

FISH
RESULTS

Fisherman's Log

DATE

WEATHER
CONDITIONS

TIDE
FLOWS

LURE

FISH
RESULTS

Also by Lawrence Galton

*The Complete Book of Symptoms and What They Can
  Mean*
The Complete Medical Guide (coauthor)
*The Complete Medical, Fitness and Health Guide for
  Men*
Executive Nutrition and Diet
Coping with Executive Stress

1,001 HEALTH TIPS

LAWRENCE GALTON

SIMON AND SCHUSTER • New York

Copyright © 1984 by Lawrence Galton
All rights reserved
including the right of reproduction
in whole or in part in any form
Published by Simon and Schuster
A Division of Simon & Schuster, Inc.
Simon & Schuster Building
Rockefeller Center
1230 Avenue of the Americas
New York, New York 10020
SIMON AND SCHUSTER and colophon are registered trademarks
of Simon & Schuster, Inc.
Designed by C. Linda Dingler
Manufactured in the United States of America

10 9 8 7 6 5 4

Library of Congress Cataloging in Publication Data
Galton, Lawrence.
  1,001 health tips.

  1. Medicine, Popular—Dictionaries.   I. Title.
II. Title: One thousand one health tips.
III. Title: One thousand and one health tips.
RC81.A2G3   1984   610'.3'21   83-27097
ISBN 0-671-47689-0
ISBN 0-671-50935-7 pbk.

It should be noted, of course, that this book in no way is meant to substitute for any specific advice from a doctor. It may often supplement such advice and can be useful in many instances when medical advice is not available.

INTRODUCTION

This book brings together—for the first time—brief, pointed tips drawn from the medical literature that are almost certain to be of use, day in and day out, in any household.

The emphasis is on everyday concerns, not esoteric problems, and a very broad range of those concerns is covered. They extend, for example, from a strategy for getting a good night's sleep before a "Big Day," Cleopatra's remedy for stubborn itching, and positions to assume to eliminate painful gas to a simple maneuver to stop air swallowing and bloating, getting an insect out of an ear, using stretch gloves to help arthritic hands and cheese to aid asthma, tilting a bed to ease chest pain, how to medicate a bottle-fed baby, and—flat-footed or not—using arch supports to relieve back pain.

Few people are aware of the following remedies:

- When you burn your tongue with hot food or drink, a few grains of sugar sprinkled on the site can sweetly undo the misery.
- Carsickness in a child often can be prevented by elevating the child's riding position ten inches.
- The pain, burning, and itching of shingles can be greatly relieved by the slight pressure of an elasticized binder worn around the chest.
- A migraine attack often can be aborted just by exhaling into and rebreathing from a bag placed over the nose and mouth.
- While swallowing a tablet is easy with the head tilted backward, swallowing a capsule that way is difficult since the capsule, being lighter than water, will float

forward. But if the head is tilted forward, the capsule will float backward for easy swallowing.

Such is the nature of the tips, which are presented in alphabetical order and immediately cross-referenced in the text to make them easy to locate.

Additionally, a separate section—Part Two: Guidelines—provides a series of useful references, including guides to foods and their makeup, vitamins and minerals, drug side effects and the specific drugs that may produce them, and a concise glossary of often-used medical terms.

CONTENTS

Six helps for eliminating constipation
One physician's simple, effective treatment

COUGHING   94
How to make it effective when it's not
Cough medicines—expectorants and suppressants

CROUP   95
A cold shower for relief

CYSTIC FIBROSIS   96
The benefits of swimming

DANDRUFF   96
Controlling it

DIABETES   97
Fiber to help
Wine drinking—four tips
Insulin before breakfast

DIAPHRAGM CONTRACEPTION   98
Avoiding risk of toxic shock

DIARRHEA   99
Four helpful measures
Three useful measures for traveler's diarrhea
Dietetic foods and diarrhea

DOG BITES   100
Six tips about them

DOUCHING   101
As an infection factor

DRINKING (NONALCOHOLIC)   102
Balance that soft drink intake
No spills in bed
Hot/cold drinks and the heart

When medicines produce dry mouth
How to halve tablets
Where to keep medicines
How long to keep leftover prescription drugs
Determining the dose for a child
Stocking your medicine cabinet

•II• GUIDELINES

·I·
HEALTH TIPS

AEROSOL MEDICATIONS

How to inhale them   Aerosol medications are often used for breathing difficulties, and the usual recommendation is to close the lips around the aerosol mouthpiece and inhale. But here's a more effective method, according to a British study: Hold the aerosol very close to and aimed at the mouth. In the study, the open-mouth method produced greater symptom improvement, apparently because less of the medication is swallowed, leaving more of it to act on breathing passages.

See also Medicine.

AIR SWALLOWING

The discomfort it can cause   Some air is unavoidably swallowed with food and drink. But large amounts may be gulped during emotional upsets, rapid eating, gum chewing, smoking, and while drinking carbonated beverages. The excessive air intake—called aerophagia—can lead to one or more of the following: excessive belching, abdominal distention, breathing difficulty, smothering sensations, heart palpitations, and chest pain resembling that of a heart attack.

A chin-to-chest maneuver to stop it   Air is swallowed when the closing mechanism at the upper end of the esophagus (the tube leading from the throat to the stomach) opens, allowing air to be sucked in. One effective measure: Hold your chin to your chest. That position makes it difficult for the mechanism to open.

Five ways to avoid it
- Each sigh means a swallow of air. Try to become aware of any sighing so you can stop it.
- Don't bolt food. And exhale just before swallowing.
- Rather than sip or gulp liquids, drink slowly—and keep your upper lip submerged by tilting the glass.

- Let very hot beverages cool before drinking. Otherwise, knowingly or not, you'll draw in air to cool them.
- Moderate intake not only of soda pop and other carbonated beverages but also of foods and drinks with air whipped in (for example, milk shakes and whipped butter).

AIR TRAVEL

To avoid/treat ankle swelling Ankle swelling can occur on long flights because of extended, uninterrupted sitting. Both the seat's continuous upward pressure against the thighs and unrelieved bent knees impair blood circulation and allow fluid to accumulate in the ankles. To avoid or relieve it, get up and walk about the plane at intervals if possible. Or exercise your toes and ankles in your seat, moving them about briefly every half-hour or so. A useful technique: Make bicycle-riding motions, one side at a time, using thigh, knee, leg, ankle, and foot.

For ear/sinus pain Ear pain occurs—mostly during descent—because of failure of pressure equalization in the ears. If you have a sinus problem, you may sometimes experience, also mostly during descent, pain over the affected sinus or sinuses because of failure of pressure equalization inside and outside the area. For both conditions, frequent swallowing and forced yawning help by equalizing pressure. Gum chewing also may be useful. Another often-valuable measure: Taking an oral antihistamine drug an hour before flight or using decongestant nose drops or inhalant just before or during descent.

And for baby on a plane Commonly infants howl when a plane begins descent for landing. The changing air pressure, often uncomfortable for adults, may be more so for babies because their mouth-to-ear (Eustachian) tubes are narrower, less able to equalize ear pressure quickly. Suggests Dr. Hans

H. Neumann of the New Haven, Connecticut, Department of Health: When flying with an infant, bottle-feed with any liquid the baby likes during ascent and especially during descent. The frequent swallowing helps pressure equalization.

Relieving an earache when usual methods fail The following simple, four-step, five-second maneuver could help alleviate the ache on an airline when yawning, swallowing, or gum chewing fails, according to a report in the medical journal *American Family Physician:*

- Take a deep breath and hold it with the mouth closed.
- Press both nostrils closed with the thumb and forefinger.
- Block the opening of the *unaffected* ear with the forefinger of the other hand.
- Exhale forcefully and briefly as if blowing the nose.

NOTE: This maneuver should be used for descents only and should not be attempted if you have a sore throat, fever, significant heart or circulatory disorder, or other serious health problem.

Fluids to fight lethargy, fatigue, and jet lag You can lose as much as two pounds of body water by evaporation through the skin during even a three-and-a-half-hour flight on a jetliner because of the rapid circulation of very dry air. Dehydration—fluid loss without adequate replenishment—can sometimes become severe enough to cause dry skin and mucous membranes, cracked lips, lethargy, fatigue, and muscle cramps. Short of that, it can contribute to jet lag and underpar feelings. Replenish fluids! Airplane water may be insipid, but drink it. Don't depend on alcohol—or on coffee, tea, or other beverages containing caffeine; all can increase fluid excretion, adding to the loss.

ALCOHOL

How much can you take and still drive safely? The question is more complex than it may seem. For one thing, weight counts. Generally, the less your weight, the higher the level of alcohol in your blood from a given amount of intake.

- For example, on an empty stomach, it may take only two drinks for someone weighing 120 pounds to have the blood alcohol level reach half the legal limit within an hour; a 150-pounder may require three drinks. Starting to drink after a full meal or its equivalent, a 150-pounder may have five drinks before reaching half the legal blood alcohol limit.

- How quickly alcohol is removed from the body also counts. A healthy liver needs an hour to handle one mixed drink, five ounces of wine, or twelve ounces of beer. If your liver isn't in the best of health, it can take longer.

- And people vary in their reactions: Some will drive dangerously at blood alcohol levels well below the legal limit.

Alcohol's role in nonhighway injuries Although excessive alcohol use's association with highway injuries is well known, its relationship with many other injuries is not.

- In a Washington state investigation, alcohol use was found in 10 percent of 1,750 persons with fall injuries seen in hospital emergency rooms and in 22 percent of those experiencing more than one fall injury in a year.

- In a Massachusetts study, alcohol-positive Breathalyzer readings of 0.01 percent and higher were found in 22 percent of 620 persons treated for injuries sustained at home.

- In a California study, high blood alcohol concentrations were found in 37 percent of persons suffering fatalities, with excessive levels present in 60 percent of those dying from falls and 64 percent of those dying of burns.

- In a Baltimore study of adult drownings, high blood alcohol concentrations were found in 47 percent of victims.

- And a New York City study found that 41 percent of deaths from falls, 46 percent of those from fires, and 53 percent of drowning deaths were associated with high blood levels of alcohol.

See also Hangover; Sleep; Guidelines: Calories in Alcoholic and Carbonated Beverages.

ALLERGIES

Wheezing, sneezing, and mattress vacuuming Asthma, bronchitis, other allergic respiratory ailments often are traceable to house dust mites—and mattress vacuuming may work as well as an antihistamine. Studying microscopic mites, a University of California, Riverside, researcher has shown that the organisms prefer to live at the *head* of human mattresses, feeding on skin scales deposited there. They're much less numerous on other home furnishings. His study indicates that twice-a-week mattress vacuuming can reduce mite populations by 60 to 80 percent.

A *dozen other helps for house dust allergies*
- Nylon carpeting (low pile) is okay, but be wary of shags and any carpets with jute- or kapok-containing pads. Best bet: hardwood, vinyl, or tile flooring.
- Use zipper covers on all mattresses.
- Use polyester fiberfill rather than foam pillows (they can absorb moisture and molds).
- Avoid Venetian blinds in favor of window shades.
- No draperies. Use washable cotton-polyester curtains.
- Monthly, in season, change furnace and air-conditioner filters.
- It may help to increase a filter's capacity. For this, suggests the medical journal *Consultant*, you can use a temporary filter made of two or three layers of cheesecloth soaked with mineral oil, changing it when it becomes discolored.
- Regularly clean a fireplace and chimney flue—and woodstove if you use one.
- Avoid carpet "fresheners" and other scented agents.
- Don't keep unused clothing in the closet; store it away from the bedroom, preferably in sealed boxes.
- Keep upholstered furniture out of the bedroom. Elsewhere in the house, polyester- or foam-filled cushions are preferable to down- or kapok-filled ones.
- If you use a quilt or comforter, it should be filled only with polyester.

Detecting your food allergies (if any) for yourself   There are other possible causes but food allergies can sometimes produce varied symptoms: crampy pain, diarrhea, hives, constipation, anal itching—even, possibly, headache, vertigo, seizurelike attacks, anxiety, depression, and mental dulling. When other causes cannot be found, you can try an "elimination and challenge" strategy devised by a Kansas allergist, Dr. Frederic Speer. In his experience, chief food offenders are cow's milk, chocolate, cola, corn, eggs, the pea family (chiefly peanut, which is not a nut), citrus fruits, tomatoes, wheat and other small grains, cinnamon, and artificial food colors.

To find out which may be responsible: If two or more foods are suspect, remove them from the diet for three weeks. Return one and, at two-day intervals, reintroduce the others, one at a time. If only a single food is suspect, similarly remove it for three weeks, then reintroduce. If symptoms improve when a suspected food is out of the diet only to reappear when the food is reintroduced, the blame is clear.

Hay fever—one physician's effective personal strategy   You'll need a doctor's prescription to try this strategy worked out by a distinguished neurologist, Dr. Donald J. Dalessio of the Scripps Clinic and Research Foundation, LaJolla, California, for his own hay fever problem, and used successfully by several other physicians for themselves.

Because he disliked consuming large amounts of antihistamines, which dulled him, and anticongestants, which made him anxious, on waking each morning during his hay fever season Dalessio tried applying a small amount of a potent corticosteroid cream—either flumethasone 0.03 percent or fluocinonide 0.05 percent—to the nasal mucous membranes, using his little finger. Only a *small* amount, he emphasizes. The cream causes a slight irritation, and he sniffs vigorously to inhale it to the upper reaches. At night he repeats the process and at bedtime takes a six-milligram dose of Polaramine, which provides antihistamine effects (at night pollen counts rise and the drug's sedative effect is no bother). The strategy works, he finds, leaving just an occasional sneeze (virtually no paroxysmal sneezing), with nasal discharge much reduced.

Four other helps for hay fever

- In pollen seasons, keep clear, if possible, of grassy areas, woods, and fields; they're apt to have high pollen concentrations.
- If ragweed is your problem, keep such ragweed-related plants as daisies, dahlias, and chrysanthemums out of the house.
- Because pollen counts are likely to be particularly high on hot, sunny, windy days, stay in an air-conditioned room as much as possible at these times. It may help, too, to keep the air conditioner's fresh-air vent closed on such days.
- Pollen allergy sufferers are often sensitive to dust as well. Keep your bedroom as free of dust as possible (see previous A Dozen Other Helps for House Dust Allergies).

Humidification for year-round nasal stuffiness Adding moisture to winter air in the home—with a room humidifier or a device attachable to the hot-air system—can be surprisingly helpful for perennial or year-round allergic rhinitis. In a three-winter study covering more than eight hundred sufferers, humidification was found to reduce, markedly, previous winter-long symptoms of dryness in the nose, throat, and deep chest; improve breathing; allow more restful sleep; and lessen the need to clear mucus from breathing passages in the morning. Significantly, too, 83 percent of patients were free of respiratory infections during the winters for the first time in years.

Avoiding mold allergy Sensitivity to molds in itself can sometimes cause nasal congestion, stuffiness, and other annoying symptoms. Mold sensitivity also tends to occur along with other sensitivities, such as to pollen. The following are useful measures for avoiding molds:

- Keep dust accumulations to a minimum (see previous A Dozen Helps for House Dust Allergies).
- Keep mold-collecting sites such as bathroom walls and discarded furniture in a damp basement scrupulously clean.
- Dry damp clothing, shoes, and boots quickly.
- Be sure your clothes dryer vents to the outdoors.
- If your basement is very damp, a dehumidifier can help combat mold growth.

Allergy shots during pregnancy A woman who, after being immunized against allergy, continues her maintenance injections during pregnancy, may do more than protect herself. Her child, too, may be protected against allergy, possibly for life. Kaiser-Permanente Medical Group physicians in Los Angeles did a study of twelve mothers who received standard maintenance doses of allergen extracts by injection at three-to-four-month intervals during pregnancy. They did well. Their children were checked, first between the ages of three and eleven years, then later as well. The youngsters had lower frequencies of hay fever, asthma, and skin-test sensitivity to rye, Bermuda grass, Chinese elm pollen, house dust, and dust mite than genetics would predict and than siblings from earlier untreated pregnancies.

Alfalfa pills and allergy The alfalfa pills being used by some allergy victims may be hazardous, according to an American Medical Association report. Actually, alfalfa, a grass, may intensify symptoms caused by grass pollen sensitivity. Alfalfa also may cause flatulence and diarrhea. In addition, while there have been no medical reports of efficacy, there is some indication that alfalfa seeds may contain a high concentration of a potentially poisonous substance, canavanine, which may have been responsible for a blood cell disorder in at least one patient reported in the medical literature. "It would seem prudent to avoid use of alfalfa in the treatment of allergies," advises an American Medical Association expert.

See also Asthma.

ANTACIDS

The best forms: six important factors Commonly used for heartburn, peptic ulcer, and digestive upsets, antacids temporarily neutralize stomach acid.

• For most purposes, liquid preparations have the edge, even if tablets win on convenience. Many tablets contain aluminum hydroxide, which may lose some of its acid-neutralizing action in the drying process used in making tablets. Also, liquids coat more of the surface of the esophagus and stomach.

NOTE: If not well chewed, tablets may do little coating and be worthless.

• Acid-neutralizing strengths vary. Among liquid antacids, the top five, according to a recent study, are Maalox TC, Titralac, Delcid, Mylanta-II, and Camalox. You get more for your money with the more potent antacids.

• Calcium carbonate antacids—such as Titralac, Tums, and Alka-2—produce quick relief. But they may later trigger a "rebound" of acid secretion and so are not recommended for ulcer patients.

• Most preferred antacids contain both magnesium hydroxide and aluminum hydroxide. The magnesium compound tends to produce diarrhea while the aluminum hydroxide tends to constipate—so one balances the other. Still, if bowel habits are affected, you may need to try several brands to find one with a balance suitable for you.

• Sodium (salt) content varies; for example, Titralac has ten times as much as Mylanta-II—something to be considered if you're on a salt-restricted diet for blood pressure, or heart or kidney disease.

• Baking soda—sodium bicarbonate—is cheap but should be used rarely, if at all. It almost instantly neutralizes acid. But, unlike many other antacids, it is absorbed through the stomach wall and may upset body chemistry when used in large amounts or over the long term. It may, for example, with chronic, heavy use, increase blood alkalinity, leading to shallow or irregular breathing, prickling or burning sensations, and muscle cramps. The sodium it contains also may not be advisable for those on salt restriction.

The best times to take antacids   Antacids are most effective in repeated doses one hour and three hours after meals and at bedtime. Immediately after a meal, stomach acid does increase, but protein in the food, an excellent buffer, acts to neutralize any excess acid. After about an hour, however, the buffering capacity disappears. Then an antacid can supply the buffering for a period of about two hours. A second dose of antacid taken three hours after eating is then effective for about another hour.

ANTIHISTAMINES

Those among the array that, happily, cause less drowsiness   Sometimes useful for allergies, antihistamines are compounds that help to keep undue amounts of a body chemical, histamine, from producing allergic sneezing, itching, and other symptoms. A major problem with the drugs: sleepiness. But, with the many antihistamines now available, you can experiment to find one that works best with the least drowsiness. Among those reported to produce relatively little:

- Tripelennamine
- Pyrilamine
- Chlorpheniramine
- Brompheniramine
- Cyproheptadine
- Phenindamine

These are generic names. Look for them in labels of trade-named antihistamine preparations.

APHTHOUS STOMATITIS (*See* CANKER SORES.)

ARTHRITIS

Three pain savers The following three tips may help at least a little in lessening day-to-day discomfort, one physician reports in the medical journal *Patient Care:*
- Open bottle containers with the heel of the hand.
- Comb hair with a long-handled comb or brush to reduce shoulder motion.
- Hug shopping bags rather than carry them by the handles.

Relief with a blanket Sleeping under an electric blanket —a good source of therapeutic heat—can be helpful for arthritic and other aches. Hot-water bottles cool quickly; heating pads on too high a setting may burn the skin. But an electric blanket can provide low, continuous heat to painful joints and muscles, resulting in less stiffness in the morning.

An ice bag for the arthritic knee For the rheumatoid arthritis sufferer with painful knees, ice "Baggie therapy" may offer significant relief. It calls for putting six ice cubes in a plastic bag to make an ice pack and placing the pack over and under the knee for twenty minutes, three times a day, for four weeks. That led to marked pain relief and improvement in knee range of motion, strength, and sleep duration in a trial with twenty-four patients. The inexpensive therapy produced no undesirable effects and reduced the need for pain-relieving drugs. Curiously, too, even as one knee was being treated, pain relief occurred in the other as well, according to a report by Dr. Peter D. Utsinger of Germantown Medical Center, Philadelphia.

Stretch gloves for arthritic hands At Albert Einstein Medical Center, Philadelphia, Dr. George E. Ehrlich, director of the Arthritic Clinic, observed that several women patients with hands affected by rheumatoid arthritis or osteoarthritis wore stretch gloves. The gloves helped so much, they reported, that they were worn at night as well. When Ehrlich set up a trial with forty-four other patients, the gloves helped forty-one, reducing or eliminating morning pain, stiffness, and joint swelling, and increasing strength. All this occurred within the first two days of wearing the gloves, with some patients reporting being able to sleep through the night for the first time in years. Both nylon-knit and Spandex-and-nylon gloves were effective; the latter were more comfortable for some patients.

Iron and arthritis Iron supplements may worsen rheumatoid arthritis in some patients. British investigators found that three of ten patients, after getting an iron dextran preparation by vein, developed acute joint inflammation. The disease got worse, too, in three of ten others with early rheumatoid arthritis given oral iron sulphate. In the United States, Dr. David G. Borenstein of George Washington University, Washington, D.C., studying the synovial, or joint, fluid of fourteen patients with several types of arthritis, found that adding an iron compound to the fluid helped bacteria there to grow. "When iron is absent," he reports, "synovial fluid may do a better job of inhibiting bacterial growth. Iron promotes the growth of the bacteria which can contribute to the inflammation associated with arthritis."

Exercise for arthritics Even in moderate amounts, exercise can help. Using stationary bicycles, fourteen women with rheumatoid arthritis took part in supervised exercise plans in a University of Michigan, Ann Arbor, study. Three times a week, during a twelve-week study period, some exercised fifteen minutes per session, others twenty-five minutes, still others thirty-five minutes. Even for those exercising the minimum time, there were improvements in exercise tolerance and functional status, according to Dr. Thomas Harkcom and other researchers. And, assessing themselves, the women reported an improvement in energy and an increased ability to carry out household and social activities.

Arthritis and food Some rheumatoid arthritis patients have long believed that certain foods worsen their disease. Some support for their belief comes from a very limited British study, involving only one woman. Seen by investigators at the Royal Postgraduate Medical School, London, the thirty-eight-year-old patient had suffered from progressive arthritis, unresponsive to treatment, for eleven years. She had a family history of rheumatoid arthritis and allergy and was allergic herself but had never noticed a worsening of arthritis after exposure to agents she was known to be allergic to. She did, however, love cheese, eating up to a pound a day. Despite lack of any clear history of allergy after cheese consumption, when, in a trial, cheese, butter, and milk were eliminated from her diet, arthritis symptoms improved within three weeks. When milk products were reintroduced, her arthritis deteriorated within twenty-four hours. Suggest the investigators: In some cases, rheumatoid arthritis may be similar to diseases such as eczema and migraine, which can be allergic manifestations of food intolerance.

A copper bracelet for arthritis? Wearing a copper bracelet to ease the pain of arthritis has long been considered an old wives' tale, but new scientific evidence is beginning to offer support. At the University of Akron, Ohio, Dr. Helmar Dollwet, associate professor of biology, has found that copper implants in rats' legs reduce swelling. The exact role of copper in joints is unknown, but the metal enters into the production of enzymes that participate in forming collagen, a material present in connective tissue.

Observes Dr. Dollwet: "I have never said, nor can I say now, that a copper bracelet or a copper implant will cure arthritis. But as we dig deeper into the problem and our efforts expand, I believe more strongly than ever that the copper reduces the pain of this disease and makes life a little more bearable for its victims."

ASPIRIN

Three ways to avoid stomach irritation Although a valued drug and one of the safest, aspirin sometimes causes stomach upsets and bleeding.

• One preventive measure: Take the drug with food or at least a glass of milk.

• Aspirin-induced bleeding appears to be the result of a local effect of aspirin particles, according to studies by Dr. Martin I. Blake at the University of Illinois, Chicago. To minimize that effect, he suggests: Never swallow aspirin tablets whole; chew them thoroughly, swallow with plenty of fluid.

• Alternatively, suggests Blake, crush the tablets to a fine powder, and take the powder in orange juice.

Aspirin and IUD contraceptives—beware Women using intrauterine devices would do well to avoid heavy aspirin use, or they may risk increased likelihood of becoming pregnant. A University of Utah, Salt Lake City, study of seventy-eight women who became pregnant while using IUDs and seventy-seven who did not found that the former used an average of forty-one aspirin tablets a month compared with only six for the others. IUDs are believed to work by stimulating production of hormonelike chemicals (prostaglandins) in the uterine lining; heavy aspirin use may inhibit that production.

Aspirin late in pregnancy—caution Aspirin use in the five days before delivery may cause bleeding complications in both mother and baby. Investigators at Upstate Medical Center, Syracuse, New York, found that only one of thirty-four (3 percent) not taking aspirin had mother or child bleeding problems. On the other hand, six of ten (60 percent) of mothers taking aspirin within five days of childbirth had excessive blood loss during or after delivery, and nine of their ten babies (90 percent) had blood in the urine or bleeding from circumcision.

Aspirin and nonaspirin pain relievers—how to choose Both aspirin and another commonly used nonaspirin•analgesic, acetaminophen, proved equally effective in relieving moderately severe headaches and did not differ markedly in side effects in a University of Texas, Austin, study with 269 patients. In selecting one or the other, suggests Dr. Bruce H. Peters who did the study, "patients with bleeding disorders should not choose aspirin and those with kidney or liver disorders should avoid acetaminophen."

Aspirin, acetaminophen, and food Taking aspirin with food is helpful for avoiding stomach upsets. But taking acetaminophen with food is unnecessary and can slow absorption and delay relief. Tufts–New England Medical Center, Boston, researchers have found that acetaminophen taken on an empty stomach is quickly absorbed and reaches peak effective blood levels in about fifty-five minutes, while the presence of food nearly doubles the time—to about an hour and forty-five minutes—to reach effective levels.

See also Toothache: Aspirin and Toothache.

ASTHMA

Cheesing it Patients can contribute to medical knowledge, and doctors sometimes pay heed. It was an asthma sufferer who noted that his asthma improved whenever he ate aged Cheddar cheese. Intrigued, physicians at the Milton S. Hershey Medical Center, Hershey, Pennsylvania, found that aged Cheddar was often helpful for other patients as well.

Apparently, tyramine—a natural ingredient in the cheese—helps by dilating air passages.

A dust-free bedroom for the asthmatic child Many asthmatic children have an allergy to house dust or house dust mites. In such cases, a dust-free bedroom can be a practical, effective method for decreasing asthma attacks.

- The value: In a Canadian study by Drs. A. M. Murray and A. C. Ferguson of the University of British Columbia, Vancouver, twenty children testing positive for house dust or dust mite sensitivity were divided into two groups matched for asthma severity. Parents of one group were shown how to make bedrooms dust-free; the other group, serving for comparison, continued with usual bedroom environments. At the end of one month, children with dust-free bedrooms had a total of only ten hours of wheezing and required only five doses of medication; the others had a total of 339 hours of wheezing and needed 224 doses of medication.
- How to achieve it: These were the instructions given in the study:
    - Launder bedroom curtains and wash blankets and mattress pads every two weeks.
    - Use zippered vinyl covers for pillows, mattresses, and box springs.
    - Clean drawers and closets with a damp cloth and use them only for storing laundered clothes.
    - Remove toys, models, books, upholstered furniture, and carpets from the room.
    - Clean the floor daily with a damp or oiled mop.
    - Seal any hot-air duct in the room, and heat, if necessary, with an electric radiator.

See also Allergies.

ATHLETE'S FOOT

Help for one kind There are, in fact, two kinds of athlete's foot. The first—and pure—form, tinea pedis, is dry and scaling, without other symptoms. It's caused by a fungus. An antifungal preparation, such as Tinactin or Desenex, often helps.

Relieving the second kind Once soggy, white, malodorous lesions appear between the toes, it's because bacteria, in the presence of perspiration, have taken over from the fungus and the infection is now bacterial. At this stage, University of Pennsylvania, Philadelphia, physicians have found, a 30 percent solution of aluminum chloride ($AlCl_3.6H_2O$) is most effective. Applied with a cotton-tipped applicator twice a day, it relieves itching, causes malodor to disappear within forty-eight to seventy-two hours, and abates other symptoms within a week. The preparation combats both bacteria and wetness, is inexpensive, and can be made up by a pharmacist.

Five preventive aids Because moisture and warmth aid the growth of athlete's foot fungus, relatively simple measures can be preventive:
- Allow shoes to dry thoroughly between wearings.
- Change socks frequently.
- You may do well to avoid deodorant soaps; they tend to remove surface-protecting oils and may irritate the skin.
- Cornstarch powder can help decrease friction on the skin and absorb perspiration.
- If perspiration is excessive, it may be reduced by cutting consumption of caffeine-containing beverages such as coffee, tea, and cola.

ATHLETIC INJURIES

Cold treatment This should come first. Applied as soon as possible after sprain, strain, and other kinds of injuries, cold not only helps relieve pain, it also restricts swelling and helps relax muscles and reduce the spasms (involuntary muscle contractions) that often accompany injury. Depending upon the injury site, apply cold either by immersion in a pail or bowl of cold water, or with wet towels, cold packs, or crushed ice in a pillowcase.

Heat treatment Heat should *not* be used *immediately* after an injury. Heat may aggravate inflammation and encourage bleeding from any torn blood vessels. Later—no sooner than twelve to twenty-four hours or even longer after injury—heat can relieve pain and spasm and may also help the repair process by increasing the blood flow to the injury site. It can be applied by immersion in hot water or by hot compresses. An electric heating pad produces dry heat, which often is not as effective for pain relief as moist heat.

"A" TYPE BEHAVIOR (*See* TYPE A BEHAVIOR.)

BABY

Medicating a bottle-fed infant When you must administer liquid medication, try this method suggested by Dr. David N. Besselman of Harrisburg, Pennsylvania: Give the baby an empty nipple to suck on, then pour medicine through the nipple. The medication bypasses most taste buds, especially those on the tip of the tongue, and the baby is unlikely to gag.

Making weaning easier Weaning a toddler from a nursing bottle can be difficult, but Dr. Robert H. Laird of Kailua-Kona, Hawaii, says he has found this technique helpful: Put only tap water in the bottle and give the child other liquids from a cup. The child may soon learn to prefer the cup, and getting him or her off the bottle can help prevent "nursing bottle tooth decay."

Taste-testing baby's skin If baby's skin tastes very salty, the possibility (only that) of cystic fibrosis may need to be investigated. Excess salt in sweat—up to ten times the normal amount—is one possible indication of the genetic problem, which affects two thousand to three thousand American children born yearly. Cystic fibrosis leads to thick, sticky mucus secretions that clog airways and obstruct pancreatic and bile ducts. Although CF is still not curable, early detection and treatment have made life more normal for CF children and their families and increased life span from the 3-to-4-year average of the 1950s to greater than twenty years now, with the possibility that further advances before long may make for near-normal life span.

When baby naps, don't tiptoe Parents who try to provide total silence and tiptoe around while a baby naps may be doing exactly the wrong thing if they want their infants to sleep. At the University of Florida, Gainesville, psychologists have found that very young babies sleep longer—and spend less time crying when they wake—if they're exposed during sleep to noise at levels up to seventy-five decibels (about the level inside a jet). "Contrary to intuition," says Dr. C. Michael Levy, one of the researchers, "repetitious noise at a moderately intense level has a calming effect on infants. The type of sound doesn't matter as long as it is repetitious and moderately loud."

Homemade baby food—saltier than you think Although making baby food at home is a labor of love—an effort to give baby the best—it isn't always the most healthful. Reason: the amount of salt in home-prepared versus commercial baby foods. Dietitian Carol Courser of the University of New Hampshire, Durham, reports that parents often tend to be more heavy-handed with the saltshaker than industry is, often salting baby foods to suit their own tastes. Also, homemade baby foods are often prepared from commercially made table foods already containing a lot of salt. Even if no salt is added in the kitchen, a serving of pureed peas made at home from canned peas, for example, has sixty times more salt than strained peas from a baby-food jar. Advises Ms. Courser: Use fresh, unsalted table foods when you make baby food at home. If preparing an infant's food from the family dinner menu, remove it from the family pot before seasoning. Better yet, don't add salt to anyone's food; we can all benefit from shaking the salt habit.

Figuring an infant's food needs You might want to consult with your pediatrician about using this information from Dr. David A. Driggers of the pediatrics department at the University of California School of Medicine, Davis.

• An infant must gain about one ounce per day in the first six months of life and a half ounce daily in the second six months to attain what is considered normal weight gain for the first year.

• To achieve such weight gain, the usual infant needs about fifty-five calories per pound of weight per day during the first six months and about forty-five calories for every pound of weight during the second six months.

• If an infant is taking only formula containing twenty calories per ounce, it's possible to determine readily whether the child is getting enough calories for normal weight gain. For example, an infant weighing 8 pounds should receive 440 calories (8 pounds × 55 calories per pound per day) divided by 20 calories per ounce of formula, or 22 ounces of formula per day in 5 to 6 equal feedings.

Buying baby shoes It's a common misconception that babies need shoes to help them learn to walk.

Here are some interesting facts from physicians at the Thomas Jefferson University Department of Pediatrics, Philadelphia, based on data collected from 104 parents, 127 pediatricians, and 36 shoe store managers:

• Infants receive their first pair of walking shoes at an average age of 8.1 months, at an average cost of $14.56. Most shoes have laces (95 percent), high tops (87 percent), hard soles (74 percent), and special arch supports (50 percent). Of the 104 children in the study, 73 had shoes before they were walking and 35 wore walking shoes before they were even standing.

- Yet there is no evidence that shoes promote walking skills or foot development—and there *is* evidence they may actually cause more deformity and less mobility of the foot.

- Although most pediatricians suggest *soft* soles, because hard soles may delay walking and aggravate in- and out-toeing, 75 percent of the salespeople surveyed recommended hard soles and 74 percent of the parents bought them.

- Most parents and shoe store managers believe wearing sneakers is unhealthy for a baby but 75 percent of pediatricians do not.

- Your best bet is to get advice from your pediatrician at baby's five- or six-month checkup to avoid buying shoes before they are really needed.

- And the Thomas Jefferson physicians have this to add: "We usually suggest a canvas sneaker that sells for approximately $10. If parents prefer a high-top shoe so that the toddler does not step out of the heel, we stress that arch supports and ankle supports, steel shanks and hard soles are neither necessary nor desirable."

See also Air Travel; Children.

BACKACHES

The right combination of steps to ease them Suddenly you have agonizing spasmodic back pain. You don't know why —and cause, at the moment, is not important; when severe pain is present, even a medical specialist couldn't determine cause. The urgent need is to relieve the pain. Often you can do that with simple measures—*provided* you use them properly and don't stop with just one or two, as most victims do, when a combination of many could help. The immediate problem is spasm, the contraction of strained muscle fibers. With spasm the fibers can't get adequate blood supply and dispose of waste. The result: more pain and a vicious cycle of more pain, more spasm, more pain, still more spasm. You have to attack both pain and spasm.

- Immediately take two aspirin or acetaminophen (aspirin substitute) tablets and lie down. Get into bed as soon as possible.

- Apply heat with a heating pad wrapped in a towel. Apply for thirty minutes, then change position to avoid stiffness.

- For some people, cold provides quicker relief than heat. If you're one of them, gently rub the painful area with ice cubes or crushed ice contained in a pillowcase.

- Next, have someone gently rub the painful site with any commercially available counterirritant (such as Ben Gay, Heet, Icy Hot, or InfraRub).

- Continue the aspirin or acetaminophen; most people can take two tablets of either every three to four hours without trouble.

- Repeat heat or cold applications. If you can make it to the bathtub, soak in a hot bath for half an hour at a time four or even more times a day.

- Repeat the gentle rubbing massage several times a day.

- Within twenty-four hours—as the pain diminishes and you continue the pain-reliever medication, hot or cold applications, and massage—begin to move your arms and legs gently and arch and curve your back gently to avoid stiffness.

- As the pain eases further, start gentle exercises—pull in your stomach muscles, hold briefly, then relax and flatten the curve of your back against the mattress. Repeat about every half-hour.

For a relatively mild attack, bed rest may not be needed. But cut back on physical activities and use aspirin or acetaminophen, hot or cold applications, and counterirritant and massage until the pain is gone.

Arch supports to help—flat-footed or not Surprisingly, arch supports are often effective for chronic back pain. Here's why and how:

• For many back pain victims, an important factor turns out to be "heel strike." Each time the heel hits the ground in walking or jogging, a shock wave passes through the body's skeletal system.

• The intervertebral discs in the spine are supposed to act as shock absorbers. But studies using special equipment to measure bone vibrations have shown that the muscle and skeletal systems of patients with low-back pain are less able to reduce the vibrations caused by heel strikes.

• When patients were asked to use commercially available arch supports, measurements showed a 42 percent reduction in incoming shock waves, and 60 percent of the patients in the study were completely free of pain after three to four weeks of use of the supports. By the end of a year, 90 percent were pain-free.

"The results surprised even us," reports Iowa State University researcher Dr. Arkady Voloshin, who conducted the study with Dr. Josef Wosk of Hillel Jaffe Hospital in Hadera, Israel. "We didn't expect such improvement. It gives us hope that we're moving in a promising direction in prophylactic treatment of low-back pains."

Seven other preventive aids
• When you sneeze, sneeze up rather than down.
• When you cough, arch backward rather than forward.
• Avoid twisting your back when you bend.
• Sit upright. If your work involves mostly sitting, use a chair that provides low-back support.
• Stand tall; it's good for the spine.
• Work at surfaces—benches, kitchen counters, the ironing board, and so on—of proper height. You can generally figure that if, standing erect, you can place the palm of your hand on the work surface without having to bend your arm or back, the work-surface height is right.

- In lifting, keep your back as straight as possible, the object close to body, and use your hips and knees rather than your back for bending.

   Three helps for homemaker low-back pain
- When doing dishes, open the cupboard door below the sink and keep one leg elevated on the cupboard ledge, thus relieving pressure on your spine by flattening your back.
- Slow down doing household chores. When vacuuming, for example, bend your knees and move your feet slowly rather than jerk them forward and back.
- In bed, to help ease pressure on your spine, curl up in the baby-in-the-womb position, with a pillow between your knees or behind your back, another hugged to your chest. Use a feather pillow (it yields more than a synthetic) to support your head.

BALDNESS

   Four bizarre old theories and a current one   Dozens of strange theories about what causes baldness in men have been offered. Not long ago, the *Journal of the American Medical Association* reprinted a paper it had first published in 1900 on "Some Theories of Baldness." Among them:
- Baldness results when an exceptionally active brain has used up the blood supply which should have nourished the scalp.
- Indigestion is the cause.
- Music affects hair growth and brass instruments—notably the cornet, French horn, and trombone—have a fatal influence and will depilate a player's scalp in less than five years. Plus, "baldness which is said to prevail among habitues of the front rows at theaters may be due to the proximity of the brass instruments or may be caught by some contagion from the players themselves."
- Loss of hair is a sign of high breeding.
   At least the last theory introduces the question of heredity

—and current scientific belief is that baldness is influenced by heredity.

According to the latest theory, each individual hair follicle is genetically programmed to respond to hormone influence. Depending upon how it is programmed, it may stop growing, grow faster, or be unaffected by hormonal activity. Beard, underarm, and chest hair are usually stimulated by hormones. But in some people the hereditary predisposition is such that scalp hair over time becomes resistant to hormone action. And if a man's forebears were bald, his chances of having such a predisposition are greatly increased.

Minimizing the progression

- Shampooing, even daily, will not increase hair loss—but vigorous scalp massage during shampooing or at other times should be avoided.
- Keep combing and other manipulation to a minimum; use a comb and brush for grooming purposes only.
- No special diet is needed or helpful; a normal balanced diet is adequate. In fact, according to Dr. Norman Orentreich, a New York University School of Medicine expert on baldness, "Excessive vitamin, mineral, and health food supplement intake can cause or aggravate hair loss. Wheat germ, for example, has the potential for aggravating loss rather than preventing it."

See also Scalp Massage.

BATHS (*See* BUBBLE BATHS; HEMOR-RHOIDS: Five Relief Aids; HOT SOAKS.)

BATH ITCH (*See* ITCHING: Relieving Bath Itch.)

BED

Choosing the type If you're planning to buy a new bed, what are the best types? Using volunteers and special instrumentation, a University of California Medical School, San Diego, researcher tested these types: the newest so-called "hybrid" waterbed, consisting of a central water core topped with foam padding; an orthopedic 720-coil mattress and box spring; a standard 500-coil bed; and a standard 10-inch-deep waterbed.

- The orthopedic bed and standard waterbed allowed desirably uniform pressure distribution over the entire body.

- The softer (500-coil) bed and hybrid bed supported only five points—the back of the head, shoulders, buttocks, calves, and heels.

- Suggests the researcher, Dr. Steven R. Garfin: Not only would any bedridden patient do well with a bed providing the most even pressure distribution to minimize the chance of tissue damage, but such a bed should be beneficial for the general public, contributing to more restful sleep.

- Garfin's own choice: "Never less than the 720 coil . . . and certainly never the hybrid type."

BICYCLE HANDS

Ending the numbness and weakness If you regularly ride a bicycle and experience numbness and weakness of one or both hands, the problem may lie with handlebar pressure on a nerve in the palm. Three measures can stop the symptoms and prevent recurrence, finds Dr. Norman Estin of Portland, Oregon:

- Install foam handlebar covers or wrap the handlebars with padded tape.

- Get cycling gloves that have extra padding on the palm area.

- Change hand positions often on long rides.

BINGE EATING (BULIMIA)

Controlling it With its episodes of huge overeating followed by self-induced vomiting, bulimia is often extremely difficult to overcome. But if you know people with the problem who haven't been helped by conventional therapy, they may want to consult with a doctor about the possible usefulness of antidepressant drug treatment.

At the New York State Psychiatric Institute, New York City, Dr. Timothy Walsh and other investigators have found antidepressant drug treatment effective in a first group of six women, aged twenty-one to thirty-seven, with three-to-fifteen-year histories of bulimia. Five binged three or more times a day, the sixth just twice a week. All had had symptoms of mental depression but had not benefited from individual or group psychotherapy.

On treatment with an antidepressant—either phenelzine or tranylcypromine—all six showed prompt improvement in mood, and bulimia frequency dropped to one or two episodes a month in one, less than once a month in another, and to no episodes at all in the remaining four (reported in the *American Journal of Psychiatry,* volume 139, page 1629).

BIRTHS

The moon's influence—or lack of it If you're expecting a child, is birth more likely to occur at the time of the full moon than any other time? Not according to a sizable study at the UCLA Hospital of all births that occurred during 51 lunar cycles. Included were 11,691 live births, of which 8,142 were natural (not induced by cesarean section or drugs). The live births included 136 sets of twins, 4 of triplets, 1 of quadruplets. There were also 168 stillbirths. In not one of four categories—all live births, natural live births, multiple births, and stillbirths—was the mean number of births above average on the date of the full moon.

BITES (*See* DOG BITES; INSECT BITES AND STINGS.)

BLADDER INFECTIONS

Shower versus bath Bladder infections (cystitis) are, for many women, a problem that recurs despite repeated antibacterial treatment. Could tub bathing be a factor in reinfection? Working with fifty women, each of whom had had as many as ten recurrences, Dr. Robert S. Gould of Wellesley, Massachusetts, prescribed a trial of showers, no tub baths. As long as they avoided the baths, thirty-four remained free of infection; twelve of the sixteen who had recurrences had resumed baths. In a second study, Gould found that only three of five hundred women with cystitis failed to benefit from antibiotics combined with showers instead of baths.

A matter of timing Although in many women bladder infections have been related to intercourse, and physicians usually advocate early voiding after having sex as a possible preventive measure, some studies have found no reduction of bacteria in the urine. Is the timing of urination critical? Yes, according to Dr. W. V. P. Hyde-Williams of the Windsor-Essex County (Ontario) Health Unit. Says Dr. Hyde-Williams: "In her book, *Understanding Cystitis*, Angela Kilmartin writes, 'There is one superb and vital piece of self-help in the incidence of cystitis related to intercourse. It cost me ten guineas in a Harley Street consulting room and saved my marriage. It is: Always pass an effective amount of urine within fifteen minutes of intercourse ending.'" Adds Dr. Hyde-Williams: "That brief interval has been found to be critical by many of the victims of postcoital cystitis I see in practice."

Other preventive measures Make it a practice always to completely empty the bladder without delay; wipe the perineum from front to back rather than back to front after voiding; drink at least six glasses of fluid daily; use adequate lubrication during intercourse.

See also Urinary Infections.

BLADDER TRAINING

Two ways to overcome stress incontinence Loss of urine on coughing, sneezing, lifting or laughing—called stress incontinence—troubles many women. Some leak urine while walking, jogging or running, jumping, climbing steps, rising from a seat, or even riding in a car over a bumpy surface. Either of two approaches can usually help:

• One involves three exercises: (1) voluntarily starting and stopping urinary strain during each voiding; (2) voluntarily closing the entrance to the vagina; and (3) squeezing the buttocks tightly together.

• The second consists of relatively simple bladder training. To begin with, urinate every hour. Then increase the interval by half an hour daily until voiding is done every four hours. More than 80 percent of women using the program have become free of incontinence, according to Dr. G. J. Jarvis of the Jessop Hospital for Women, Sheffield, England.

See Prostate *for bladder training for men.*

BLANKET, ELECTRIC (*See* ARTHRITIS: Relief with a Blanket.)

BLEEDING (*See* NOSEBLEEDS.)

BLISTERS

Preventing them They're especially common on the feet, more so in athletic people than in others. If you're prone to them, these three measures can help:

- Make sure your shoes fit properly—there should be one-quarter inch between the tip of your toe and the end of the shoe, and your heel should not slide upward.
- Apply petroleum jelly to areas prone to blistering before beginning activities.
- Wear two pairs of socks—the inner pair of a form-fitting, thin material; the outer of bulkier wool or a wool blend.

Treating them Don't. Leave them alone if they can be protected against breaking. The fluid within will gradually be absorbed by deeper skin layers and the skin surface will return to normal.

But if a blister is large or in an area, such as the foot, where it is likely to be broken:

- With soap and water, gently clean the blister and the area around it.
- With a needle sterilized over a flame, puncture the edge of the blister.
- Gently press the edges of the blister opposite the puncture site to force the fluid out slowly.
- Apply a sterile gauze pad and adhesive.

If a blister has already broken, wash the area with soap and water and apply a sterile gauze pad and adhesive.

BLOATING

Ear-y relief Next time you feel overstuffed and bloated after a meal, try placing a cold cloth over an ear for relief. It works because a branch of the same nerve, the vagus, which supplies the gastrointestinal tract, also serves the ear—and stimulating it in the ear has helpful effects in the gut, providing some relief for the bloated feeling.

BLOOD PRESSURE

Relaxing for a true reading Tense feelings when having your blood pressure measured can make the reading inaccurate and may suggest hypertension when, in fact, under normal conditions, your blood pressure is not elevated. To relax quickly, try deep breathing. Just two breaths, possibly because they serve both to relax muscles and create diversion, have produced a marked reduction of pressure in apprehensive patients, reports Dr. Hans H. Neumann of the New Haven, Connecticut, Health Department.

Taking your own blood pressure The instrument you use —a sphygmomanometer—consists of a column of mercury or other measurement indicator, a cloth bag to be wrapped around your arm, just above the elbow, and a rubber bulb. You'll also need a stethoscope.

• As you pump the bulb, the bag swells with air, squeezing the underlying artery in the arm until blood flow through the artery stops. At the same time, the air forces the level of the mercury or other indicator up.

• Now place the cone-shaped end of the stethoscope just below the bag on the inside of the arm; you will hear nothing since no blood is flowing through the artery.

• Next, turn the valve on the bulb, releasing air slowly from the bag; the mercury will begin to fall.

• As the air is released, a point is reached where the pressure of blood pushing against the bag overcomes the pressure from the bag that has been cutting off the flow. At this point, you will hear a sound through the stethoscope. The mercury reading at this moment is the upper blood pressure measurement—systolic pressure, which is the pressure in the artery during the beat of the heart.

• As you release still more air from the bag, the sound of blood pushing through the artery first becomes louder but then begins to fade.

• At the point where you no longer hear any sound, the mercury reading shows the diastolic pressure, the lower level of pressure reached when the heart relaxes between beats.

• You record the two pressure measurements in the form of a fraction, systolic over diastolic—for example, 140/80.

Taking pressure a simpler way   With a little practice, the standard method (just described) becomes simple to use. But if you find it cumbersome, a simplified method eliminates the need for a stethoscope.

• After inflating the bag on the arm, allow air to escape slowly until you feel a throbbing rhythmic pulsation in the arm under the bag. The reading at this point is the systolic pressure.

• At the point when, after further deflation of the bag, you no longer feel the pulsation, the diastolic pressure is indicated.

• The simplified technique can be as valid as the standard, according to Drs. M. L. Gelman and Cyrus Nemati of St. Elizabeth's Hospital and Tufts University School of Medicine, Boston.

Salt reduction to control blood pressure   Cutting back on salt intake can often be valuable. For example, 90 patients—all on medication for mild hypertension (up to 200 systolic, 95 to 109 diastolic)—participated in an Australian study. While half continued on their usual diets, half ate unsalted foods, including unsalted whole-meal bread and cakes made with potassium baking powder. Over the twelve-week period of the study, those on usual diets had to remain on full medication to control pressure; the low-salt group finished on half the initial amount of medication adequate for control, and one-third of them were able to go off medication entirely.

Pressure, potassium, and the kitchen   Although most of us get more than enough salt in our food, we may not get enough potassium. And recent studies indicate that a better potassium-to-salt ratio may help control blood pressure—and adult-onset diabetes as well. As the following results show, food preparation can influence the ratio for the better:

• When potatoes, peeled or unpeeled, are boiled, they lose as much as 50 percent of their potassium—and, if peeled, they absorb about half of the sodium (salt) in cooking water.

- When potatoes are steamed, however, as little as 3 percent of natural potassium is lost and no sodium is absorbed.
- The same is true for carrots, beans, and peas.
- Further studies are expected to find the same for fish with its very high potassium content.
- Overall, say the University of Lund, Sweden, investigators who did the food preparation studies, if steaming or use of a microwave oven were a general habit, we'd get 33 percent more potassium in relation to sodium.

Dietary fat and pressure Changing the amount and kind of fat appears to be a promising way to treat and prevent high blood pressure without drugs. In a study by U. S. and Finnish researchers, a group of hypertensive patients undertook a diet low in fat and with a high polyunsaturated-to-saturated fat ratio, using margarine high in polyunsaturates, skimmed milk, lean meat, low-fat sausage, and low-fat cheese. Over a six-week study period, blood pressures fell from a mean of about 151/99 to 139/88.

See also Salt; Weight.

BOILS

Five keys to effective home treatment
- Don't squeeze. Don't handle roughly. A boil is a local staphylococci bacteria infection that starts under the skin, forms a pus-filled pocket, and eventually ruptures, drains, and heals. Squeezing or rough handling, however, may push the infection in deeper.
- Apply warm, moist soaks to hasten bringing the infection to a head. The soaks also soften the skin for rupture. Apply several times a day.
- Once rupture occurs and drainage begins, continue soaks.

- Wash the entire skin often, soaping thoroughly, to help avoid reinfection.
- If fever accompanies the boil, or the boil occurs on the face or is very painful and slow in coming to a head, your physician may prescribe an antibiotic or lance the boil to permit drainage.

Stopping recurrent boils The bacteria producing repeated boil outbreaks may lie too deep within the skin for removal by soap and water, but not deep enough to respond to antibiotics taken by mouth. In that case, your physician can prescribe applications of an anhydrous ethyl alcohol solution of aluminum chloride (Xerac AC). University of Pennsylvania, Philadelphia, dermatologists have found it consistently effective for patients previously treated ineffectively with topical antibiotics, antibacterial soaps, and antibiotics by mouth. It has eliminated boils on the buttocks, an area where moisture, rubbing, and pressure encourage growth of boil-producing bacteria.

BONE THINNING (*See* OSTEOPOROSIS.)

BOWEL RUMBLING

Four measures to help undo it when it's undue All bowels rumble to some degree. "Borborygmus" is the descriptive, onomatopoetic medical term for the sounds. They stem from intestinal wall contractions and the movement of gas and liquid. Some quieting steps you can try when the normally soft, gurgling sounds become something more:
- Eat something. Although you may not be hungry, bowel growl sometimes arises from anticipation of eating.
- If possible, lie down briefly—on your back or right side —and apply light pressure to the abdomen.

- Minimize your intake of carbonated beverages.
- As much as possible, avoid air swallowing (see Air Swallowing).

BREAKFAST (*See* FATIGUE: Fatigue and the Slighted Breakfast).

BREAST CANCER (*See* CANCER.)

BREAST ENLARGEMENT IN MEN (*See* GYNECOMASTIA.)

BREAST DISEASE, FIBROCYSTIC

What it is The most common noncancerous breast condition in women of childbearing age, fibrocystic breast disease is estimated to affect 20 percent of women aged twenty-five to fifty. It produces breast lumps, tenderness, and pain, which tend to worsen just before the menstrual period begins and to subside after it ends. The disease appears to be an exaggerated response to the hormones that regulate the menstrual cycle, and it usually clears up after the menopause.

Medical help A medical examination can make certain that breast lumps are noncancerous.

Relieving discomfort Aspirin or the nonaspirin pain reliever, acetaminophen, can provide relief.
Some women have found that by eliminating substances containing caffeine and similar chemicals (called methylxan-

thines), they are less likely to have pain and tenderness and to develop cysts (fluid-filled lumps).

Note that coffee, tea, and most cola and many other soft drinks have caffeine in them and many drugs, both prescription and nonprescription, contain methylxanthines. Here is a list of common substances with these chemicals:

- Foods: chocolate, cocoa, coffee, colas, tea, and other beverages containing caffeine (read labels).
- Prescription drugs: Cafergot, Darvon Compound, Empirin with Codeine, Emprazil, Fiorinal, Migral, Percodan, Repan, Soma Compound, and Synalgos.
- Nonprescription drugs: Anacin, Anorexin, Appedrine, Aqua-Ban, Bromo Seltzer, Cope, Dexatrim, Dristan, Empirin, Excedrin, Midol, No Doz, Sinarest, Stanback Analgesic Powders, Triaminicin, Vanquish.

Vitamin E   According to some recent medical reports, vitamin E may be helpful in about 70 percent of women in combating fibrocystic disease. You may wish to check with your doctor about this. The dosage used successfully in trials by Dr. Robert London of Sinai Hospital, Baltimore, has been six hundred international units daily.

BREAST PROSTHESIS

An inexpensive, homemade one   For use after mastectomy, many types of prostheses are available. But the *British Medical Journal* reports an inexpensive—and effective—one that can be made at home. A cotton bag roughly the shape of the breast is filled with bird seed until it matches the size of the remaining breast. Held in place under the normal brassiere, it has five advantages:

- It can be made to the exact size required.
- It is the same weight as the normal breast.
- The seed falls into the shape of the breast.

- The prosthesis alters its shape and position with movement as the normal breast does.
- The cost is inconsequential.

BREAST SELF-EXAMINATION

How to proceed   A good time for self-examination is immediately after menstruation has ended, when the breasts are normally soft. Follow these steps:
- Looking in a mirror, raise both arms over your head so the sides of the breasts become visible. Note whether one breast looks higher than the other or one seems larger than it was the previous month.
- Using the right hand on the left breast and vice versa, gently push the breast back against the chest, feeling for any small lumps.
- Feel the armpits for any swelling.

A helpful tip   If you're not quite clear about what a breast lump or cyst would feel like, you can try this practical "tongue in cheek" demonstration suggested by Dr. Marvin H. Levick of Pittsburgh, writing in the professional journal *Consultant*. Just press your tongue against your cheek and feel the bulge with your fingertips; a lump or cyst in the breast feels much the same.

The value   How useful breast self-examination can be— even when done as infrequently as three times a year—can be seen in the results of a State University of New York Downstate Medical Center, Brooklyn, study that included 996 breast cancer patients.
- More than 48 percent of women who had examined their own breasts at least three times a year were diagnosed before cancer had spread to underarm lymph nodes—compared with 38 percent who rarely did self-exams and 33 percent who never did.

- Distant spread of disease occurred in 2.7 percent of women examining their breasts monthly compared with 14.6 percent among those who never examined themselves.
- The earlier diagnosis made possible by self-examination translated into a 10 percent reduction in death rates within five years (after which cure is considered likely) for white women and a 17 percent reduction for nonwhites, in whom, generally, breast cancer has been found later than in whites.

BREATHING, EXCESSIVE (HYPERVENTILATION)

A dozen symptoms Hyperventilation—breathing too deeply or too rapidly, or both, without conscious awareness— is often responsible for one or many of the following: seeming shortness of breath, pounding heart and racing pulse, light-headedness and giddy feelings, numbness or "pins and needles" sensations, abdominal cramps, weakness or even fainting, chest pain, anxiety and tension, swallowing difficulty or a sensation of a lump in the throat, muscle pains, trembling, and blackouts. The symptoms are caused by abnormal alkalinity in the bloodstream created by the excessive loss of carbon dioxide, which is given off during hyperventilation.

A double-check you can do If you experience any of the symptoms just noted and suspect that hyperventilation might be responsible:
- Deliberately overbreathe, taking deep and rapid breaths. Commonly, if hyperventilation is responsible, this will bring on the usual symptoms within a few minutes.
- If the symptoms appear, confirm they're from hyperventilation by rebreathing in a paper bag held over the mouth and nose. That forces you to inhale back the excess carbon dioxide

blown off during hyperventilation, and the symptoms should subside.

Five aids for stopping hyperventilation
- Use rebreathing in a paper bag to relieve an attack.
- Breathe slowly through the nose with the mouth tightly closed when an attack threatens.
- If slow breathing fails, try breath holding.
- Running in place briefly may provide relief.
- If you're a frequent hyperventilator, you're likely to benefit by changing your method of breathing to the diaphragmatic type, emphasizing use of the abdominal muscles and diaphragm.

Diaphragmatic breathing—how to achieve it For this kind of breathing the abdomen and lower chest are relaxed and the abdomen is pushed out with each breath. As the abdomen protrudes, the diaphragm—the dome-shaped muscle of breathing that separates the chest from the abdomen—has more room to descend, thus allowing more room in the chest for the lungs to expand. Diaphragmatic breathing is slow, deep, and effective. It takes some conscious effort for a time before it becomes habitual.

BREATHLESSNESS

Leaning forward to help When emphysema or some other chronic lung disease produces breathlessness, a simple form of relief is to take a "leaning forward" position while sitting, with the hands or elbows resting on the knees. That helps, according to studies at the Hines (Illinois) Veterans Administration Hospital, by compressing the abdomen, which then stretches the diaphragm upward, improving its ability to make breathing more effective for someone with this condition.

BRUXISM (*See* TEETH: Tooth Gnashing.)

BUBBLE BATHS

A risk for children Bubble bath products may be harmful unless their use is supervised by parents. A Stanford University (Palo Alto, California) dermatologist finds that bubble bath materials, especially their detergent components, can cause skin irritation and outbreaks and even bladder inflammation and blood in the urine in young children who use excessive amounts of bubble bath or who soak too long in the tub. The products are probably safe if used according to label directions, but youngsters should not be allowed to mix their own bubble baths or to remain in the tub much longer than for an ordinary bath.

BURNS

Understanding the three degrees
- A first-degree burn—for example, from sun exposure, light contact with a hot object, brief scalding with water—is superficial. Only the skin's outer surface—red, dry, painful, mildly swollen—is involved.
- A second-degree burn—for example, from severe sunburn, a flash from gasoline or kerosene, a spill of boiling water —penetrates deeper, into lower skin layers, and produces redness or mottling, blisters, oozing, wetness, swelling, and pain.
- A third-degree burn—for example, from ignited clothes, exposure to a flame, an electrical current, or a hot object—involves not only the skin but tissues below. Often, because pain nerves are destroyed, there may not be severe pain in the burn area itself, but the burn margin may be painful. The skin is swollen, usually pale white or charred black, and often underlying tissue is exposed.

Home treatment *A third-degree burn must have imme-diate medical attention.* This is seldom necessary for a first-degree burn and may not be for a second-degree burn that is not extensive and does not involve face or hands. For first- and second-degree burns:

- Apply cold water or immerse the burned area in cold water until the pain stops.
- Reapply cold if pain returns. Besides providing relief, cooling may speed recovery.
- Do not break any blisters and do not apply antiseptic or anesthetic sprays or ointments.
- If necessary, after the cold applications, apply a layer of nonadherent sterile gauze, such as petrolatum gauze (avail-able in most drugstores).

Easing a burned tongue with sugar Next time you ex-perience that common discomfort—a tongue burned by hot food or drink—try sprinkling a few grains of sugar on the painful site. An Arizona physician reports that it's a practical way to relieve the misery and you can repeat it as often as necessary.

Reset that water heater Scalding is the most frequent cause of burns, with children under five most at risk, adults over sixty-five coming next. And thousands of devastating burn injuries could be prevented each year if home water heaters were set at lower temperatures. Here are facts from a study by Dr. Murray L. Katcher of the University of Wiscon-sin, Madison:

- Parents often are unaware that young children can turn on potentially fatal hot water—and unaware, too, of the dan-ger of burns from hot tap water.
- Older people with slower reaction times—and, in some cases, with decreased strength or disability—can find it diffi-cult to get away from hot-water exposure rapidly enough.
- The problem: Many water heaters are preset by manu-facturers at dangerously high temperatures—commonly, 150°

F for electric heaters and 140° F for gas heaters. At these temperatures, third-degree burns destroying the entire skin layer may occur after just two to five *seconds* of exposure. In contrast, at 120° F, it would take ten *minutes* of exposure to cause a third-degree burn.

• Reset a gas heater to the "low" setting, an electric heater to 120°, urges Dr. Katcher.

• To be safe, check water temperature with a thermometer before placing a child in the tub—and turn off hot water first so cold water can cool the faucet and help prevent hot drips onto the child.

• Note, too: Although it is commonly thought that high temperatures are needed for automatic dishwashers, the majority of dishwashing detergents tested in recent studies, according to the *American Journal of Public Health,* provided good to excellent cleaning results and met public health germ-kill standards at temperatures as low as 100° F.

BUTTERMILK (*See* GAS PAINS: Eight Helps for an Acute Gas Episode.)

CAFFEINE (*See* BREAST DISEASE, FIBROCYSTIC; HEADACHES; GUIDELINES: CAFFEINE IN BEVERAGES, FOODS, AND DRUGS.)

CALCIUM (*See* OSTEOPOROSIS.)

CALLUSES

Safe, simple home treatment for even thick types
Calluses—dead, hard, thickened skin—are caused by contin-

ued injury. In turn, they produce pain through pressure on sensitive underlying areas. To treat them:

• Don't try to pare them with a knife or blade; that can be hazardous.

• Instead, use fine sandpaper or an emery board to reduce them. Even thick calluses respond well. They can be sanded as often as necessary, stopping short of exposing sensitive skin, advises Dr. Peter H. Gott of Lakeville, Connecticut.

CALORIES

Figuring ideal weight and calorie needs

• For a woman, a simple rule of thumb to determine ideal weight: Begin with a base weight of 100 pounds for 5 feet of height and add 5 pounds for each additional inch. That's the ideal weight for an average body frame—for example, 120 pounds for a 5'4" woman. For a small body frame, subtract 10 percent from the total; for a large frame, add 10 percent.

• For a man, use 106 pounds as base weight for 5 feet of height, add 6 pounds for each additional inch. That's the ideal weight for an average body frame—for example, 166 pounds for a 5'10" man of average build. For a small frame, subtract 10 percent; for large, add 10 percent.

• For your basal calorie need—the number of calories you burn up at complete rest—just add zero to your ideal weight. For 166 pounds, for example, you need 1660 calories a day to maintain your weight if, theoretically, you remain at complete rest.

• Actual calorie need will be larger than basal. If you're sedentary, add one-third again to basal calorie need. If you're moderately active, getting about ninety minutes of exercise a week, add half again. If you're athletic, running or jogging about five miles a day, you can double your basal calorie requirement and still maintain weight.

Eight painless calorie cutbacks If you're overweight, it's remarkable how much you can reduce with some not-likely-to-be-missed omissions. Examples of what you can accomplish over the course of a year:

- Eat one less pat of butter or margarine daily and you lose three and a half pounds.
- One less slice of bread a day can mean a six-pound loss.
- Omit a single twelve-ounce can of beer once a week and you eliminate two and a half pounds.
- Skip ten potato chips a week for a loss of one and a half pounds.
- Forgo half a slice of pie twice a week for a three-and-a-half-pound loss.
- Omit two slices of bacon once a week and you lose one and a half pounds.
- Omit two doughnuts a week for a four-pound loss.
- Cut two teaspoons of sugar a day and you lose three pounds.

Eight easy calorie-saving substitutions

- Instead of a 3-ounce hamburger on a bun (400 calories), try 3 ounces of roast beef on a roll (300 calories) for a saving of 100 calories.
- Take your shrimp boiled (6 ounces, 200 calories) rather than fried (6 ounces, 380 calories) for a saving of 180 calories.
- Have broiled chicken (6 ounces, 257 calories) instead of fried (one-half chicken, 464 calories) for a saving of 207 calories.
- Rather than a granola-type cereal (500 calories), take, say, a cup of cornflakes (95 calories) for a saving of 405 calories.
- Eat a sweetened baked apple (160 calories) instead of apple pie (410 calories) for a saving of 250 calories.
- Replace twenty French fries with a medium-sized baked potato for a 180-calorie saving.
- Poach or boil an egg for a 35-calorie saving over fried.
- Nibble on five sticks of raw carrot instead of five crackers for an 85-calorie saving.

Seven tactics for calorie cutting in restaurants

• Start with sipping club soda with a twist of lemon instead of a mixed drink before dinner.

• Instead of snacking from the bread basket while waiting for your meal, sip water.

• Order roasted, baked, grilled, or broiled meats, and avoid casseroles or mixed dishes with gravies or sauces.

• Ask for a dish of "au jus" from the meat to have with your baked potato instead of sour cream, butter, and bacon bits.

• Choose a green salad instead of a cream soup—and ask for oil-and-vinegar dressing in cruets so you can add dressing sparingly.

• If possible, ask for children's portions; otherwise, leave part of your food.

• Don't take the dessert just because it comes with the meal.

See also Guidelines: Calorie Content of Foods; Calories in Alcoholic and Carbonated Beverages.

CANCER

Breast cancer risk and diet A number of factors influence risk, but the following possible diet influences emerge from a National Cancer Institute study of dietary histories of 577 women, aged 30 to 80, with breast malignancy, and of 826 disease-free women:

• The more frequent the consumption of beef and pork, the greater the risk.

• The more frequent the eating of sweet desserts, the greater the risk.

• Risk was also increased with the use of butter at the table and frying with butter or margarine as compared with use of vegetable oils.

• 77

Breast cancer detection measures Final results of a five-year screening of more than 280,000 American women for breast cancer show that 88.9 percent of the 3,557 malignancies uncovered were found by mammography. And mammography (breast X-ray)—recently much improved, with the radiation dose greatly diminished—was especially valuable in discovering the smallest cancers responding most favorably to treatment.

Based on the findings, the American Cancer Society now makes these recommendations:

• Any woman with a breast mass or persistent discomfort, nipple discharge, or other symptoms should have a thorough breast examination including mammography.

For other women without symptoms:

• Those twenty years old and older should perform breast self-examination monthly.

• Women aged thirty-five to forty should have a baseline mammogram to serve for comparison later.

• Those under fifty should consult their physicians about possible need for mammography.

• Women over fifty should have a yearly mammogram when feasible.

• Women with personal or family histories of breast cancer should consult their physicians about possible need for more frequent examinations or about beginning periodic mammography before age fifty.

Carotene and cancer—a protective dietary factor Beta-carotene, a natural pigment in some foods, can be converted by the body to vitamin A. Studies indicate that inadequate amounts of dietary vitamin A—and, particularly, of the provitamin A, beta-carotene—may markedly increase susceptibility to lung cancer.

This is the best current advice of cancer authorities:

• Avoid excessive amounts of either beta-carotene or vitamin A. Undue quantities of the provitamin can cause skin yellowing; undue quantities of vitamin A can have poisonous effects.

- The prudent course for all apparently healthy adults—and especially those who are current or former cigarette smokers—is to include in the daily diet one or two servings of the vegetables or fruits rich in beta-carotene.
- Here is the carotene content of common foods in international units:

CAROTENE-RICH FOODS

Food	Serving	Carotene
Papaya	½ medium	8,867
Sweet potato	½ cup, cooked	8,500
Collard greens	½ cup, cooked	7,917
Carrots	½ cup, cooked	7,250
Chard	½ cup, cooked	6,042
Beet greens	½ cup, cooked	6,042
Spinach	½ cup, cooked	6,000
Cantaloupe	¼ medium	5,667
Broccoli	½ cup, cooked	3,229
Squash, butternut	½ cup, cooked	1,333
Watermelon	1 cup	1,173
Peaches	1 large	1,042
Squash, yellow	½ cup, cooked	900
Apricots	1 medium	892
Squash, hubbard	½ cup, cooked	667
Squash, zucchini	½ cup, cooked	600
Prunes	½ cup, cooked	417
Squash, acorn	½ cup, cooked	234

A vitamin to help prevent cervical cancer Vitamin C, according to preliminary evidence, may be of some value in reducing the risk of cervical cancer. Investigators at Albert Einstein College of Medicine, New York City, studied vitamin C intakes of a group of women with positive or suspicious Pap smears (a test for cervical cancer) and another group—comparable in age, race, number of children—who tested negative.

- Almost six times as many of the Pap-positive women as the others had daily intakes of vitamin C lower than the usual recommended daily allowance of sixty milligrams.
- More studies are needed but the investigators headed

by Dr. Sylvia Wassertheil-Smoller conjecture that women who are susceptible to cervical cancer might be able to protect themselves by taking vitamin C supplements so they get at least ninety milligrams daily.

Cervical cancer and the protective condom   Cancer of the cervix appears to be a venereal disease transmitted by intercourse, although the nature of the cancer-causing agent is still not established. And when the cancer is present, use of a condom may help stop progression and may even lead to regression of the disease, according to a study by Drs. A. Cullen Richardson and James B. Lyon of Atlanta of women with *premalignant* or *early malignant changes* in the cervix.

• Of 147 who were treated by surgery, all showed regression of the disease.

• But so did 136 of 139 women instructed to use a condom throughout intercourse and not otherwise treated.

• Any program for conservative treatment of cervical cancer, recommend the physicians, should include use of a mechanical barrier at intercourse.

Cancer and cooking methods   It's a complex area, but a clearer picture of how different cooking methods may produce substances with cancer-causing potential is coming from University of California, Berkeley, studies. These are the findings:

• Definite links between cancer and foods cooked in certain ways have not been found. But studies do show that high temperatures and longer cooking times for foods such as beef and eggs produce substances (called mutagens) that cause genetic mutation in bacterial test cells, suggesting that in sufficient doses these substances may contribute to causing cancer.

• Frying, grilling, and broiling have been found to produce the greatest mutagenic activity, followed by baking and roasting.

• On the other hand, very few mutagens have come from cooking methods that tend to retain the foods' own juices—such as simmering, stewing, boiling, or microwave cooking.

• Since we don't all have cancer from ingesting the mutagens in our diets, we either may not be absorbing them or we have defenses in our cells that protect us from their effects.

• One theory proposes that other foods, such as broccoli and Brussels sprouts, provide substances that stimulate defenses against the mutagens.

• Until more is known, researchers recommend, whenever possible, using slow, low-temperature cooking methods (from 280 to 360° F) that tend to boil foods in their juices.

Cancer—the quality of life afterward With improved treatments providing better cure rates for some cancers and increased length of survival for others, how well do patients do in terms of quality of life after treatment? In a major study, investigators at a leading cancer hospital, Roswell Park Memorial Institute, Buffalo, New York, followed up more than 1,500 patients treated there for various types of cancer: head and neck, colorectal, breast, urinary tract, leukemia, lymphoma, and malignant melanoma. Two-thirds report now being able to perform all usual activities; 61.9 percent consider themselves fully employable, another 14.7 percent employable on a limited basis. Only 1.5 percent require full-time nursing care; 89.6 percent have no need at all for such care.

See also Breast Prosthesis; Breast Self-Examination.

CANKER SORES

Four tips from dentists Responding to one dentist's plea for help, other dentists have reported favorite remedies for canker sores in the *American Dental Association News*:

• For fifty years, one reports, he has used an inexpensive, old-time preparation—tincture of myrrh and tincture of benzoin. Dabbed on as often as necessary with a cotton applicator, it provides immediate relief. Your pharmacist might compound it.

• Just rinsing with a weak solution of sodium bicarbonate is good for lessening pain until the sores disappear on their own, reports another.

• A third advises his patients to use a silver nitrate pencil, obtainable in almost any pharmacy. Applied to a sore, it immediately turns it white and ends pain.

• A fourth reports that after finding vitamin E oil useful for lip sores, he is getting good results with the oil for canker sores.

A physician's suggestion The only measure in his experience that reduces pain and speeds healing, a University of Pennsylvania, Philadelphia, physician has found, is a specific way of using the prescription antibiotic tetracycline. Empty the contents of one 250-milligram capsule into an ounce of water to make a solution. Saturate a cotton compress with it and apply it to the sores for fifteen minutes four to six times a day. Use a fresh solution daily. Healing usually occurs within a couple of days.

Using vitamins for canker sores Investigators at the National Institute of Dental Research report finding that nutritional deficiencies appear to be involved in at least one-seventh of people who suffer repeatedly from canker sores. Among 330 patients studied, 23 proved deficient in iron, 7 in the vitamin folic acid, 6 in vitamin B_{12}, and 11 others in combinations of such nutrients. Of 39 followed up over a 6-month period for response to iron or vitamin treatment, 34 benefited.

CARING FOR THE SICK

Thirteen ancient rules—still useful The following rules were found in an eighth century Irish manuscript and reprinted recently in the medical journals *Pediatrics* and *American Family Physician*

- No games are played in the house.
- No tidings are announced.
- No children are chastised.
- Neither women nor men exchange blows.
- There is no fighting.
- The patient is not suddenly awakened.
- No conversation is held across him or across his pillow.
- No dogs are let fighting in his presence or in his neighborhood outside.
- No shout is raised.
- No pigs grunt.
- No brawls are made.
- No cry of victory is raised. Nor shout in playing games.
- No shout or scream is raised.

CAROTENE (*See* CANCER.)

CARSICKNESS

Preventing it in children Car seats may help. A Baltimore City Hospital's pediatrician, Dr. Edward L. Schor, reports that one of his patients, a five year old, had suffered from nausea and vomiting during car travel but only when riding in the rear seat, not in front. Once a child's car seat was bought and placed in back, the sickness stopped.

"The only obvious change," notes the physician, "was an elevation of some twenty to twenty-five centimeters (about ten inches) in the child's riding position. This was enough to enable her to see out the front window. Before, the child's only view was of bobbing and vibrating objects within the car or of fast-moving scenery out the side window. Enabling her to see through the front window provided relatively still objects on which to fix her eyes."

See also Heat; Motion Sickness.

CHARCOAL (*See* GAS PAINS: Eight Helps for an Acute Gas Episode.)

CHEST PAIN

A bed tilt to help When a heart condition causes chest pain attacks during the night, a small tilt of the bed may help. Israeli physicians, working with ten patients experiencing as many as seven attacks per night, prescribed elevating the head of the bed by about ten degrees (blocks can be used) so that their feet were in a down position while they rested in a relatively flat position, head comfortably on a pillow. Eight of the patients experienced no further episodes; the other two had only one attack per night each.

CHILDREN

Treasured object attachments Worried because your youngster has formed a persistent attachment to some soft object—blanket, pillow, stuffed animal, or the like? Do such attachments, when they last for years, indicate emotional problems? No, report Dr. Miriam Sherman and other New York Hospital–Cornell Medical College investigators. When they checked on 171 normal children, they found that 54 percent had formed an object attachment in infancy and, of these, 49 percent still maintained the attachment until nine years of age. There were no significant behavioral differences between children who were and those who were not attached to an object, or between those who continued to use a soft object even after age nine compared with those who never used one at all.

Toy box accidents   If you're buying a toy box for your youngster, avoid one with a heavy, hinged lift-up lid. If the lid should fall accidentally, it may cause considerable injury to the child's head or neck. It did in four children treated by Tufts University School of Medicine, Boston, physicians. When they then went on to survey 312 families, the physicians found that 30 percent of those with hinged-lid toy boxes reported injuries compared with only 5 percent of those with open bins and 9 percent of those with sliding-door boxes. The latter two types, the physicians say, are best for children under five, who are at greatest risk.

See also Baby; Growth in Children; Obesity; Puberty; Running; Walkers, Infant.

CHOLESTEROL

Fiber cuts absorption   A clue came from the finding that in some guinea pigs unaffected by cholesterol in the diet (presumably due to genetics), intestinal transit time—the time for food to pass through the GI tract—was more rapid than in other guinea pigs that developed high blood cholesterol levels. High cholesterol levels in the blood, of course, have been linked with coronary heart disease. Following up the guinea pig clue, Italian researchers gave measured doses of radioactively labeled cholesterol to thirty-three volunteers—eight women and twenty-five men. On average, when the subjects received the drug metoclopramide, which speeds transit time, the time was reduced by 40 percent—and cholesterol absorption was cut by half. Dietary fiber—from vegetables, fruits, and whole grain breads and cereals—is known to speed intestinal transit. There have been medical reports, too, that it reduces blood cholesterol levels. Fiber's speedup of intestinal transit, it appears, can account for the potentially healthy effect on how much cholesterol is absorbed.

See also Shellfish; Guidelines: Cholesterol Content of Common Foods and Dietary Fiber Content of Some Foods.

CIRCULATION (*See* RAYNAUD'S (Finger) PHENOMENON.)

CLEANING AGENTS, HOUSEHOLD

A *mixture to beware of* Combining household cleaning agents is a common practice, but it can be dangerous. Never mix ammonia with a bleach containing sodium hypochlorite (such as Clorox). A resulting chemical reaction can release substantial amounts of irritant gases. In one recent incident, a woman who made such a mixture suffered severe lung inflammation and needed nine days of hospitalization.

CLUSTER HEADACHES (*See* HEADACHES.)

COFFEE

A *help for nasal stuffiness* Caffeine, a coffee ingredient, may help allergic rhinitis, the inflamed, stuffy nose accompanying hay fever and other allergic reactions. Recently, in a fortuitous discovery, an American medical student took two tablets of a caffeine-containing pain reliever for a headache and noticed that he also had relief from the nasal stuffiness he had been suffering. He then experimented on himself, sometimes using 140-milligram caffeine doses packed in gelatin capsules, at other times identical-looking capsules containing only sugar, not knowing which he was taking until he later broke a code he had set up. Sure enough, the caffeine significantly reduced the number of sneezes and overall discomfort. Soon after he reported this in a medical journal, Italian physicians noted that a cup of strong black coffee had been an accepted treatment for allergic asthma a century ago. And, they added, if today "coffee treatment" for allergic disorders may sound dubious, "the scientific evaluation of former treatments can sometimes advance medical knowledge."

No help "for the road" Despite the common notion, coffee does not counteract intoxication. Finnish scientists gave ten medical students three ounces of alcohol followed by the caffeine equivalent of four cups of strong coffee. Ten others received the alcohol plus decaffeinated coffee. In both groups, equilibrium, hand–eye coordination, simulated driving skills, and visual reflexes were impaired. Caffeine failed to lower blood alcohol concentration and to counteract alcohol's effects on the nervous system. The effects of alcohol peaked 90 to 120 minutes after drinking, dissipated slowly, and alcohol blood levels had not fallen below the legal intoxication level by three hours later in both groups.

See also Hangover; Heartburn; Guidelines: Caffeine in Beverages, Foods, and Drugs.

COLDS

The contagious period It lasts from two days before cold symptoms appear up to three days after they appear.

Preventing the surprising, most common form of spread Although the common cold may be spread by coughs and sneezes, it's more likely to be by fingers or hands through direct skin-to-skin contact or even through touching surfaces contaminated with cold viruses. To reduce the risk of catching a cold, especially when someone in the family has one:

- Consider hand washing as at least as important, maybe even more so, as covering up coughs and sneezes.
- Avoid eye rubbing and nose picking as much as possible.

Studies have found that in only 8 percent of people with colds is any virus expelled in a cough or sneeze, but in 40 percent the virus is shed onto their hands. And active viruses have been retrieved as long as three hours after being deposited on wood, stainless steel, and Formica surfaces and on such synthetic fabrics as Dacron and nylon. (Viruses seem to last for shorter periods on porous fabrics such as cotton cloth and facial tissue.) Nor does drying affect virus viability. In one study, four of eleven people got colds after touching their nasal mucous membranes with fingers contaminated by rubbing a dried drop of virus.

What vitamin C may do Controversy continues over the vitamin's ability to combat colds. Some investigators report little, if any, value. Nevertheless:

- According to Nobel Laureate Dr. Linus Pauling, the original proponent of the anticold value of the vitamin, regular intake of at least 200 milligrams a day for everyone, possibly 1,000 milligrams or more for some, provides some protection, almost halving the amount of common cold illness. And, according to Pauling, a high intake—1,000 to 2,000 milligrams hourly at the very first sign of a cold (the first shiver, sneeze, or sniffle) can often help the body to throw it off.
- In one study by another investigator, 622 volunteers were divided into two groups. One group received 500 milligrams of vitamin C once a week plus 1,500 milligrams on the first day and 1,000 on the next four days of any illness. They had less severe illness and spent 25 percent fewer days indoors because of sickness than members of the other group who, for comparison, received a look-alike but inert preparation.

When a cold strikes Aspirin or acetaminophen (aspirin substitute) is helpful for a fever and muscle aches. Standard treatment for adults is two five-grain tablets every four hours, especially in the afternoon and evening when fever, aches, and other discomfort tend to be most pronounced. Drink fluids. More fluid is needed when fever is present. Fluids also make mucus more liquid and may help avoid bronchitis, ear infection, or some other complication. A vaporizer can also help to liquefy secretions.

To shorten the life of a cold-associated cough Drape a dry towel over your head and stand over a steaming tea kettle, being very careful not to burn yourself. Inhale the steam deeply for several minutes. Do this every two hours and it's likely to help loosen up your chest, liquefy your cough, and make you more comfortable.

What chicken soup can really do Scientific studies indicate chicken soup—often called "Jewish penicillin"—*does* have value.

• One example: Expectorant drugs are often used for bronchitis and other respiratory diseases because they stimulate secretions and increase expectoration. At UCLA Medical Center, Dr. Irwin Ziment has shown that chicken soup—if it has pepper, garlic, and maybe some curry powder in it—has the same effects.

• Another: At Mt. Sinai Medical Center, Miami Beach, Dr. Marvin A. Sackner, using special measuring instrumentation, has demonstrated that chicken soup speeds nasal mucus flow during the common cold, helping to get rid of the disease organisms. Other hot beverages speed the flow, but chicken soup works best.

Surprising results of cold studies
• Contrary to the popular notion, becoming chilled apparently does not influence susceptibility to, or the course of, a

cold. In one study, volunteers stood either naked in 60° F temperatures for four hours or clothed in 10° F temperatures for two hours. When both groups were exposed to cold viruses, there was no difference in either the incidence of colds or degree of severity.

• Parents are commonly supposed to get more colds because of their children. Not so. Adults with no children have been found to experience about the same incidence of colds as those who have children.

See also Flu or Cold?; Nasal Congestion.

COLD SORES/FEVER BLISTERS

A *possible help* Lysine—one of the building blocks of protein—may inhibit growth of herpes viruses that cause cold sores and fever blisters.

• In a study by a UCLA School of Medicine investigator, 43 of 45 people, aged 4 to 60, all with frequently recurring sores, stopped having them when given lysine in doses of 312 to 1,200 milligrams daily. Lysine is not a cure; it only suppresses the viruses. After remaining infection-free while on lysine, patients had lesions return within one to four weeks after stopping use. Is lysine safe? No known adverse reactions occurred in up to three years of follow-up.

• Actually, the human diet contains another protein building block, arginine, which may be involved. Some foods are relatively low in lysine, high in arginine; others have the opposite ratio. It appears that a high intake of chocolate, nuts, seeds, and possibly cereals can produce a high arginine-to-lysine ratio, which may favor herpes virus lesions. On the other hand, foods such as dairy products and yeast, which are high in lysine, may discourage herpes infection—which may be why infants have little trouble prior to weaning from a predominantly milk diet.

• Victims of repeated cold sore/fever blister outbreaks can help themselves by selecting foods with lysine in mind.

Lysine also is commercially available in capsule and tablet form.

COLD THERAPY (*See* ATHLETIC INJURIES.)

COLIC

Relieving it with a formula change Cow's milk—and, to a lesser extent, soy formulas—may be responsible for colic in some babies. Swedish investigators studied sixty infants hospitalized because of severe colic—with such symptoms as intense, convulsive abdominal pain, severe crying for several hours, gas formation and abdominal distension, and the desire to suck often. Eleven (18 percent) became symptom-free after a change from a cow's milk formula to soy fomula. An additional thirty-two (53 percent) continued to have symptoms on either cow's milk or soy formula but were freed of symptoms when fed a formula (Nutramigen) containing neither milk nor soy.

Relieving it with a change in mother's diet When a breast-fed baby develops colic, a diet free of cow's milk for the mother should be the first treatment tried, urge Swedish pediatricians. In their study, reported in the American medical journal *Pediatrics*, when mothers of sixty-six colicky, breast-fed infants stopped drinking milk, the colic disappeared within one to three days in thirty-five of the babies. And when, as a further test, milk was reintroduced into the mothers' diets, most of the thirty-five became colicky again within eight hours.

COMPUTERS (*See* TV–COMPUTER HOOKUPS.)

COMPRESSES, HOT

Slow-cook them If you have a "slow cooker" or crock pot, next time you need to apply hot moist compresses, turn the pot on "high," drop in a damp towel, and leave the lid off. The cloth will heat to the proper temperature almost immediately, reports Dr. Janice F. Gable of Konnarock, Virginia. And if two compresses are needed, one can be kept hot and within reach while the other is being used.

CONSTIPATION

A surprising finding—a relationship to breast disease Severely constipated women often have damaged cells in their breast fluids that may indicate increased risk of developing breast disease. Studying nearly fifteen hundred women, University of California, San Francisco, investigators found that those who moved their bowels fewer than three times a week—the most constipated group in the study—had abnormal cells in their breast fluid more often than did other women in the study. Most women with such abnormal cells probably never go on to develop breast cancer, but the new findings add severe constipation to a long list of factors believed to be associated with breast cancer.

Tea and constipation If you're a heavy tea drinker and also suffer from constipation, there could be a connection. In a study with twelve healthy volunteers, Danish physicians allowed them unrestricted diets except for beverages. For one week, they were allowed two quarts of water daily; for another week, they drank two quarts of tea daily. The tea had marked constipating effects. Apparently a chemical found in tea, theophylline, can, in large amounts, expel a lot of fluid via the kidneys from the spaces between body cells where it is normally present. To compensate, the body absorbs more water from intestinal fluid, which leads to stool hardening, slowing of intestinal transit time, and constipation.

Six helps for eliminating constipation   Although it can be a symptom of disease, it rarely is. Common constipation is correctable, usually without drugs. Try the following:

- Add fiber to your diet—via vegetables, fruits, whole-grain breads and cereals, and bran (the kind available in health-food stores). This is a most important step.
- Get daily exercise—walking, jogging, swimming, or another activity.
- Drink plenty of fluids—eight or more glasses daily.
- On awakening, drink coffee or another hot beverage to stimulate the reflex that will produce a sense of urgency to defecate—and heed the call.
- Cut down and eliminate any laxatives if you're taking them.
- Use a bulk preparation, such as Metamucil, if ever you do need a laxative.

One physician's simple, effective treatment   For years Dr. Judith Weinstein of Los Angeles has used the following treatment in her pediatric/teenage practice with great success:

- Use equal proportions of bran and Metamucil—in amounts ranging from one to four tablespoons of each, once or twice a day, depending upon age, the size of patient, and the degree of constipation.
- In the morning, fill a glass halfway with cold juice, add the bran and Metamucil, stir well, then fill glass with more juice. It is easier to mix if the glass is only half full and, if not thoroughly mixed, the bran will remain dry and tend to stick in the mouth.
- Follow the mixture with a full glass of water; this is very important and must not be omitted.
- If there's no satisfactory relief in a few days, add one tablespoon each of bran and Metamucil. If necessary, increase by one tablespoon every other day until reaching a maximum of four tablespoons of each.
- If necessary, repeat the program in the evening as well, starting with one tablespoon each of bran and Metamucil and

increasing the amount daily by one tablespoon up to a maximum of four tablespoons of each.

- Once bowel movements become soft, wait two weeks, then decrease the proportions by half a tablespoon every week over a period of four to six months.
- Restart the program if, for any reason, the constipation recurs.

Says Dr. Weinstein, writing in the *American Family Physician:* "I have never had a patient who did not respond to this treatment unless some underlying pathology (disease state) was involved."

CONTRACEPTION (*See* ASPIRIN: Aspirin and IUD Contraceptives—Beware; CANCER: Cervical Cancer and the Protective Condom; DIAPHRAGM CONTRACEPTION; HEADACHES: Headaches and the Pill.)

COOKING (*See* CANCER: Cancer and Cooking Methods; MICROWAVE COOKING.)

COUGHING

How to make it effective when it's not It was a Chicago physician—himself subject to allergic asthma attacks complicated by bronchitis—who experimented until he found a coughing technique that could clear large numbers of mucus plugs. The technique:

- Exhale as completely as you can—forcing air out.
- With all the air expelled, cough hard a couple of times.
- Now take in a small amount of air and cough again a couple of times.

• Take in a little more air, cough again—and take in a little more air and cough again—and keep taking in still more air and coughing until large amounts of air are taken in and coughing is done in the usual way.

Using this technique, you should be able to feel the secretions moving up the air passages and being coughed out.

Cough medicines—expectorants and suppressants Expectorants are usually advised; they liquefy secretions and help get rid of unwanted material. Suppressants should be avoided as long as coughing is bringing up material or if there is a lot of mucus. Later, if the cough turns dry and hacking, a suppressant may be useful.

Read labels. Expectorant action is provided by such compounds as glyceryl guaiacolate, potassium iodide, and chloroform. Suppressant action comes from codeine or a codeine relative such as dextromethorphan hydrobromide.

See also Colds: To Shorten the Life of a Cold-Associated Cough.

CRAMPS (*See* LEG CRAMPS, NOCTURNAL.)

CROUP

A cold shower for relief Frightening for both parents and child, acute spasmodic croup attacks typically occur suddenly at night in two to four year olds after a relatively mild upper respiratory infection, producing hoarse, croupy voice or cough and breathing difficulty.

For quick initial relief until the child can be seen by a physician, do this, advises Dr. Adam G. N. Moore of Squantum, Massachusetts: Turn on the cold shower and sit in the bathroom with the child held comfortably in a sitting position on your lap. The cold mist and upright posture both help immensely.

CYSTIC FIBROSIS

The benefits of swimming Regular swimming can produce substantial benefits for children with cystic fibrosis. The inherited disease involves the pancreas, sweat glands, and respiratory system and leads to abnormally thick mucus that clogs the lungs. Chronic cough, rapid breathing, and persistent respiratory infection are among the symptoms.

Austrian investigators report a seven-and-a-half-week trial in which ten boys and girls, aged six to eighteen-and-a-half years, from the cystic fibrosis clinic of the University Children's Hospital, Graz, participated in seventeen hour-long swimming sessions in a heated pool. Nonswimmers were trained in shallow water, then integrated into the floating, swimming, diving, and group games.

Tests showed marked improvement in both the clearing of mucus and breathing function of these subjects. Both parents and children were enthusiastic, and in subsequent months, after the special program ended, most youngsters continued physical activity.

CYSTITIS (*See* BLADDER INFECTION.)

CYSTIC MASTITIS (*See* BREAST DISEASE, FIBROCYSTIC.)

DANDRUFF

Controlling it
• Ordinary dandruff is an excessive shedding of scalp skin cells, with moderate itching. It sometimes stops on its own. If not, there's no cure, but control is usually possible with an over-the-counter dandruff shampoo. Some of the

shampoos contain zinc pyrithione or selenium sulfide to help slow production of the scaling cells; others contain sulfur or salicylic acid to help lift the scales off more readily.

• If redness or inflammation occurs along with greasy scaling and itching, you may have more severe seborrheic dermatitis. A tar shampoo may help. If not, see a dermatologist.

DENTAL DECAY (*See* TEETH.)

DERMATITIS, SEBORRHEIC (*See* DANDRUFF.)

DIABETES

Fiber to help A high-fiber diet may help control blood sugar levels—and cholesterol levels as well. In a Temple University School of Medicine, Philadelphia, study with adult-onset diabetics, added fiber (ten grams—about one-third of an ounce—of wheat bran and twenty grams of guar daily) led to blood sugar level declines from a high of as much as 327 to a low of as little as 212, with blood cholesterol decreases from a high of as much as 287 to a low of as little as 170. The added fiber was well tolerated and improved blood sugar levels in patients whose levels were poorly controlled with usual diabetes treatment.

Wine drinking—four tips If you're diabetic and enjoy wine, most likely you can drink it in moderation, provided you take certain precautions:
• Choose dry vintages.
• Adult-onset diabetics requiring close control of carbohydrate (sugar and starch) intake should stick to low-carbohy-

drate dry types such as Burgundy, zinfandel, Chablis, dry Riesling or sauterne, rosé, or dry sherry.

• Because chronic excessive wine intake may lead to nerve inflammation in diabetics, wine intake should be held to no more than two glasses (four ounces) a day, recommends Dr. Peter H. Forsham of the University of California Medical School, San Francisco.

• Some diabetics taking the oral antidiabetic drug chlorpropamide may experience flushing, head and neck throbbing, headache, vomiting, sweating or chest pain when drinking wine, and should avoid it.

Insulin before breakfast The tendency for blood sugar to shoot up after eating can be reduced significantly in insulin-dependent diabetic children if insulin is injected thirty minutes before rather than immediately prior to breakfast, British doctors have found. Studying a group of diabetic children, aged ten to seventeen, they reported blood sugar concentrations significantly lower in blood samples taken up to three hours after breakfast when daily insulin injections were given half an hour instead of five minutes before the meal. So try giving the morning insulin injection before washing and dressing, rather than afterward.

DIAPHRAGM CONTRACEPTION

Avoiding risk of toxic shock Keeping a diaphragm in place for a prolonged period after intercourse may promote the growth of certain staph bacteria and increase the risk of toxic shock syndrome (high fever, vomiting, diarrhea, confusion, and skin rash), according to the following findings:

• At the State University of New York Medical Center, Buffalo, Dr. Elizabeth Baehler and other physicians reported that nineteen healthy, nonpregnant women showed significant increases in the bacteria after wearing sterile diaphragms covered with a spermicide for more than twelve to eighteen hours.

- Although none of the nineteen developed toxic shock syndrome, a patient seen previously developed the syndrome after wearing a diaphragm for forty-eight hours.

- For safety women should not leave their diaphragms in for longer than twelve to eighteen hours after intercourse.

DIARRHEA

Four helpful measures

- Loss of fluid, which leads to losses of sodium, chloride, and potassium, is one of the worst effects of diarrhea on the body. Adequate fluid intake is essential. Soup, crackers, toast, soft drinks, and mineral-fortified beverages all help, but overall fluid replacement is what really counts, so drink plenty of water, too.

- During bouts of diarrhea, certain foods should be avoided: those containing gastrointestinal stimulants such as caffeine, and anything served very hot or cold. In some people, beer and milk may aggravate diarrhea; and it may be wise to avoid fried and spicy foods.

- Chronic diarrhea sufferers often benefit from regular intake of bran, which tends to normalize bowel motility.

- If necessary, drugs can be used to relieve diarrhea. Kaolin-pectin mixture and bismuth subsalicylate (Pepto-Bismol) are old and helpful standbys in many cases. In more severe diarrhea, a prescription drug—such as diphenoxylate or loperamide—can provide substantial relief.

Three useful measures for traveler's diarrhea

- Used properly, an antibiotic, Vibramycin, can be an effective preventive measure. Your doctor can prescribe it in a dose of one hundred milligrams per day before you leave— and, advises Dr. Richard B. Hornick of the University of Rochester, you should take it the day *before* you leave since studies show that travelers are most likely to be contaminated the first day in a foreign environment.

● Pepto-Bismol may also be effective, but a large amount is needed. Two ounces, four times a day, has been used to prevent diarrhea in adults. For treatment, one to two ounces every thirty minutes for a maximum of eight doses has been found to decrease diarrhea.

● If diarrhea develops, this practical way to replace the fluid loss when abroad is recommended by the U.S. Center for Disease Control. Combine the following in one glass: eight ounces of orange, apple, or other fruit juice (rich in potassium which is lost in diarrhea); half a teaspoonful of honey or corn syrup (useful for absorbing essential salts); and a pinch of salt (contains sodium and chloride lost in diarrheal stools). Combine in a second glass: eight ounces of boiled or carbonated water and one-quarter teaspoon of baking soda. Drink alternately from each glass. Supplement with carbonated beverages, boiled water left to cool, or tea made with boiled or carbonated water. Avoid solid food and milk until you have recovered.

Dietetic foods and diarrhea If you eat a lot of dietetic foods and experience diarrhea, there could be a cause-and-effect relationship. Dietetic foods commonly contain substances known as hexitols (such as sorbitol and mannitol). On reaching the colon or large bowel, hexitols in large quantities can have a diarrheal effect. In one case, a young man experienced severe diarrhea for two weeks beginning at the time of daily use of dietetic foods. This diarrhea stopped when the dietetic items were discontinued.

DIET (*See* GUIDELINES.)

DOG BITES

Six tips about them Dogs are responsible for about 85 percent of all animal bites and most victims are children.

- The most likely age: Surveying 455 Denver families with 960 children, Eleanor A. Lauer, R.N., of the University of Colorado found that 194 of the youngsters had been bitten, more than half of them under five years of age.

- The biter: Contrary to what most parents believe, the biting dog was usually not a stray but belonged to a neighbor or the victim's own family.

- Breeds: A large proportion of the bites were by German shepherds, shepherd mixes, and mixed breeds weighing more than thirty pounds.

- To reduce risk: Small children should always be supervised when around dogs, including family pets.

- Also to reduce risk: Parents should use good judgment in choosing a pet—and in deferring their purchase until children are old enough to be trusted not to provoke an animal, either deliberately or by innocent activities that might seem threatening to a dog.

- If a large dog is desired, the Labrador retriever would be a good choice. In the Denver study, this breed lived up to its reputation for gentleness.

DOGS (*See* PUPPY FAT.)

DOUCHING

As an infection factor Excessive douching may be a factor in pelvic inflammatory disease and inflammation of the fallopian tubes. Studying 101 women with those diseases and 743 others free of them, researchers in New Haven, Connecticut, found that almost 90 percent of the afflicted women were vigorous douchers, compared with half that many among the others. Three times as many of the diseased women habitually douched more than once a week. There's a strong suspicion, the investigators note, that douching may contribute to ascent up the genitourinary tract by whatever disease organisms happen to be present in the vagina.

DRINKING (NONALCOHOLIC)

Balance that soft drink intake Soft drinks commonly contain phosphorus, an essential nutrient. When soft drink consumption is excessive, however, the phosphorus can deplete another essential material—calcium, in the bones. Over time, this can lead to the softening of bones (osteoporosis) and fractures; it can also shrink jawbones, leading to tooth loss or poorly fitting dentures. In a Washington State University, Pullman, study of thirteen soft drinks, all the colas and powdered drink mixes contained phosphorus while root beers, noncolas, and fruit-flavored carbonated beverages contained little or none of it. If cola drinks and beverages made from powders are part of your daily routine, make sure you get an ample supply of foods with a high calcium content. Top calcium sources include milk, cheese, and whole-grain breads.

No spills in bed For a bedridden patient, an ordinary aluminum beer or soda can with a keyhole top makes a practical drinking vessel, advises Dr. Maurice Rotbart of Torrance, California. The can is not likely to spill contents even when used without a straw, and it can be washed, sterilized, or thrown away after use.

Hot/cold drinks and the heart Hot and cold liquids are commonly considered bad for heart patients because of potentially dangerous effects on heart rate, heart rhythm, and blood pressure. But investigators at the Naval Regional Medical Center, San Diego, closely monitored a group of patients with severe anginal chest pain who were given hot and cold drinks, and another group who was given them within thirty-six hours after heart attacks. In no case in either group was there any change in heart rhythm or significant change in heart rate or blood pressure.

See also Alcohol; Coffee; Hangover.

DROWNING

Survival beyond six minutes For years it has been assumed that a drowning victim would die or have permanent brain damage if not revived within five or six minutes. But a number of recent medical reports show that individuals can survive without permanent disabilities for a much longer time, especially if the water is icy cold.

• One example: A twenty-three-year-old woman immersed for twenty-five minutes in Boston's Charles River. Resuscitation started immediately. Upon arrival at the hospital, her body temperature was still 14° F below normal. After two weeks of hospitalization, she had complete mental and physical recovery.

DRUGS

Should you use them beyond their expiration dates? A date of expiration appears on the label of many drugs. But is a drug dangerous after the expiration date? Here's the advice of an official of the Consumer Safety Office, Bureau of Drugs, U.S. Department of Health and Human Services, Food and Drug Administration:

We make no allegations that a product is "dangerous" if used beyond its expiration date. Rather, our position is that stability data submitted by manufacturers guarantee the potency to the expiration date and not beyond. Usually there is a margin of safety, so drugs generally retain varying degrees of potency for some time after the expiration date. Of course, storage conditions are important.

We feel that products should not be used beyond the expiration date, not only because of potential loss of potency but also because of the greater lack of assurance of other qualities, such as sterility, for example.

See also Antacids; Antihistamines; Headaches: Drugs and Headaches—Fourteen Possible Culprits; Heartburn: Certain Drugs May Bring on Heartburn; Medicine; Skin: Skin Rashes from Drugs; Guidelines: Drug Side Effects.

EARS

Itching—three helpful measures Possibly the most common reason for ear canal itching is a relative shortage of ear wax, finds Dr. Jeffrey C. Reynolds of Hays, Kansas. Because of a lack of adequate lubrication by wax, the skin becomes red and itchy, and may also be sensitive to cold or to wind blowing into the ear canal. The following simple treatment can be effective:

• Make certain all soap getting into your ears is cleaned out. Tilt your head to help.

• Use a mild saltwater solution to get out any soap that doesn't come out with head tilting.

• Apply an emollient such as baby oil or glycerine or an ointment such as 10 percent boric acid in lanolin, using your little finger. *Don't* use cotton-tipped applicators, such as Q-tips.

Ear noises and hearing problems—zinc to help In sensorineural hearing loss, inner ear structures undergo changes that interfere with perceiving or discriminating sounds. Ear noises—known as tinnitus—can result from the sensorineural changes or other hearing disorders or allergies. After first trying zinc treatment successfully with a tinnitus patient three years ago, Dr. George E. Shambaugh, Jr., of Northwestern University, Evanston, Illinois, has reported observing improvement in more than twenty other patients with hearing loss and tinnitus who were given six hundred milligrams of zinc sulfate daily by mouth.

Ear noises from a hair in the ear   As bizarre as it may seem, a hair lying free in the ear canal can be responsible for loud, disturbing noises. Three people with the problem were seen recently by Dr. George Goldman of the Massachusetts Institute of Technology Health Services, Cambridge. In one case it was as a result of a haircut two days before symptoms developed. When a hair intermittently brushes against the eardrum, it can produce a "distant, thunderous noise," which may be intensified by chewing or yawning. The hair may fall out on its own. If not, it can be removed readily by irrigation, forceps, or a cotton-tipped applicator.

"Swimmer's ear"—two preventive measures   This is an ear canal infection so common among swimmers that it got the name "swimmer's ear." It's caused by water remaining in the ear canal, containing organisms able to set up infection, with itching and pain. Once the infection develops, antibiotics are needed to eradicate it so you should see a doctor. To avoid the condition, try the following:

• For prevention, water must be removed from the canals after swimming or diving. Don't use cotton-tipped applicators. Rather, allow the canals to dry gently by fanning the openings to help. Even more effective, use a hair dryer. If necessary, shake your head vigorously or jump with your head tilted to one side to remove any trapped water.

• Another measure: One physician reports completely controlling swimmer's ear among his patients by suggesting they use a low-cost solution that can be made at home. Just add thirty drops of white vinegar to two tablespoons of boiling water. After swimming, put two drops of cooled solution in each ear.

Getting an insect out of an ear   Your best bet: Since insects are attracted to light, use light. If you're outdoors, turn the ear to the sun and gently pull the ear backward to help straighten the ear canal. If the sun isn't bright, turn on a bright light indoors and do the maneuver. It's important to use the light technique immediately. Don't poke in the ear with your finger or a cotton-tipped applicator; that decreases the likelihood the insect will fly out. If you get no results, it may be because the insect is stuck in ear wax; get medical help.

See also Air Travel; Hearing; Insect Bites and Stings.

EATING (*See* BINGE EATING; FATIGUE; GALLSTONES; GAS PAINS; MEDICINE.)

ECZEMA

Controlling the outbreak Itchy, sometimes oozing, sometimes blistering, an eczema skin outbreak may be caused either by contact with some material to which you are sensitive or by fungus infection. If it's skin sensitivity and the sources can be determined, avoiding them usually ends the problem. Some suggestions:

• To relieve mild eczema, try an over-the-counter cortisone cream, suggests Dr. Gary Brauner of Albert Einstein College of Medicine, New York City.

• If oozing is present, also apply warm tap water or Burow's Solution (obtainable in drugstores) compresses to help dry the eruption.

• If such treatment fails or if scabs form, infection may be present and medical attention is needed.

See also Skin.

ELBOW (*See* TENNIS ELBOW.)

EMPHYSEMA (*See* LUNG DISORDERS.)

ENEMA

The proper equipment The standard enema bag, also called a fountain syringe or douche bag, includes a bag, hose, shut-off clamp, a long plastic or hard-rubber douche nozzle that is fluted and has perforations, and a shorter smooth, straight enema nozzle. Another kind, a hot-water bottle, comes with a stopper to which accompanying hose, clamp, and nozzles can be attached. Rather than use the plastic or hard-rubber enema nozzle, many physicians recommend a soft-rubber rectal tube, size 22 French, which is more comfortable and provides better protection against injury. This can be ordered through your druggist.

Giving yourself an enema With the shut-off clamp closed, fill the bag about half full with lukewarm water.
- Raise the bag by its tab and, opening the clamp, direct the rectal tube into the washbasin until water comes through in a steady stream; then close the clamp. This removes air in the hose which otherwise can flow into the rectum and cause cramping.
- Hang the bag so its lower end will be about twelve inches above your hips when you administer the enema.
- Lubricate the rectal tube tip with lubricating or petroleum jelly or salad oil, or moisten it with water.
- Seated on the toilet or in the bathtub, or if you prefer lying on your side on bathmat, slowly and gently insert the lubricated tip with a twisting motion into anus, aimed toward navel, until it is two to three inches deep. To relax anal muscles it often helps to breathe deeply through the mouth or bear down as if to have a bowel movement.
- Open the clamp. You should feel fullness inside but no discomfort. If cramps develop, lower the bag (clamp still

open) to below hip level so gas and liquid can return into the equipment, thus relieving pressure and cramping. Relax with deep breathing and, when cramps are gone, hang the bag up again and finish the enema.

• Once the bag is empty, or you're at a point where you are unable to hold more water, close the clamp and withdraw the tube. If possible, wait a few minutes before expelling stool.

EPILEPSY

Outgrowing childhood seizures Many children do outgrow epilepsy. For fifteen to twenty-three years, Dr. Jean H. Thurston and other Washington University School of Medicine, St. Louis, physicians followed up 148 people who had been treated for seizures in childhood and taken off anticonvulsant medication after being free of seizures for at least four years. Of the 148, 107 (72 percent) have remained free ever since.

Increased risk of relapse, the study found, is associated with certain factors: epilepsy persisting for more than six years before being controlled; seizures involving half of the body (Jacksonian seizures); combinations of various types of seizures; and neurologic problems such as motor handicap or mental retardation. In such cases it is questionable whether medication should ever be withdrawn.

EXERCISE

Determining your "target zone" for exercise Any sound exercise program should start slowly and increase gradually in strenuousness over a period of weeks or months until a level that conditions the heart is reached. The optimum conditioning level should exercise the heart at 70 to 85 percent of your maximum heart rate.

Your physician can tell you what that rate is on the basis of a stress test. Or you can approximate it for yourself this way:

- From the number 220, subtract your age in years. For example, if you are 35, the maximum rate would be 185.
- Your "target zone"—the heart rate to be aimed for in exercising—would be 70 to 85 percent of 185, or in the range of 129 to 157 beats per minute.
- Below the "target zone" rate, you would get little heart conditioning effect from exercise; above that rate, the burden on your heart could be excessive and dangerous.

Measuring your heart rate It's simple but can be awkward at first. The heart rate—the number of heartbeats per minute—is essentially the same as the pulse rate.

- To take your pulse, apply the index and middle fingers of one hand to the upturned wrist of the other hand, at the thumb side where you can feel the pulse beat.
- Count the beats for ten seconds, then multiply by six.
- Take your pulse within fifteen seconds after you stop exercising to get a close approximation of the beat during exercise.

Breathing properly during exercise Although there is a tendency to hold the breath when you exercise against resistance—as in sit-ups, chin-ups, weight lifting, isometrics, and similar activities—it should be avoided. Breath holding interferes with normal blood flow by building pressure within the chest and abdomen. The proper procedure: Exhale while exerting force—for example, blow out while lifting a weight—and then inhale on completion—when the weight is brought down.

The need to keep going Physical activity, to be valuable, can't be sporadic; it has to be a regular, lifelong habit. Its benefits include an increase in the ability to clear fat from the blood and raised levels of a blood element, HDL_2 (high density lipoprotein), which is protective against heart disease and heart attack. But if you stop exercising for as little as three weeks, the blood may become "milky" with fat after each meal and HDL_2 levels may decline. Both the benefits—and the need to keep vigorous—have been demonstrated in a three-year study at Baylor College of Medicine, Houston.

Exercise as antidote for tension and stress "It has been said that a five-mile walk will do more good to an unhappy but otherwise healthy man than all the medicine and psychology in the world." That observation was made years ago by Dr. Paul Dudley White, distinguished heart specialist and physician to U.S. presidents.

More recently, at the University of Southern California, Los Angeles, Dr. Herbert de Vries compared the effects of exercise with those of tranquilizing drugs. In tense, emotionally upset people, muscles almost invariably become tense. Measuring the muscle tension provides an objective way to determine someone's emotional state and changes in it. De Vries found that as little exercise as a fifteen-minute walk provides more relaxation than a tranquilizer.

Exercise for weight loss—two little-known aspects
• Quite obviously, you burn more calories when you exercise. Not so obviously, you keep burning more afterward. For four to six hours after you stop exercising, body temperature and metabolism are higher and you continue to burn extra calories. It has been estimated that over a period of a year, the extra calories can amount to a weight loss of five to ten pounds for the average person.

• An appetite control center in the brain is responsive to blood sugar level, signaling hunger when blood sugar drops. During exercise, fat is released into the bloodstream and the body tends to burn more fat, less sugar. With less of a fall in sugar level, you won't be as hungry and won't eat as much.

Exercise for weight loss—how much, what kind
Analyzing twenty-seven studies in which people lost weight through exercise without dieting, Dr. Michael Pollock of the University of Wisconsin School of Medicine, Madison, found that you need to burn at least three hundred calories in workouts of at least thirty minutes each, at least three times a week, before the weight-loss effect begins.

Best for weight loss are continuous-exercise sports such as fast walking, swimming, cycling, ice or roller skating, disco or aerobic dancing, rope jumping, and cross-country skiing.

Exercise after childbirth—four tips

- Most women can safely resume jogging or other exercise within six weeks of delivery as uterus muscle tone and position return to normal, reports Dr. Edward C. Hill of the University of California School of Medicine, San Francisco.

- And, contrary to the fears of many women, postpregnancy exercise usually does not lead to prolapse—downward displacement of the uterus—advises Dr. Hill. Prolapse, in fact, is almost always traceable to tissue weakening or injury in childbirth, and if this has not occurred, exercise will not be harmful.

- Even if uterine prolapse is already present, there is no evidence that jogging worsens it, reports Dr. Christine E. Haycock of the New Jersey Medical School, Newark.

- Resume activities gradually, advises Dr. Haycock. If you're a runner, for example, proceed like a beginner. Start with a ten-to-fifteen-minute stretching routine—and, before going back to distance running, alternate between walking and jogging until reaching prepregnancy athletic condition.

Exercise and digestion Mild exercise soon after eating shortens stomach emptying time and may help relieve discomfort from overindulgence. But strenuous exercise at that time can temporarily stop stomach activity.

Exercise and celery—watch out Peculiarly, exercise soon after nibbling celery may not work out well for some people. Dr. Jordan Fink of the Medical College of Wisconsin, Milwaukee, has reported on a group of patients who experienced feelings of apprehension, itchy palms, wheezing, and faintness whenever they exercised vigorously—such as playing tennis for an hour or jogging for thirty to forty-five minutes —within three hours after eating celery. All proved sensitive to celery by skin test and all responded to treatment with epinephrine. But a good precaution—if you're one of the sensitive and have noticed discomfort during exercise that could be celery related—is simply to wait three hours after indulging in the nibbling before indulging in the exercise.

Exercise and proteins It is commonly thought that vigorous exercise demands an increased protein intake. But many investigations have failed to show any beneficial effect of a high-protein diet. These facts from the studies:
- Muscles actually hang on to their protein a little bit better when exercised.
- Protein is never a source of immediate energy and the body has no way to store extra protein as protein; if not used immediately, it is broken down by the liver and excreted by the kidneys. If you take in extra amounts, you not only may deny yourself other important nutrients but may make your liver and kidneys work harder needlessly.
- An amount of protein reasonable for a nonathlete is quite adequate for the athlete.

Preventing exercise injuries These tips from Dr. Gabe Mirkin, a sports medicine authority:

• Listen to your body. If you experience pain in one part and it gets worse as you exercise, quit and go home. If "exercising through pain" sounds romantic, "it's closer to stupid," says Mirkin. More than 70 percent of runners dropping out do so in the first six weeks because of an injury, and as many as 70 percent of women taking up aerobic dancing develop shin splints (pain in the muscles on the front of the lower legs). The reason for the high injury rates? "In these two activities and in others as well," says Mirkin, "beginners often don't stop exercising at the onset of pain."

• Space hard workouts two days apart. Vigorous activity takes a temporary toll on muscles—which is the reason for familiar morning-after stiffness. You ask for trouble when you repeat strenuous activity without a day's break. Alternatively, you can use different muscles on different days—for example, biking one day, swimming or running the next.

The fourteen most beneficial sports Under the auspices of the President's Council on Physical Fitness and Sports, seven medical experts evaluated fourteen popular forms of exercise in terms of their benefits for (1) heart and lung endurance, (2) muscular strength and endurance, (3) flexibility, (4) balance, (5) weight control, (6) muscle definition, (7) digestion, and (8) sleep. The following were judged, in order, to be most beneficial:

1. Jogging
2. Bicycling
3. Swimming
4. Skating
5. Handball or squash
6. Skiing—Nordic
7. Skiing—Alpine
8. Basketball
9. Tennis
10. Calisthenics

11. Walking
12. Golfing
13. Softball
14. Bowling

Six special notes about beneficial sports

• Jogging, running, swimming, and bicycling are especially valuable for improving cardiovascular fitness. When vigorous enough, skating and other activities can also be useful for that purpose.

• Handball, with its fast movements, can be superior to tennis for endurance and improving heart function and breathing. But it's exacting—not for anyone who is not in good condition.

• Skiing, which uses arm and leg muscles, improves balance and agility but may not do much for endurance, especially if downhill runs are short and a chairlift is used. Best for total body strengthening: cross-country skiing, both uphill and down.

• Tennis singles can be strenuous. Unless you've played recently, it's wise to get heart and leg muscles in shape with brisk walking and jogging before starting to play. Tennis can build endurance even in unskilled players who run all over the court to reach the ball. Doubles tends to be less valuable for endurance.

• Golf, while good exercise, doesn't do much for improving fitness since little more than one-third of playing time is usually spent walking. According to some studies, it may take twelve hours of golf to get the same conditioning effect as a one-hour brisk walk. Helpful: brisk walking, even jogging, between shots.

• Bowling is good for vision coordination, sometimes for relieving postural backaches from long hours at a desk—but it's too intermittent and not taxing enough to help with endurance and heart conditioning.

See also Arthritis; Breathing, Excessive (Hyperventilation); Fertility/Infertility; Fitness; Jogger's Nipples; Osteo-

TWENTY-FIVE RECREATIONAL ACTIVITIES AND THE ENERGY THEY USE

Light exercise 4 calories a minute	Moderate exercise 7 calories a minute	Heavy exercise 10 calories a minute
Dancing (slow step)	Badminton (singles)	Calisthenics (vigorous)
Gardening (light)	Cycling (9.5 mph)	Climbing stairs (up and down)
Golf	Dancing (fast step)	Cycling (12 mph)
Table tennis	Gardening (heavy)	Handball
Volleyball	Stationary cycling (moderately fast)	Squash
Walking (3 mph)	Swimming (30 yards a minute)	Paddleball
	Tennis (singles)	Jogging
	Walking (4.5 mph)	Skipping rope
		Stationary cycling (fast)
		Stationary jogging
		Swimming (40 yards a minute)

porosis (Bone Thinning); Pregnancy; Sleep; Tennis Elbow; Walking; and Guidelines: Sports and Activities Best Liked by Americans; Jogging and Running; Calories Expended Per Mile of Running/Jogging.

EYES

Five common misconceptions Not only the public but many medical professionals who are not eye specialists have these misconceptions, according to a University of Michigan, Ann Arbor, quiz of 300 doctors and 250 medical students:

• People who wear glasses need a yearly check to determine if a change of prescription is needed—believed by 83 percent of the physicians, 43 percent of the students. In fact, as long as you're satisfied with vision with present glasses, checking yearly for a change of prescription would be like going to a shoe store each year to see if you need a new pair of shoes.

● Children with reading difficulties are likely to have eye coordination problems and can be helped by special exercises —believed by 60 percent of the doctors, 80 percent of the medical students. Not so.

● Children sitting too close to a TV set may permanently harm their eyes. No.

● Wearing too strong glasses can cause permanent harm. No.

● Reading in dim light for prolonged periods can harm the eyes. No, a dim picture will no more hurt the eyes than it would a camera—though reading in dim light may be difficult, uncomfortable, and may even cause headaches.

Bloodshot eyes from swimming—relieving/preventing them This is a common problem after swimming in chlorinated pools, but no instance of permanent damage—even among professional swimmers practicing many hours a day—has ever been reported as the result of the inflammation. Here is a suggestion from a physician member of the American Medical Association Committee on Medical Aspects of Sports: A few drops of methylcellulose (obtainable in drugstores) into the eyes is often valuable for relieving irritation and even as a preventive agent.

Dry eyes—relief measures Eye irritation and pain caused by reduced tear production or poor quality of tears can occur at any age but is most common after age sixty, more so in women than men. Replacement tears often help. More than two dozen brands are available in drugstores.

Also useful for some but irritating to others: a cellulose product (Lacrisert) which a physician can prescribe for insertion under the lower eyelid, where it dissolves slowly over a twelve-hour period, making tears thicker and aiding lubrication.

See also Swimming.

EYE DROPS

Cool them   It helps to store them in the refrigerator. By using cooled drops, you can feel them as they go into the eye, or if they accidentally fall on lashes or cheeks instead.

Using them properly—three steps   These steps will make certain eye drops get where they're supposed to go and stay there to work:

- Pull the lower lid away from eye at a right angle, forming a pouch. Drop the medication into the pouch.
- Immediately look down, gently close the eye, and keep it closed for a minute or two. Closing the eye prevents blinking, which can pump part of the medication into the nose where it does no good.
- To place drops under the upper lid, lie down with head tilted back, then follow the same procedure as above.

EYE PUFFINESS

Reducing it   Puffiness under the eyes may occur at menstruation, apparently related to water retention. Bananas and grapefruit, which act as natural diuretics, often reduce the retention and the puffiness. Water retention sometimes may be relieved, too, by sleeping on two pillows. If these measures fail, you may want to have a medical check for a possible underfunctioning thyroid gland.

EXAMINATIONS (*See* CANCER, HEALTH CALENDAR FOR A LIFETIME.)

FAT

The pinch test for body fat   With thumb and forefinger, pinch a fold of skin at various body sites—waist, stomach, upper arm, buttocks, and calf. At least half of all body fat is directly under the skin. The under-skin layer—which is what you measure with the pinch since only fat, not muscle, pinches—generally should be one-quarter- to one-half-inch thick. Since you get a double thickness with a pinch, it normally should be one-half- to one-inch thick. Anything over an inch indicates excess body fat.

The ruler test Lie on your back and place a ruler on your abdomen along the midline of the body. If there is no excess fat, the abdominal surface—between the flare of the ribs and front of the pelvis—normally is flat and the ruler should not point upward at the midsection. If your stomach holds up the ruler so it doesn't lie flat, you're carrying excess fat.

See also Obesity.

FATIGUE

Is it psychogenic? A helpful clue: People with psychogenic or emotionally or psychologically induced fatigue commonly feel tired on awakening in the morning—and, if they feel better at all, it is usually later in the day, finds Dr. Harry F. Klinefelter of Baltimore. On the other hand, people with fatigue related to organic disease almost always feel best in the morning, worst later in the day.

Fatigue and the slighted breakfast If you find yourself unduly fatigued, consider what you eat or fail to eat for breakfast. In one study of 138 generally healthy men and women, 79 percent were found to skip or slight breakfast, eating at most some juice, cereal, bread, and coffee, getting little protein. Forty-nine of the breakfast slighters experienced fatigue and, in some cases, puzzling fluid retention. They undertook to try to include in breakfast more protein—either fish, meat, cheese (cottage, mozzarella or provolone), or the whites of four or five eggs—along with at least two tablespoons of brewer's yeast while also reducing sugar and bread intake. Forty-seven of the forty-nine experienced clear—in some cases, dramatic—reductions in fatigue and fluid retention.

Space your eating   Some fatigue sufferers are helped by eating four, five, or six smaller meals a day instead of three large ones. Eating spaced in this way often can do more to maintain energy levels.

FERTILITY/INFERTILITY

The underwear factor   When infertility is a problem for a couple and the husband wears Jockey briefs, a switch to boxer shorts may save money that would otherwise go for laboratory tests. Also worth trying: sleeping without underwear. The fact is, sperm production is temperature dependent and works best at below body temperature. Because they hold the testicles closer to the body and thus have a warming effect, briefs may decrease sperm counts or sperm quality or both.

The sitting-position factor   For a man, sitting with legs apart can drop scrotal temperature by 1.6° C compared with sitting with the thighs together—which in some cases may help to increase fertility, according to the *British Journal of Urology*.

The jogging factor   Women who jog and have an infertility problem due to failure of ovulation may want to consider giving it up for a while. An Irish medical report tells of two women, both in their mid-twenties, both enthusiastic joggers, neither of whom menstruated for a year after giving up contraceptives to try for pregnancy. Neither responded to a fertility drug, clomiphene citrate, even in sizable doses. After jogging was stopped, both conceived.

A curable infection   For a substantial number of childless couples, detection and treatment of a seemingly innocuous infection may permit conception. The infection—caused by a bacterium known as T-mycoplasma—may produce no symptoms. Yet, in as many as one-third of the childless couples seeking help at New York Hospital–Cornell Medical Center, New York City, investigators recently have found T-mycoplasma in husbands' semen specimens.

In 80 percent of the cases (129 out of 161) the infection was eradicated when both partners were treated with an antibiotic, doxycycline, for four weeks. Thereafter, 60 percent of those successfully treated were able to conceive—in a median time of 10.6 months—without additional fertility tests or use of drugs.

FIBER, DIETARY (*See* CHOLESTEROL; CONSTIPATION; DIABETES; HEMORRHOIDS; OBESITY; SURGERY; ULCER, PEPTIC; and GUIDELINES: DIETARY FIBER CONTENT OF SOME FOODS.)

FITNESS

Four ways to check for it

• Take your pulse while resting comfortably. (For how, see Exercise: Measuring your heart rate.) A trained athlete often has a resting pulse rate below fifty a minute. If you're in good condition, the figure need not be that low, but it should be less than seventy.

• Stand quietly in one place for two to three minutes, then take your pulse. If the rate increases more than fifteen beats a minute over the resting pulse rate, or goes above one hundred, you're likely to be in poor physical condition.

- Do an exercise for one minute—for example, running in place. Lie down and immediately take your pulse. If it exceeds one hundred a minute, your condition is poor.
- See if you can cover a mile and a half in twelve minutes by a combination of walking, jogging, and running. Sound easy? According to some studies, less than 10 percent of American men over age twenty-one can do it.

FLU OR COLD?

Which is it It's not always easy, even for a physician, to be absolutely certain. But, generally, if you're *suddenly* afflicted with dry cough, fever, and fatigue, flu (influenza) is likely. If symptoms begin *slowly*—with a slight headache or a feeling of "being out of sorts"—and then progress to a scratchy throat, runny nose, and possibly a slight elevation of temperature, you probably have a common cold.

What to do for flu Often, you can take care of a bout of influenza on your own.
- To relieve muscle aches, headache, sore throat, fever, take either aspirin or the aspirin substitute, acetaminophen, as directed on the label.
- Drink plenty of fluids to help loosen secretions and relieve nasal stuffiness. A vaporizer often helps. An over-the-counter decongestant drug can be used, following label directions.
- Get as much rest as possible.
- If your doctor determines you're a victim of a Type A flu outbreak, he or she may prescribe a drug, amantadine, which can be effective for the Type A flu virus but not for other flu-causing viruses. It can be useful for prevention and treatment.

Flu vaccine A vaccine is recommended especially for people at high risk of developing serious complications—such as the elderly and patients with lung or heart problems or other chronic illness.

When to definitely call the doctor Do so if any of the following applies:
- You have a chronic condition—such as bronchitis, asthma, emphysema, or heart disease—which might be worsened by flu.
- You experience chest pain or shortness of breath.
- Your temperature reaches 102° F or higher and is present for twenty-four hours or more.
- You cough up mucus.
- Your throat is very sore.
- You note excessive sleepiness, confusion, slow thinking, or other change in mental status.

FOOD (*See* ALLERGIES; ARTHRITIS; BABY; HEADACHES; ITCHING; MEDICINE; MILK INTOLERANCE; SALT; SHELLFISH; GUIDELINES.)

FEET

Relieving dry skin conditions Persistent dry skin conditions of the feet can have a variety of causes, including fungal infections and ichthyosis (dryness, roughness, and scaliness stemming from the failure of normal shedding of the keratin produced by skin cells).

The compound urea may be helpful since it increases water uptake by the skin and has a mild, useful peeling action on the horny skin layer. In one study, every one of seventy-five patients benefited from use of a urea preparation (Carmol Cream, available without prescription), with relief of itching, heel fissuring, cracking, and promotion of healing.

Foot odor—five ways to combat it   In general, you need to keep your feet dry and cool in order to reduce the growth of bacteria that break down the skin and produce odor. To do this:

- Expose your feet to air as much as possible. Whenever you can, go barefoot or wear light sandals.
- Choose leather for shoes; it breathes.
- Alternate shoes to permit them to dry out thoroughly.
- Wear absorbent light cotton socks rather than heavy ones or socks made of synthetics.
- Dry your feet thoroughly after showers or baths—and apply ordinary talcum powder.

GALLSTONES

An eating schedule to prevent them   The length of overnight fasting—the interval from dinner to the first meal the next day—apparently can influence gallstone formation. The shorter the interval, the less likely a gallstone problem, French physicians have found. They studied twenty-four women, aged twenty to thirty-five, twelve with gallstones, twelve without. For those with the stones, the time from dinner to the first meal next day—whether breakfast or lunch—was significantly longer (fourteen hours, forty-one minutes on average) than for those without stones (twelve hours, forty-one minutes on average). Many of the gallstone patients skipped breakfast or limited it to coffee. Short-term fasting is known to be associated with an increase of cholesterol in gallbladder bile—a necessary condition for forming cholesterol gallstones, the most common kind.

GAS PAINS

What they can mimic   Excessive gas can produce abdominal pain, bloating, and distention. In some cases, the gas can lead to pain in the lower-left chest that can radiate to the left side of the neck and the left shoulder or arm, much as does angina pectoris, the chest pain associated with coronary heart disease.

Where the gas comes from   Gas in the gut is normal and inevitable, coming from three sources.

Some air is swallowed with food and drink. Belching up of the swallowed air may follow—but only when you're in upright position or lying on your left side. In these positions, gas is near the upper opening of the stomach, and belching can take place when the circular muscle of the opening relaxes.

Unbelched air descends the gut, arriving at the upper part of the colon, or large bowel, in six to fifteen minutes. It may be expelled as flatus in as little as thirty minutes. Normally half a quart is expelled daily as part of defecation or independently.

Some people are aerophagics—air eaters. Unknowingly, they swallow large amounts of air because they eat too fast, chew gum, are emotionally upset, or do a lot of sighing. Carbonated drinks, often taken to foster burping, can actually increase air swallowing. (For more on aerophagia and what to do about it, see AIR SWALLOWING.)

A second source of gas is a certain amount that diffuses into the gut from the bloodstream.

The third source—accountable for less than many people suppose but up to about 30 percent—consists of bacterial fermentation and food ingredients.

Culprit foods   Because individual reactions to foods vary greatly, no one food can be indicted as an excessive gas producer for all people all of the time. But gas sufferers often are aware that for them some foods don't sit well. A recent study of five hundred found the following to be the worst culprits: onions, raw apples, radishes, baked beans, cucumbers, milk, melon, cauliflower, chocolate, coffee, lettuce, peanuts, and eggs, in that order. Other foods as well may play a role in excessive gas: soufflés, beaten omelets, cake, fresh bread, and meringues, all containing more gas than other foods; also, malted milk, effervescent drinks, and whipped egg white. If you're a chronic sufferer from excessive gas, a trial of eliminating some foods may be in order.

Eight helps for an acute gas episode

- A hot-water bottle or heating pad applied to the abdomen may provide relief.
- Gently massaging the abdomen, especially when combined with heat application, may help.
- For some people, a pint-sized lukewarm tap-water enema works.
- Gas elimination may be hastened by the "telephoning teenager position": Lie stomach-down on a bed with the legs bent at the knees at a ninety-degree angle, arms bent at the elbows and turned toward each other and stretched out ahead and supporting the head.
- Another useful position for stubborn flatulence is a headstand. It reverses the gravitational pull and may roll back any fecal obstruction so gas can move on. Make the stand brief. You can prop your feet against a wall or support your body in a corner while standing on your head. Return immediately to a reclining position and take advantage of nearness of the gas to the rectum to expel it.
- Some commercial preparations marketed for gas relief contain simethicone, a silicone material that theoretically should—and sometimes does—help by stimulating the release of entrapped gas.
- Charcoal tablets or capsules may help by adsorbing gas. They are not always immediately available in drugstores, but you can request that your pharmacist order them for you.
- Also helpful for chronic sufferers: buttermilk. Says Dr. Eddy D. Palmer, one of the country's top gastroenterologists: "History tells us that every society since New Testament days

has found that buttermilk preparations are helpful for gas problems and for colon function in general. One useful move is for the gassy patient to add large amounts of buttermilk (at least a quart a day) to his diet. If he or she cannot stand buttermilk, the commercial lactobacillus preparations (available in drugstores under such trade names as Bacid and Lactinex) are the next best, although not really a good substitute for the real thing."

GELATIN (See NAILS.)

GLASSES (See SUNGLASSES.)

GROWTH IN CHILDREN

When it stops for good Studying hundreds of children from birth to age twenty-two and beyond, investigators at the Fels Research Institute, Yellow Springs, Ohio, have found that full-adult stature is reached and growth stops at a median age of 21.2 years in boys, 17.3 years in girls. After age 18, little further growth occurs: a median of slightly under half an inch in boys, still less in girls.

When it may stop temporarily At some point, some children experience a temporary growth delay. Why growth stands still for a period is not clear, Fels researchers report. Occasionally it appears to be related to a stressful event such as an illness or a family move. As inexplicably as it may stop, growth usually starts again and thereafter its rate is normal. In such children the point at which growth finally stops is often delayed, so they ultimately do achieve normal or near-normal height.

See also Puberty.

GYNECOMASTIA (BREAST ENLARGEMENT IN MEN)

The link with estrogen-containing vaginal creams   When a healthy seventy-year-old man complained of breast enlargement and sensitivity, investigating physicians found laboratory tests to be inconclusive. But they learned that the man's wife had been using vaginal cream containing 0.01 percent dinestrol (an estrogen) two or three times a week as a lubricant to facilitate intercourse. Apparently a sufficient amount of estrogen was absorbed through the penis to cause the gynecomastia. Within three months after the cream was discontinued, the gynecomastia disappeared.

In a separate study of 306 normal men over age 44, the occurrence of breast enlargement was found to increase with advancing age. The investigating team of physicians speculate that the increase could also be caused by exposure to estrogen in sexual partners' vaginal creams.

HAIR

A new way to stop excessive growth   Because of excessive amounts of facial and body hair, some women undergo as many as two or three electrolysis treatments a week and others shave daily. For them, checking with a physician about a new treatment could be very worthwhile.

Treatment with the medication spironolactone (previously used for an entirely different purpose—to lower mildly elevated blood pressure) reduces abnormally high levels of androgen (male sex hormone), which may lead to excessive hair growth. At the University of California School of Medicine, San Diego, a team headed by Dr. Samuel S. C. Yen has reported dramatic improvement in 95 percent of women with moderate to severe hirsutism.

Hair spray reactions—choosing your spray Although most people are unaffected by brief exposure to hair spray, some sprays interfere almost immediately with breathing in those with sensitive airways associated with asthma, allergic rhinitis, or viral respiratory infection. In a study in which two hair sprays were tested, a twenty-second exposure of both sprays caused no problems for healthy people. But among the sensitive, one of the sprays temporarily impaired breathing—and this appeared to be due to a difference in the perfume used. So if you have trouble with one spray, try another.

Green hair Swimmers often get this when swimming in pools, the green color deriving from algaecides or copper in pipes. To remove it:
• Wash the hair immediately—or it becomes difficult to get rid of the color.
• For color difficult to remove, suggests one dermatologist, your pharmacist may be able to supply a chelating agent such as Metalex, which combines with the greening agent so it's more readily removed. Apply to the hair for thirty minutes, then wash out.
• An alternative for stubborn green: Wet the hair with hydrogen peroxide, allowing it to remain for three hours. Then wash it out.

See also Baldness; Scalp Massage.

HAND

Freeing a stuck one safely When a child gets his or her hand stuck in a glass jar, a safe way to free it is suggested by

Dr. Ben Kritchman, a Jamaica, New York, pediatrician. Wrap cloth or cardboard around the child's wrist for protection, then submerge the hand and jar in a bucket of water. Using a hammer you can control easily—preferably a small-headed one—tap the jar smartly above its base. Because glass will break but not shatter under water, you should be able to remove the jar without injuring the child.

HANGOVER

What's good, and not good, for it—eight useful insights

- Coffee, believed by many to counteract alcohol effects, may in fact postpone recovery from a hangover. That's because one effect of large amounts of alcohol is dehydration—and coffee acts as a diuretic, further adding to the dehydration.
- Along with dehydration, excessive alcohol produces three other effects: It dilates blood vessels, disrupts metabolism, and alters dream state sleep.
- To speed the body's return to normal metabolism, advises Dr. James Dexter, a neurologist and alcohol researcher at the University of Missouri, Columbia, take in fluids and carbohydrate calories in the form of fruit juice.
- For a moderate to severe hangover, a quart of fluid is needed immediately on waking to counteract dehydration. Then, over the next twenty-four hours, drink an additional quart, beyond what you would normally consume.
- An alcohol-irritated stomach may interfere with eating. A forced-fluid regimen of fruit juices can counteract the double whammy of dehydration and stomach irritation. Fruit juice adds calories along with fluid, giving the body what it needs.
- Only the passage of time, unfortunately, can be counted on to counteract the two other alcohol effects—allowing blood vessels to return to normal and the recovery of normal sleep.
- The need for sleep the day after heavy drinking indi-

cates that normal sleep patterns were disrupted during a seemingly full night of sleep. "If in a night you normally have an hour of REM [rapid eye movement—dream state] sleep," reports Dexter, "during high levels of alcohol you would have maybe ten minutes of REM. Then the next night you would recover the loss by having nearly two hours of REM sleep."

• It's the REM sleep recovery phenomenon, when accompanied by an adequate amount of food and fluids, that signals the end of a hangover.

See also Coffee: No Help "for the Road."

HAY FEVER (*See* ALLERGIES.)

HEADACHES

Avoiding the bedcover ("turtle") type These otherwise puzzling headaches, which occur on waking and affect both sides or even the whole head, have been traced by one physician—who calls them "turtle" headaches—to a habit of some sleepers. On first waking, wanting to go back to sleep but finding the daylight bothersome, they pull bedcovers over their heads or retract their heads beneath blankets. The headache, on second awakening, results from not enough oxygen and too much carbon dioxide in the blood. The solution: Avoid the turtlelike, back-to-sleep maneuver. An effective measure: Install light-proof window shades or draperies in the bedroom.

Help for "cluster" headaches Painful, one sided, involving the eye, temple, neck, and face, cluster headaches get their name because they appear suddenly, recur for days or weeks, and disappear suddenly, only to return in another cluster. One surprising help: an over-the-counter decongestant preparation, Sinutabs. A Yale physician reports that one of his patients, a cluster victim for fifteen years, unresponsive to many measures such as ergot alkaloids, propranolol, methysergide, and codeine, discovered he got relief in five to ten minutes with Sinutabs. When several other patients tried two Sinutabs at the first indication of cluster headache, their pain persisted only ten to twenty minutes in contrast to a usual duration of several hours. Excessive amounts—more than four to five tablets a day—should be avoided, especially by anyone with high blood pressure.

Drugs and headaches—fourteen possible culprits

• For some women, the estrogen contained in oral contraceptives and other preparations may lead to migrainelike headaches. A study of three hundred such women noted marked reduction in headache frequency when estrogen-containing preparations were eliminated or reduced in dosage.

• For both men and women who happen to be sensitive to them, these drugs also can be responsible for headaches:

Valium—a tranquilizer
Equanil—a tranquilizer
Miltown—a tranquilizer
Benadryl—an antihistamine used for allergies
Chlor-Trimeton—an antihistamine for allergies
Periactin—an antihistamine for allergies, other purposes
Aldactazide—a drug for hypertension (high blood pressure)
Aldomet—an antihypertensive
HydroDIURIL—an antihypertensive
Reserpine—an antihypertensive
Ser-Ap-Es—an antihypertensive
Indocin—a pain reliever and antiinflammatory agent
Demerol—a pain reliever

• If persistent headaches develop after starting use of any drug, check with your physician. If the drug is responsible, dosage reduction or a switch to an alternative medication could solve the headache problem.

Foods and headaches—sixteen that may trigger migraine Although there are other possible triggers for mi-

graine, foods are sometimes involved. These are common culprits. A trial of avoidance may be useful.

Red wines
Champagne
Aged or strong cheese (especially Cheddar)
Pickled herring
Chicken livers
Pods of broad beans
Canned figs
Frankfurters
Bacon
Ham
Salami
Monosodium glutamate in excess amounts

And, especially if taken on an empty stomach:

Pretzels
Potato chips
Nuts
Other salted snack foods

Forecasting a migraine—a tip Although medications can often stop short a migraine attack, success depends on good absorption of the medication—and a nauseated stomach absorbs poorly. Waiting to take medication until nausea is already present can account for failure. A useful maneuver for helping to determine whether a migraine or an ordinary headache is coming on is to sit down and place your head between your knees. If your head then throbs, a migraine episode is on the way and medication for it should be taken without delay.

For migraine—try a simple maneuver Place a paper bag over your nose and mouth, exhale into it, and rebreathe from it. How this works is not clear, but a British physician reports that all of a group of migraine patients who tried the maneuver succeeded in aborting many oncoming migraine episodes. One patient, for example, whose attacks usually persisted for eighteen to twenty-four hours, was able, two out of three times, to cut the migraine short to ten to fifteen minutes.

Migraine and the sun Exposure to the sun can trigger headaches in many people, especially migraine sufferers. In a study of 250 headache patients, sun exposure proved to be a frequent reason for attacks in 30 percent of those with migraine, 7 percent of those with tension headaches.

Swimmer's headaches—a helpful switch Swimmers who experience headaches and who use goggles could benefit from a switch of goggles. A Johns Hopkins Medical School, Baltimore, physician, on taking up swimming, began to experience throbbing headaches an hour or two after the exercise but not on nonswimming days. Puzzled, he recalled that at about the time the headaches first began he had taken to wearing a type of swim goggles that require the rubber head strap be shortened so the individual eye pieces fit tightly. When he stopped using the goggles, the headaches stopped. They returned when he tried the goggles again. His final solution: use of goggles with a single soft rubber rim that fits around both eyes and does not require a tight head strap to be watertight.

Headaches and the pill For reasons not yet well understood, some women with a history of chronic headaches experience a striking improvement while taking birth control pills while others note a worsening of existing headaches or the onset of new headaches.

There are two main types of pill-associated headaches. There may be tension-type headaches occurring at any time throughout the menstrual cycle. Or migraine-type headaches may occur, predominantly midcycle or during the seven-day period when the pill is not taken.

Although diuretics and conventional headache medications have been used to treat pill-related headaches, they are often ineffective until the pill has been discontinued in favor of another method of birth control.

Weekend/holiday headaches Headaches that occur on weekends and holidays are often blamed on emotional factors —inability to relax, need to keep busy. That may be true in some cases but not necessarily in others.

• One other reason, suggested by recent studies: Some people are used to consuming caffeine-containing beverages starting early in the morning on weekdays. Caffeine has a vasoconstrictive, or blood vessel narrowing effect, to which they may become accustomed. When they sleep later on holidays and weekends, the early morning deprivation of caffeine may cause widening of blood vessels, which can trigger headaches.

• Another possible reason: Studies have shown that when headaches begin during sleep, they ususally do so during the REM (rapid eye movement), or dream phase, of sleep, which occurs at intervals during the night. Holiday and weekend headaches may stem from increased REM sleep at these times because of longer sleeping periods, allowing more time for REM sleep.

HEALTH CALENDAR FOR A LIFETIME

How to have your health evaluated on a regular basis— twelve principles These are suggested by Dr. Donald B. Louria, chairman of preventive medicine at the New Jersey Medical School, Newark:

• After age eighteen, have your blood pressure checked every two years.

• Also every two years, get a check of your blood cholesterol and HDL (high density lipoprotein) levels.

• If you insist upon smoking, stay below ten cigarettes a day, filter type, to help reduce the risk of lung and other cancer and coronary heart disease.

- After twenty-five, women should have a Pap smear every two years to screen for cervical cancer.
- Beginning at age thirty, breast self-examination should be carried out by every woman at least once every three months and there should be a medical examination of the breasts yearly or every other year.
- Beginning at age forty, every woman should also have a mammographic breast examination at least every two years.
- For both men and women after forty, there should be a yearly test of stool for blood, which could be an indication of bowel cancer.
- After fifty, both men and women should have a sigmoidoscope examination of the large bowel every six to seven years to detect any polyps that might become cancerous.
- Weigh yourself monthly. If your weight is 20 percent or more above what is considered desirable for your height and build, it's a risk to your health.
- After thirty-five, have a simple eye tension test every five years to check for possible glaucoma.
- Between the ages of twenty and forty, have your blood hemoglobin level checked every two years for anemia detection—and after sixty, have the check yearly.
- At least four times in adulthood have a general physical examination—one between ages of twenty and thirty, a second between forty and fifty, a third at sixty, and again at seventy.

HEARING

A curable loss Some hard-of-hearing patients who are told they need hearing aids may not need them at all. If they have serous otitis media, which is commonly diagnosed and corrected in children, but often overlooked in adults, there is an alternative treatment that may restore hearing. In serous otitis media, fluid accumulates in the middle ear as the result of ear infection, allergy, or enlarged adenoids. The fluid may impair hearing. Temple University, Philadelphia, physicians reported a study of thirty such adult patients, most coming in for hearing aid prescriptions after being told their hearing loss was incurable. The same treatment used for children—puncture of the eardrum to release fluid and insertion of a small ventilation tube through the drum—brought improved hearing in 75 percent.

Hearing aids—they don't increase hearing loss Although that's a common concern, hearing aids can help without adding to loss. Veterans Administration Hospital, Tucson, investigators studied 175 patients with sensorineural deafness and 86 with conductive deafness fitted with hearing aids during a ten-year period. In each case, difference in hearing between aided and unaided ear was measured before and after hearing aid use. No significant shift in hearing or detrimental effect of the devices was found in patients with either type of hearing loss.

Headphones and hearing loss Portable earphone FM and stereo cassette players (of the Walkman type) *do* have a potential for causing permanent nerve-type hearing loss if used at volume settings of 4 or above for extended periods. Testing users, Tufts–New England Medical Center, Boston, researchers found sound intensity at volume setting 4 ranging between 93 and 108 decibels and at setting 8 predominantly above 115 decibels. For comparison, government industrial standards limit worker exposure to a maximum of 8 hours at 90 decibel noise, 4 hours at 95 decibel, 2 hours at 100, and no exposure is allowed to continuous sound above 115 decibels.

See also Ear.

HEARTBURN

Fourteen helps for chronic sufferers

• Remember that heartburn mostly results from what happens at the lower end of the esophagus, or gullet, where it joins the stomach. There, a circular muscle, known as the lower esophageal sphincter (LES), is supposed to close snugly after food and drink pass into the stomach. With improper closure, some stomach acid can reflux, or move back up, to the esophagus, producing burning discomfort.

• It helps to minimize intake of certain foods that tend to unduly relax the LES. Among them: alcohol, garlic, onion, peppermint, chocolate, food containing derivatives of chocolate, fried foods, fatty meats, olive oil, and salad oil.

• Make use of foods rich in protein or carbohydrates (starches), which leave LES strength unaffected.

• Check on how coffee may affect you individually. In most people, it has no undesirable action on LES pressure and may even increase it. In some, however, it has no effect on LES pressure but does increase stomach acid secretions and thus may lead to heartburn discomfort. Note, too: decaffeinated coffee, while largely free of caffeine, still may increase acid secretions.

• Avoid smoking cigarettes, especially right after meals. There's a 40 percent fall in LES pressure within one to four minutes after lighting a cigarette.

• Avoid lying down soon after a meal. It can take several hours for the stomach to empty its contents into the intestine. Once that happens, regurgitation—and heartburn—are less likely.

• Avoid eating near bedtime—for the same reason.

• Certain drugs may bring on heartburn. They include antispasmodics and anticholinergics often used for peptic ulcer and irritable bowel; also, for some people, aspirin-containing medications and other antiinflammatory agents used for arthritis. If you're taking medicine for any purpose, check with your physician about whether it could be contributing to your discomfort and whether a reduction in dosage or change in the medication could help.

- Obesity contributes to heartburn by increasing abdominal pressure; weight reduction could help.

- Tight garments with a cinched in waistline or belt also increase abdominal pressure. Avoid wearing them or at least loosen them after meals.

- Avoid bending over soon after meals; that can facilitate flow of stomach contents back up into the esophagus.

- Antacids? You may need them only if the above measures are inadequate. An antacid—in the form of two tablets chewed or one to two tablespoons of a liquid preparation—is best taken an hour after meals and at bedtime to help neutralize stomach acid during the period when reflux is most likely. Maalox, Gelusil, and Mylanta-II are the most effective, according to Dr. Sidney Cohen of the University of Pennsylvania School of Medicine, Philadelphia, a top heartburn expert.

- For especially stubborn heartburn, one of these two prescription drugs may be useful: bethanechol increases LES pressure; cimetidine, often used for peptic ulcer, helps prevent excess stomach acid production.

- Surgery? When heartburn accompanies hiatus hernia— an abnormally large opening in the diaphragm (the muscle of breathing) that allows part of the stomach to slide up from the abdomen into the chest—repair of the hernia may help. But experts now generally believe that surgery is needed only in about 5 percent of all cases, only after the measures noted above have been tried for at least three months and haven't worked.

Heartburn in pregnancy As many as 70 percent of mothers to be experience heartburn, usually in the last six months but sometimes earlier. Although long supposed to result from increased pressure within the abdomen from the expanding uterus, recent studies point to hormone changes that overrelax the LES muscle.

- For some women, frequent small meals rather than three large ones, and avoidance of bending or lying down flat soon after eating, can help.
- Antacids may harm the fetus if taken in the first three months but apparently cause no harm later in pregnancy.
- In stubborn cases, metoclopramide, a drug your physician can prescribe, tones up the LES muscle and has been reported to be effective in more than 90 percent of cases.

HEART DISEASE (*See* CHEST PAIN; DRINKING; TYPE A BEHAVIOR.)

HEAT

The dangerous buildup in a parked car   Temperatures can go surprisingly high in a car parked in the sun. A recent special study by Dr. J. S. Surpure of Oklahoma Children's Memorial Hospital, Oklahoma City, found the interior temperature reaching 111.2° F in the shade, 172.4° F in the sun! Such temperatures can mean potentially hazardous stress for pets, children, and older people left sitting in a car under such conditions. If possible, park in the shade. Leave both doors open for ventilation; open windows may not be enough.

HEMORRHOIDS

What they are   Often called "piles," hemorrhoids are enlarged veins, either outside the anus (external hemorrhoids) or inside the rectum (internal hemorrhoids). They may become inflamed and swollen or clotted, producing itching, pain, and sometimes bleeding. The flare-ups may result from constipation and straining at stool, heavy lifting, or pregnancy. Inflammation, swelling, or clots usually begin to disappear within a few days.

When to call your doctor Call your physician if pain is severe and persists for more than twenty-four hours or if bleeding occurs.

Five relief aids
- Increase fiber in your diet (bran and whole-grain cereals are good sources) and drink a lot of liquids—if possible, two quarts a day. The liquids are needed if fiber is to produce a soft stool, easy to pass without straining.
- Use sitz baths—sitting in a warm tub—two or three times a day if possible, to get some relief of pain and itching.
- Use witch hazel compresses; they can be soothing.
- Avoid sitting and standing for prolonged periods. Lying down even briefly can help.
- A commercial hemorrhoid salve, ointment, or suppository may not be necessary if you use the measures above. If you've found one that works for you, use it—provided it doesn't contain a "caine" ingredient, such as benzocaine or dibucaine. Anesthetics in the "caine" family may add to irritation with continued use.

Six helps for avoiding recurrences
- Establish a regular time for bowel movements and never delay when there is an urge.
- Avoid straining at stool, and spending long periods on the toilet, which can aggravate hemorrhoids.
- You may do well to avoid using toilet tissue when possible; instead cleanse the anal area with warm, soapy cotton or cloth followed by rinsing.
- Drink plenty of fluids and get more fiber into your diet. Two tablespoons of bran daily can help. You can get more fiber, too, through whole-grain breads and cereals, and vegetables and fruits.
- Avoid heavy lifting.
- Get exercise every day. It can help ease pressure on the hemorrhoidal veins due to standing and sitting. And lie down,

relaxed, two or three times a day for five to ten minutes at a time.

HERPES SIMPLEX (*See* COLD SORES/FEVER BLISTERS.)

HERPES ZOSTER (*See* SHINGLES.)

HICCUPS

Half a dozen and more stoppers to try

• Swallow a teaspoon of granulated sugar; the back-of-the-throat irritation may interrupt the hiccup cycle.

• Eat dry crackers; they may also work through irritation.

• Drink many small, quick sips of ice water.

• Breathe into a paper bag.

• Hold your breath.

• Fill a glass to the top with water, bend over from the waist as far as you can, then drink all you can from the far side of the glass.

• Take a teaspoonful of white corn syrup (a lesser amount for children).

• Eat a lemon wedge soaked in angostura bitters (all but the rind).

• Induce sneezing by sniffing a small pinch of pepper.

HOT SOAKS

An effective homemade cushion For anyone with rectal or similar pain needing hot tub soaks, sitting on the hard tub surface can be painful. This suggestion from Dr. Paul D'Amico and Gerald N. Unger of Livingston Manor, New York:

Fold two bath towels in fourths, or roll them, and place one under each buttock. "There's no need," they say, "to purchase a surgical doughnut or attempt to stuff an automobile inner tube into the bathtub."

HOUSE DUST (*See* ALLERGIES.)

HYPERVENTILATION (*See* BREATHING, EXCESSIVE.)

ICE

A flexible, homemade ice pack Next time you want to apply ice to an injured muscle or joint, try this: Soak a small bath towel in water, wring it out until it stops dripping, place it folded on aluminum foil in the freezer, and let it stay there until crystals form but the towel is not frozen solid. Then you can apply the towel-pack and make it conform effectively to the injured area.

Ice massage simplified Ice massage can be helpful for bursitis, back pain, bruises, and other problems. A simple way to carry it out, suggested by Dr. Thomas J. Morrow of Fort Washington, Maryland: Fill a polystyrene plastic cup with water, freeze it, then peel the cup to below ice level. The remainder of the cup then can serve as a cold-resistant handle. In applying the ice, be sure to keep it moving in order to avoid skin damage.

Ice massage for chronic pain Massaging a chronically painful area with ice often provides relief. At the Boston Pain Center of the Massachusetts Rehabilitation Hospital, where ice massage has been used for one thousand patients with chronic pain of various types—low back, rheumatoid arthritis, osteoarthritis, cancer—78 percent have had significant relief, another 8 percent have had some benefit. In the procedure used at the center, ice is applied to an affected area for five to ten minutes but is stopped immediately when numbness occurs. Relief lasts up to three hours.

See also Arthritis; Sunburn.

IMMUNIZATION

Latest official seven-step recommended schedule Published in January 1983 by the U.S. Center for Disease Control, these are the newly revised recommendations for normal infants and children.

Age	Vaccines	Comments
2 months	Diphtheria-tetanus toxoids-whooping cough; oral polio	Can be given earlier in areas of high-disease incidence.
4 months	Diphtheria-tetanus toxoids-whooping cough #2; oral polio #2.	
6 months	Diphtheria-tetanus toxoids-whooping cough #3.	An additional dose of oral polio vaccine is optional in high-risk areas.
15 months	Live measles, mumps, and rubella (German measles) viruses in a combined vaccine.	
18 months	Diphtheria-tetanus toxoids-whooping cough #4; oral polio #3.	This completes the primary series of immunizations.
4–6 years	Diphtheria-tetanus toxoids-whooping cough #5; oral polio #4.	Preferably at or before school entry.
14–16 years	Adult tetanus toxoid and diphtheria toxoid in combination.	Repeat every 10 years throughout life.

INCONTINENCE, STRESS (*See* BLADDER TRAINING.)

INFANT WALKERS (*See* WALKERS, INFANT.)

INFERTILITY (*See* FERTILITY/INFERTILITY.)

INJECTIONS

Taking the sting out Try this yourself if you have to administer intramuscular injections—and suggest it to a nurse or technician giving shots and unfamiliar with the technique: After wiping the skin with alcohol before an injection—a usual procedure—wait a few seconds before giving the injection. When the alcohol is allowed to dry, the pain of injection is markedly reduced.

INJURIES (*See* EXERCISE; TAPING INJURIES.)

INSECT BITES AND STINGS

A vitamin for avoiding them Vitamin B_1—thiamine—as a means of combating mosquitoes was recommended by one U.S. physician as far back as 1943. Some years later, another recommended it. The dose: two hundred milligrams a day for adults, one hundred for children. When taken by mouth, some of the vitamin is excreted via the skin—enough, according to the reports, to act as an effective insect repellent.

More recently, Mexican physicians reported a study with children with insect prurigo—a hivelike condition resulting from bites of mosquitoes, flies, bedbugs, and other insects. The hives, or skin wheals, persist for weeks, itch intensely and constantly, often lead to secondary infection from frenzied scratching. Of 100 children given 200 to 300 milligrams of thiamine daily, 89 had their prurigo controlled.

Six other avoidance measures

• If there are any Hymenoptera (yellow jacket, bee, hornet, wasp) nests around house or yard, they should be destroyed—but by someone not allergic to insect stings. Wasps tend to nest under eaves and windowsills; their nests should be knocked down with a broom handle. Yellow jackets often take up residence in old stumps and holes in the ground and can be discouraged by fumes of kerosene or gasoline, or by lye—applied at night when they are not home.

• Wear shoes and socks outdoors—and, as much as possible, keep from looking like a flower to insects. Avoid floral prints, bright colors, perfumes, scented hair, and scented soaps, lotions or shampoos. Also avoid floppy clothing, which may entangle and infuriate insects.

• Favor light colors such as white, light green, tan, and khaki.

• Be especially cautious near garbage cans, which attract insects. Also attractive to them: watermelon and melting ice-cream cones. On picnics, keep food covered until you're ready to eat it and pack any leftovers immediately afterward.

• If you encounter a bee or other stinging insect, don't swat; move away slowly. If you can't retreat, lie face down and cover your head with your arms.

• If an insect gets trapped in the car, stop the car, open the window carefully, and open the door as well so the insect may fly out. Or, moving slowly and carefully, get out yourself. It's a good idea to keep an aerosol can of insecticide in the car and use it if necessary.

Meat tenderizer for relief Next time you're stung by a bee or other insect, you might want to try this—but you have to do it immediately; the next day is no good: Make a paste by adding about one-fourth of a tablespoon of household meat tenderizer to about one or two teaspoonfuls of water. Rub the paste into the stung area. Repeat in an hour if necessary. The tenderizer contains papain, an enzyme that can break down insect venoms, making them harmless.

Relieving itchy bites An often-effective and inexpensive remedy for itchy mosquito bites is a dab of ammonia. Useful for old but still-annoying mosquito, flea, and chigger bites is a preparation your pharmacist can prepare for you: a combination of 1 percent phenol and 10 percent benzocaine in fifteen grams of flexible collodion. It should be applied to bites twice a day with a glass rod or plastic toothpick. But do *not* use it if you happen to be sensitive to benzocaine, suggests Dr. Jerome Z. Litt of Beachwood, Ohio.

INSULIN (*See* DIABETES.)

IRON (*See* ARTHRITIS; GUIDELINES: GUIDE TO VITAMINS AND MINERALS.)

ITCHING

Hot water relief For itching from mild poison ivy (no blisters)—as well as insect bite itching—the brief application of hot water may provide almost instant relief lasting as long as three hours. The water has to be fairly hot—120 to 130° F —or the itching may worsen. Just a few seconds under such hot running water or a few applications with a hot washcloth should do the trick, according to dermatologist Dr. M. B. Sulzberger of New York City.

Cleopatra's remedy When nothing else helps itching from a skin disorder, Cleopatra's remedy may. Just dip clean linen or cotton cloth compresses in cool milk and apply. According to a report in the medical journal *Consultant*, the treatment is especially effective for severely itching eczematous eruptions and unyielding vulvar itching and soreness. Note, too: In many cases, a substitute for milk—either a solution of cornstarch in water or water-diluted laundry starch—works well.

Relieving jock itch For this mostly male fungus infection in the pubic region:

• It's essential to eliminate friction and moisture, which are contributing factors, by using boxer shorts rather than Jockey briefs.

• Change underclothes often.

• Use a powder to dry the area after bathing.

• A medicated powder, Tinactin, containing the antifungal agent tolnaftate, can be effective, often relieving burning, itching, and soreness within twenty-four hours.

Rectal itching—six diet culprits While it can have many possible causes, including bowel or rectal disease or even the use of some drugs, such as antibiotics, otherwise unexplainable recurrent rectal itching may be caused by any of these six items in the diet: coffee, tea, cola, beer, chocolate and tomatoes.

It's when a certain "threshold" amount of one or more of the items is consumed that itching occurs—not immediately but twenty-four to forty-eight hours afterward. Stay below the threshold amount and all is well.

For example, says Dr. William G. Friend of the University of Washington, Seattle, the most common culprit is coffee. The average threshold for anyone sensitive to it is two and a half cups a day. Three cups may cause itching; but two will not.

Relieving bath itch Intense itching—without noticeable skin changes—after a shower or bath with water of any temperature may be a common problem that has often been mistakenly labeled as "neurotic." British researchers, studying all otherwise healthy after-bath itchers, found raised blood levels of a body chemical, histamine, after exposure to water. An antihistamine drug stopped the itching in two-thirds of the group.

See also Antihistamines; Ears.

JET LAG

Minimizing it Jet lag, the effect of crossing time zones rapidly, can make you feel exhausted yet unable to sleep, irritable, and forgetful for a day or two or longer. But there are ways to minimize the impact. These are suggested by an expert, Dr. Charles F. Ehret of Argonne National Laboratory, Argonne, Illinois:

• There's no jet lag effect on north–south flights, no matter how long. The problem arises upon crossing one or more time zones when the body resists adjusting to new cycles of sleep and wakefulness.

• Start speeding the adjustment as soon as you board the plane. If it will be night when you land, pull down your window shade, wear dark glasses or a sleep mask, and doze if possible. If you depart at night and will arrive during the daytime, try to remain awake, keep your eyes open and the seat light on, trying to make it seem as if you're already in the new time zone.

• On landing in daylight, don't go to your hotel and take a nap. You'll just let your old rhythms keep working. Stay outdoors if possible. If indoors, keep lights on and stay awake.

• On arriving at night, do go to your hotel room and try to sleep.

• Diet is important. High-protein foods, such as fish, fowl, eggs, meat, and dairy products, can provide up to five hours of energy; high-carbohydrate foods, such as pasta, salad, fruit, and rich desserts, provide an hour's energy surge but then tend to make you drowsy. If you arrive at your destination in the morning after a long flight and need to get into action without delay, start with a hearty high-protein breakfast, and eat a high-protein lunch to keep you going through the afternoon. For dinner, go heavy on carbohydrates to help assure sleep.

• Caffeine—from coffee or tea—can help keep you alert on arrival. It works best, according to Dr. Ehret, if you avoid caffeine-containing beverages for several days before your flight.

• Reset your watch immediately after takeoff. It helps get you in tune with the new periods of day and night you'll face on arrival.

• If your rescheduling calls for sleeping on the plane, don't try to force sleep with sedatives or alcohol. Just resting, with your eyes closed, can be almost as useful as sleep.

• While you may be out of step on the plane—staying awake while others doze or vice versa—the payoff will be fewer jet lag symptoms on arrival.

See also Air Travel

"JEWISH PENICILLIN" (*See* COLDS.)

JOCK ITCH (*See* ITCHING.)

JOGGER'S NIPPLES

Preventing them A now common problem because of the enthusiasm for jogging and running is sore nipples that become red, fluid-logged, and sometimes slightly eroded as a result of friction. Women get them when they jog or run without brassieres and wear shirts made of rough fabrics. Men can suffer, too. To prevent them:

- Women should wear brassieres; men should tape the nipples or lubricate them with petrolatum.
- Both should wear shirts made from silk, polyester, or another fabric with a smooth, hard finish.

JOGGING (*See* FERTILITY/INFERTILITY; GUIDELINES: JOGGING AND RUNNING: THE DIFFERENCES; CALORIES EXPENDED PER MILE OF RUNNING/JOGGING.)

KNUCKLE POPPING

It's usually harmless Although it's generally supposed that cracking or popping knuckles can cause bigger finger joints, that's not usually the case.

Says Dr. John Gould, chief of hand surgery at the University of Alabama Medical Center, Birmingham: "When people crack their knuckles, they are causing the nitrogen that normally is present in the joint tissue to be displaced with enough force to be audible. This causes no real harm, and the nitrogen naturally builds back up to the point that there is enough to 'pop' the knuckle again. If it is not painful, you're not causing big knuckles. But if it hurts, that could mean that cartilage has been sheared off and a prearthritic condition could result. And arthritic joints do increase in size; these are the cases in which popping knuckles causes big knuckles."

LEG CRAMPS, NOCTURNAL

The knot of pain You're sound asleep, paying attention to your dream life, when the agony suddenly strikes. A muscle in your leg or foot has bunched up into a tight knot, painful enough to wake you, keep you awake, and maybe make it difficult, for fear of recurrence, to fall asleep the next night. It can strike anyone—healthy young people as well as the elderly, diabetics, arthritics, and those with other ills.

A *simple exercise for relief*
• With your shoes off, stand two to three feet away from, and facing, a wall.
• Place your hands against the wall and lean forward— using your arms to regulate the leaning—while keeping your heels on the floor. Lean until you feel a moderately intense but not painful pulling sensation in your calf muscles.
• Hold this position for ten seconds. Repeat after five seconds of relaxation.
• Carry out the sequence three times a day until the nightly attacks stop.

In one trial with forty-four sufferers, some of whom experienced the leg cramps as often as twice a night, the cramps disappeared in twenty-one of them within twenty-four to seventy-two hours, in all the rest within a week, with no recurrence in up to a year of follow-up.

Other helpful measures
• Massaging the legs after walking or exercise may help prevent cramps.
• Sometimes preventive: sleeping with a small pillow under bent knees or wrapping the legs with a warm (not hot) towel for a time.
• If cramps do occur, relief may come from massaging, stretching, or walking, applying more warm towels, or immersing the feet in cold water.

LINIMENT

What it's good for   Liniment is useful for ordinary, run-of-the-mill, self-limited muscle aches and pains. A common principal ingredient in liniment is methyl salicylate, and there may be additions of camphor or menthol (oil of wintergreen). These ingredients act to bring more blood to the skin, produce warmth, increase temperature of deeper muscle layers, and reduce discomfort. According to Dr. Ernest W. Johnson of Ohio State University, Columbus, liniments also increase the time needed to fatigue a muscle, thus increasing muscle capacity for work. *Caution:* Do *not* apply heat during or immediately after using a liniment because of danger of a skin burn.

LONG LIFE

The seven simple rules   Since 1965, the California Health Department has been studying seven thousand residents of Alameda County, looking into the influence of what it calls "the seven simple rules of clean living" on health and longevity. The study indicates that women can add seven years to their lives and men can add eleven years by following the rules. Here they are:

• Get the right amount of sleep (eight hours for men, seven for women).

• Eat a good breakfast each day.

• Eat three meals a day at regular times and avoid snacks.

• Exercise regularly (preferably by participating in a sport).

• Control your weight.

• Drink moderately (one or two drinks a day).

• Don't smoke cigarettes.

LUNG DISORDERS

Breathing to help   Emphysema patients can often make themselves more comfortable by learning to use the diaphragm more than the stomach muscles for breathing. Diaphragmatic breathing requires simply relaxing the abdomen and lower chest so the abdomen can protrude during inhalation. That allows the diaphragm—the dome-shaped muscle separating the chest and the abdomen—to descend, enlarging the chest cavity, allowing for better expansion of the lungs, and reducing the work of breathing. One recent study has found that even as diaphragmatic breathing markedly reduces breathing rate and work involved, it significantly improves ventilation of the lungs.

Overcoming two irritants Postnasal discharge and the return of stomach contents into the esophagus (esophageal reflux) are two common airway irritants in emphysema and other chronic-lung-disease patients. And both can be overcome, finds Dr. Reuben M. Charniack, a Denver lung specialist.

• Lung function, he reports, improves when the back of the throat is kept clear of secretions with a treatment as simple as drinking a glass of water with a pinch of salt in it, morning and night. An alternative: Close one nostril and sniff into the other a weak saltwater solution from a cupped hand, then cough until only the clear salt solution is expectorated.

• To improve reflux, sleep with the head elevated about eight inches; avoid lifting and bending and remain upright for at least two to three hours after meals; avoid evening snacks. Also useful for some: avoidance of coffee, cola drinks, alcohol, chocolate, fatty foods.

Spices to help Well-spiced foods may help bronchitis and emphysema patients. Reason: a spicy diet stimulates reflexes that loosen breathing passage secretions, making it easier to cough up mucus.

• Recommends Dr. Irwin Ziment of UCLA Medical Center: horseradish on hamburgers, liberal use of garlic, chili, mustard, and other hot condiments.

- An alternative for any who get indigestion from spicy foods: gargling with ten to twenty drops of Tabasco sauce in a glass of water.
- "Hot spicy food," says Dr. Ziment, "clears your sinuses, clears your nose, and may help clear your lungs."

L-TRYPTOPHAN (See SLEEP.)

LYSINE (See COLD SORES/FEVER BLISTERS.)

MASSAGE (See ICE MASSAGE.)

MEDICINE

Take it upright If you've experienced heartburn or nausea after taking pills or capsules, next time try this: Take your medication with at least three and a half ounces of fluid while standing—and remain upright for at least ninety seconds afterward.

- Danish researchers had 121 healthy volunteers take tablets and capsules containing barium so the medication could be traced by fluoroscope after swallowing. When taken with little fluid or while lying down, the medication was much more likely to produce discomfort by remaining in the esophagus for more than ninety seconds, sometimes even disintegrating there, before reaching the stomach.
- Other recent studies have found that many drugs can irritate if they remain long in the esophagus. Among them: potassium chloride, quinidine, cromolyn sodium, fluorouracil, phenylbutazone, prednisone, iron tablets, vitamin C, and antibiotics such as tetracycline, doxycycline, and clindamycin.

The studies have also shown that even tablets no bigger than aspirin size can remain in the esophagus for more than five minutes almost 60 percent of the time. Plenty of fluid and remaining upright help move medication along in shorter time, reducing the risk of inflammation of the esophagus, burning pain, and swallowing difficulty.

Two ways to swallow   If you have difficulty getting capsules down but do well with tablets, or vice versa, it may be because you're using the same swallowing technique for both.

• For a tablet, place it in the mouth with a small amount of water, tilt the head backward, and you can swallow readily. Follow with more water.

• But that method doesn't work well for a capsule which, being lighter than water, will float frontward and be difficult to swallow. Instead, tilt the head or upper part of the body *forward;* then the capsule will float backward to be swallowed easily.

When to take medications in terms of food   Some drugs may impair food absorption, while some foods may impair drug absorption. Some medications are best taken on an empty stomach, and some should not be taken with particular foods.

• Erythromycin, for example, should be taken on an empty stomach—and, like other medication, should be taken with plenty of fluid, more than just a swallow of water. Important?

In a British study, some patients took erythromycin on an empty stomach, others with a meal. Tests found that the empty-stomach patients had twice the essential blood levels of the drug as the others. And among the empty-stomach patients, those taking the drug with a full glass of water had significantly more of the drug in their blood than those taking it with a few sips. Clearly, for erythromycin, absorption is impaired by eating beforehand and using little water for wash down; a considerable portion of the drug passes through un-absorbed and does no good.

• It's also a fact that antibiotics such as penicillin, ampi-cillin, and erythromycin can be partially destroyed in the stomach when taken with fruit juices. And if most tetracy-clines are taken with milk or dairy products, the calcium in these products can bind the drug and prevent it from being absorbed completely.

Here are useful guidelines:

Take on an empty stomach (two to three hours before meals)
    benzathine penicillin G
    cloxacillin (Tegopen)
    erythromycin
    lincomycin (Lincocin)
    methacycline (Rondomycin)
    potassium phenoxymethyl penicillin (penicillin V)
    tetracyclines, except Declomycin

Take a half hour before meals
    belladonna and its alkaloids
    chlordiazepoxide hydrochloride (Librax)
    hyoscyamine sulfate (Donnatal)
    methylphenidate (Ritalin)
    phenazopyridine (Pyridium)
    phenmetrazine hydrochloride (Preludin)
    propantheline bromide (Pro-Banthine)

Take with meals or food
    aminophylline
    antidiabetic drugs
    APC (aspirin, phenacetin, caffeine)
    chlorothiazide (Diuril, HydroDIURIL)
    diphenylhydantoin (Dilantin)
    mefenamic acid (Ponstel)
    metronidazole (Flagyl)
    nitrofurantoin (Furadantin, Macrodantin)
    prednisolone

prednisone
rauwolfia and its alkaloids
reserpine (Serpasil)
triamterene (Dyrenium)
trihexyphenidyl hydrochloride (Artane)
trimeprazine tartrate (Temaril)

Do not *take with milk*
bisacodyl (Dulcolax)
potassium chloride
potassium iodide
tetracyclines except doxycycline (Vibramycin)

Do not *take with fruit juices*
ampicillin
benzathine penicillin G
cloxacillin (Tegopen)
erythromycin

Avoid alcohol while taking
acetohexamide (Dymelor)
antihistamines
chloral hydrate
chlordiazepoxide (Librium)
chlorpropamide (Diabinese)
diphenoxylate hydrochloride (Lomotil)
monoamine oxidase (MAO) inhibitor antidepressants
  (Eutonyl, Marplan, Nardil, Parnate)
meclizine hydrochloride (Antivert)
methaqualone (Quaalude)
metronidazole (Flagyl)
narcotics
tolbutamide (Orinase)

When medicines produce dry mouth Excessive mouth drying is an unpleasant effect of some medications. A good way to combat the problem: Use ice chips. They're longer acting and often more effective than cold water, don't have the bloating effect of large quantities of water, and help more than chewing gum or mints.

How to halve tablets   If you often have to halve scored medication tablets, try using a steak knife or other knife with a serrated edge. Place the serrated blade in the tablet groove, and tap it sharply with the handle of another knife. The tablet should be separated neatly, without wasteful crumbling.

Where to keep medicines   Because dampness and heat can speed their deterioration, drugs don't belong in the bathroom. The best place is in a separate small cabinet or closet outside the bathroom, and some, which say so on the label, belong in the refrigerator.

How long to keep leftover prescription drugs   It's safest to throw away any leftovers immediately. Although there's a temptation to reason that you've spent money on them and they should be useful again, that can be dangerous. Drugs shouldn't be given to anyone for whom they were not prescribed; that person might have a serious allergic reaction to a drug. You shouldn't take them again yourself because they were prescribed for a specific illness, one that may not be present next time around. Prescription drugs also have a limited shelf life and can have toxic effects if taken after they've begun to decompose. Tetracycline, for example, a commonly used antibiotic for bronchitis, ear, and other infections, has a short shelf life and can cause kidney problems if taken after decomposition has set in.

Determining the dose for a child   You'll do best to consult your physician about the right dose of a medication for a child.

One formula for determining the dose was first published

back in 1813 by an English physician, Thomas Young. It's still in use today. The Young rule is that the dose of a drug for a child over two years of age is calculated by dividing the child's age by the age plus twelve. The result is the fraction of the adult dose recommended for the child. For example, a four-year-old child would require $\dfrac{4}{4+12}$ = ¼ of the adult dose.

Stocking your medicine cabinet   The following are useful basic supplies for many types of minor emergencies and even some major ones:

• Attached to the inside of the cabinet door, a sheet or card of emergency information, including what to do in case of poisoning, phone numbers of the poison control center, hospital, ambulance squad, pharmacy, and physician.

• Syrup of ipecac, one-ounce bottle, to induce vomiting in case of poisoning.

• Activated charcoal, helpful for gas.

• Calamine lotion for minor bites, rashes, sunburn, and so on.

• A tube of petroleum jelly.

• Sterile gauze dressings, individually wrapped, for cleaning and covering wounds.

• A roll of two-inch gauze bandage for securing dressings over wounds.

• A roll of half-inch-wide adhesive tape.

• Cotton-tipped applicators, such as Q-Tips, for removing a foreign body from the eye.

• Band-Aids, or their equivalent, in assorted sizes.

• Aromatic spirits of ammonia, a small bottle.

• Aspirin or acetaminophen (aspirin substitute).

• A mild, nonstinging antiseptic such as Merthiolate, Zephiran Chloride, or Betadine.

• Tweezers for splinter removal.

• Scissors with blunt tips for cutting tape and gauze.

- An antacid, preferably liquid.
- An antidiarrhea agent such as Kaopectate.
- A thermometer.

See also Aerosol Medications; Antacids; Antihistamines; Baby; Coughing; Drugs; Eye Drops; Headaches; Injections; Mouth Irritations; Nasal Congestion; Nitroglycerin; Prescriptions; Skin; Sleep; Snoring; Suppositories; Ulcer, Peptic.

MICROWAVE COOKING

Nutritional values In addition to saving time and energy, microwave oven cooking conserves nutrients. These are the findings of Cornell University, Ithaca, New York, researchers:

- Microwave oven cooking results in 50 percent less vitamin C lost from fruits and vegetables because of the need for less water, and up to 70 percent less cooking time.
- More nutrients of many kinds are retained in foods defrosted in a microwave oven than at room temperature because nutrients have less time to degrade.
- A higher protein content is retained in flour-based foods because fewer proteins are damaged during shortened microwave cooking time.

MIGRAINE (*See* HEADACHES.)

MILK INTOLERANCE

Three ways to detect it If you experience bloating, cramps, and diarrhea, the reason could lie with intolerance to a milk ingredient, lactose. How can you make certain?

- A physician can tell from a blood test done after you've consumed a specified amount of milk.
- You can test yourself by cutting back on milk or stopping its use entirely for a week to see if symptoms disappear.
- Alternatively, you can drink two glasses of cold milk, which seems to produce symptoms more often than warm milk, on an empty stomach and see if your typical symptoms appear.

Four helps in overcoming it
- Most lactose-intolerant people, although unable to consume large quantities of milk without experiencing symptoms, can take milk in reasonable quantities in cereal or coffee.
- You may also find you have no problems when you take your milk with a meal rather than by itself—and when you avoid ice-cold milk.
- You can also eat hard or fermented cheeses in which lactose has been reduced during processing. Cultured buttermilk and cultured yogurt may also be tolerated.
- You can use an enzyme product called LactAid, available in stores. Added to milk, it takes the place of the missing or inadequate body enzyme needed to handle the lactose in milk.

MOLDS (*See* ALLERGIES.)

MOLES (*See* SKIN.)

MOTION SICKNESS

A *folk cure* Ginger tea is an old folk remedy for upset stomach. Now it appears that capsules of powdered ginger root can ward off motion sickness even more effectively than an antimotion sickness drug. In a study reported in the British medical journal *The Lancet* two capsules of powdered ginger (940 milligrams in all) proved to be twice as effective as 100 milligrams of the drug Dramamine. Ginger capsules are available in health-food stores. Ginger root, the researchers emphasize, must be taken in capsules to avoid severe irritating effects. The researchers recommend two or three capsules for avoiding motion sickness.

A wrist-point cure Pressure on an acupuncture point called nei-kuan may help relieve seasickness or other motion sickness. The point is located on the surface of the inside of the forearm, three finger widths away from the crease of the wrist and in the center, between the two flex tendons.

Based on that principle, a "seasick strap" has been devised by a New York City physician, Dr. Daniel Shu Jen Choy, an internist affiliated with Lenox Hill and Columbia-Presbyterian hospitals. The strap is a four-inch piece of elastic, two-thirds of an inch wide, with one-inch pieces of Velcro stitched on the ends so it can be readily closed around the wrist. In the center of the strap is a rounded plastic button worn against the skin to exert constant pressure on the nei-kuan point.

Reportedly the strap has been 70 percent effective in preventing seasickness—and 60 percent effective as well in preventing the nausea accompanying pregnancy.

Ten other aids for coping with motion sickness

- Because the balance system in the brain may be involved, it may help, if you're a chronic sufferer, to take up jogging or swimming as a means of acclimating the balance system to movement.

- When riding in car or train, focus on distant objects rather than nearby ones moving past you.

- On a ship, stay on deck as much as possible and keep busy.

- On a plane, pick a seat over the wheels rather than in the tail, which moves more than the rest of the plane.
- Keep your head as still as possible. When seated, brace it against the back of the seat. In moving the head, do so slowly.
- Avoid reading if it makes your motion sickness worse; it does for some people.
- Avoid tobacco smoke if possible.
- Avoid eating or drinking for an hour before a trip.
- An alcoholic drink may help; more than one is likely to make matters worse.
- Taken as long as an hour before departure, over-the-counter drugs for motion sickness—such as Dramamine and Bonine—can be helpful although they do tend to cause drowsiness.

See also Carsickness.

MOUTH IRRITATIONS

A helpful rinse   For minor mouth sores not related to any specific disease, you can try frequent rinsing with a solution of half water and half hydrogen peroxide. Usually the irritations respond quickly, finds Dr. R. E. Couch of Watkinsville, Georgia. If necessary, rinsing once a day thereafter may prevent recurrences.

See also Canker Sores.

MUSCLES (*See* LINIMENT; TENSION.)

NAILS

Some help for the brittle   Fragile nails that break easily may be hereditary or the result of inadequate protein in the diet. Although gelatin has been pooh-poohed as a remedy, recent studies indicate that three or four teaspoons daily of plain, unflavored, powdered gelatin do help make for stronger nails, with results noticeable in a month or five weeks.

More help for the brittle   This from a Tulane Medical School, New Orleans, dermatologist: Your companions may find it a bit nerveracking but tapping your fingernails, drumming them on tabletops and other surfaces, does toughen the nails. Witness the strong nails of guitar players.

NASAL CONGESTION

The stuffy nose, nose drops, and nasal sprays   Drops and sprays used to relieve nasal congestion can, ironically, cause it too—and are often-overlooked reasons for chronic stuffiness. Here's why: When applied to the nasal mucous membrane lining, drops and sprays shrink the tissue. Fine. But prolonged or frequent use results in rebound swelling that often exceeds the original. Commonly, then, more drops are applied, resulting in a vicious cycle. Stopping the use of drops or sprays normally will reverse the swelling in five to seven days. To prevent recurrence, future use of drops or sprays should be limited to three to five days. (See Using a Spray More Effectively, which follows.)

The stuffy nose and other medication   Sometimes medications used for other purposes can be responsible for nasal congestion. They include:
- Medications for high blood pressure: guanethidine, Hydralazine, methyldopa, prazosin, Reserpine.
- Beta-blocker medications used for high blood pressure and other purposes: nadolol, propranolol.
- Antidepressant medications: chlordiazepoxide-amitriptyline, perphenazine, Thioridazine.

Many of these drugs are prescribed under a variety of

trade names. If you're taking medication and are experiencing nasal congestion, check with your physician or pharmacist about whether the medication could be the source of your problem. If so, a switch to a different drug could help.

Using a spray more effectively This advice from Dr. Frank J. Marlowe of the Medical College of Pennsylvania, Philadelphia: Spray each nostril once, wait five to ten minutes, then spray once more in each nostril. The first spray will shrink membranes in the front part of the nose, allowing the second spray to penetrate deeply to the back of the nose. Used this way, a spray can provide more prolonged relief, and there's less tendency to remedicate at too frequent intervals.

Salt solution nose drops Properly made, a salt solution can be useful for irrigating a stuffy nose. But beware an excessively strong solution. Stir one-fourth of a teaspoon of salt in an eight-ounce glass of water. That provides an 0.5 percent solution. But don't exceed that strength. When one mother, for example, mixed a whole tablespoon of salt in a glass of water, producing a 6 percent solution, twelve times the proper strength, her infant became severely ill and had to be hospitalized.

Exercise may help One effect of exercise is to stimulate the movement of blood from the nose to muscles. Another is to increase the body's production of adrenaline. Both effects tend to decrease congestion, report Columbia-Presbyterian Medical Center, New York City, physicians.

See also Allergies; Coffee; Colds: What Chicken Soup Can Really Do.

NITROGLYCERIN

How to tell if it's stale and useless Nitroglycerin tablets can be valuable for relieving and even preventing episodes of anginal chest pain associated with coronary heart disease. But often when they prove ineffective, it's because they're stale. The tablets lose potency during extended storage or exposure to sunlight. A simple way to tell if nitroglycerin is still useful: Look for an immediate burning sensation when you begin to dissolve a tablet under your tongue. If there's no burning, you need a new supply.

NOSEBLEEDS

Three wrong ways of trying to stop them   These methods can delay normal healing:
- Stuffing cotton, tissue, or gauze into the nose.
- Applying cold towels to the back of the neck.
- Inserting a paper towel under the upper lip.

The right way
- Clasp the nose between the thumb and index finger and squeeze—just hard enough to stop the bleeding, not enough to cause pain.
- Breathe slowly through the open mouth.
- Continue the finger pressure for five minutes—no less —without interruption. If bleeding is not controlled after five minutes, press again once or twice more. In most instances, bleeding stops after the first properly done pressure application.
- Once bleeding stops, sit quietly, leaning forward—or, if you prefer, lie down with the head and shoulders propped on three or four pillows.
- For three or four hours after bleeding has stopped, do not blow the nose and, preferably, do not talk or laugh. This is to avoid disturbing the blood clot.
- If bleeding is not controlled after three attempts, get medical help.

OBESITY

Preventing it in childhood　Don't overfeed infants and children. The tendency to do so is remarkably common. The results can be a lifelong problem.

- A check of food consumed by 130 Maryland babies at ages two, seven, and eighteen months in a Johns Hopkins University School of Hygiene and Public Health, Baltimore, study found a calorie excess of 70 percent at all three ages over recommended allowances. In some infants, the excess ran to 250 percent.

- In another study, when children nine to fifteen years old were given skin fold tests, those with the largest skin fold measurements, indicating excess fat, proved to be the same as those overweight at age one year.

- Currently, an estimated 20 percent of all American children are obese.

- Whereas a slim adult may have only about twenty-seven trillion fat cells, obese adults who were overweight in childhood have been found to have as many as seventy-five trillion. Fat cells—which demand nourishment and, when in excess, demand excess nourishment in terms of the body as a whole —can be reduced in size but not in numbers. This may be why childhood obesity is often the precursor of extreme adult obesity.

- Don't overfeed. More than what a child really needs is *not* better.

Self-curing obesity—better results than commonly supposed　If you're discouraged by all the reports—popular and medical—that overeating (and smoking as well) are extraordinarily difficult habits to correct, take heart. Surprisingly, many people are curing themselves without professional therapy, for long periods of time—in many cases, apparently permanently.

- Dr. Stanley Schachter of Columbia University, New York City, interviewed 161 people on their weight and smoking histories. They included university people and blue-collar residents of a small Long Island town. Overall, 62 percent of those with a history of obesity who had tried to lose substantially on their own had been successful, a far higher percentage of success than reported in medical and other professional literature.

● And of those who had attempted to quit smoking on their own, without treatment, 63 percent had succeeded and, on average, had been off smoking for seven years, contrasted with as few as 10 percent of people given treatment who remained nonsmokers after one year.

● Suggests Dr. Schachter: People who cure themselves do not see therapists. So the therapeutic literature tends to report only the most difficult cases and is based largely on success or failure in a single attempt. Success rates among the nontreated may be higher because they may make multiple, long-term efforts to stop overeating or smoking.

Four ways dietary fiber can help take off excess weight
● Fiber-rich foods—vegetables, fruits, and whole-grain breads and cereals—have to be chewed more, which slows eating, and the slower the eating, the more chance for satiety to set in before there is overeating.

● Fiber has a space-filling effect that helps bring about satiety—and fiber is not absorbed and does not supply calories.

● Fiber also helps promote satiety because chewing stimulates secretion of both saliva and gastric juices, and these help fill the stomach.

● And fiber, unabsorbed itself, helps reduce absorption of other food. While in a typical modern diet of refined foods, 93.2 percent of the available energy in foods is absorbed, alteration of the diet to include brown instead of white bread, plus more fruits and vegetables, cuts absorption to 91.2 percent. And, on whole-meal bread, very high in fiber, the absorption is cut to 88 to 89 percent.

Soup for obesity Soup can act as a calorie intake regulator to help the overweight. University of Nebraska, Omaha, researchers examined the three-day dietary records of twenty-eight thousand Americans of all ages surveyed by the U.S. Department of Agriculture.

• Some eight thousand Americans ate soup at least once during the three-day period—and, on soup days, each person consumed an average of five percent fewer calories than on other days.

• The calorie reduction was even greater for those eating soup twice in one day.

• Notably, too, 8 percent more grams of food were consumed on soup days—but soup, while high in nutrients, is low in calories, unlike a piece of pie, which may weigh only two hundred grams but contains five hundred calories.

• Remember, however, that all soups are not low in calories; those containing real cream or lots of fat are loaded with calories.

How to assess true obesity   Weight alone is a poor measure of obesity because it is not a real measure of the amount of excess body fat. The simplest way to assess your degree of obesity is by means of the *body mass index*. The index is calculated metrically, and here is how to arrive at it:

• Convert your nude weight in pounds to kilograms. Since there are 2.2 pounds to a kilogram, divide the pounds by 2.2.

• Convert your barefoot height to meters. Since there are 39.371 inches to a meter, divide your height in inches by 39.371.

• Square your height in meters; that is, multiply the height by itself.

• Divide your nude weight in kilograms by the square of your barefoot height in meters and the result is the body mass index.

• For example, if you weigh 154 pounds, that's equivalent to 70 kilograms. If your height is 5'9", that's equivalent to 1.8 meters. The square of 1.8—1.8 × 1.8—equals 3.24. Seventy divided by 3.24 equals 21.6, the body mass index.

The body mass index range for normal-weight men is 20

to 25; for women, 19 to 24. Above that range, there is some degree of obesity. When body mass index is greater than 30, both sickness and death rates begin to rise steadily in both sexes.

See also Fat; Weight.

OSTEOPOROSIS (BONE THINNING)

Combating it with exercise and calcium A common problem, especially in postmenopausal women, osteoporosis involves loss of bone mineral content, bone thinning, and easy bone fracture. It can be a painful disorder, particularly when it strikes the spine. But studies show that bone loss in elderly women may be reversed or at least controlled through physical activity and/or calcium–vitamin D supplements.

• Osteoporosis is common because women over age thirty-five lose bone mineral content at a rate of about 1 percent a year.

• To see if the loss could be slowed, stopped, or possibly even reversed, a three-year study included 80 women, aged sixty-nine to ninety-five years, who were divided into groups.

• Group I received only doses of a placebo (an inert preparation). They served as a control, or comparison, group.

• Group II was given 750 milligrams of calcium daily— and, to help absorption of the calcium, 400 international units of vitamin D daily.

• Group III engaged in light physical activity three times a week, thirty minutes at a time, and received the placebo.

• Group IV engaged in the same physical activity as Group III and also received the calcium–vitamin D supplement used in Group II.

• Results after three years: Group I showed a continued significant decline in bone mineral content of 3.29 percent. Group II showed an actual increase in bone mineral content of 1.58 percent, and in Group III the increase was higher: 2.29 percent. Group IV showed a reduced loss of bone mineral—0.32 percent—but didn't do as well as Groups II and III; probably, the researchers believe, because they were older and had a higher rate of overall decline during the three years.

PAIN

When you feel it most Chances are you tolerate pain less well in the afternoon than in the morning. This is what University of Chicago researchers have found after noting it takes more mild electrical current to produce pain in volunteers in the morning than later in the day—apparently because the pain threshold varies according to natural biological cycles. The practical value: You may do better to schedule dental appointments for the morning—and if your physician prescribed a pain reliever, you might be well advised to check with him or her on using larger doses in the evening than the morning.

How long various pains should last Here are the average durations of pains from various causes. If they last longer, an additional problem or complication may be involved and medical attention is needed.

Sprain
```
Ankle . . . . . . . . . . . . . . 1 week
Knee  . . . . . . . . . . . . . 3 days
Wrist . . . . . . . . . . . . . 3 days
Finger . . . . . . . . . . . . 1 day
```

Low back strain
```
Minor  . . . . . . . . . . . . 1–2 days
Major . . . . . . . . . . . . . 3–5 days
```

Burn
```
Small . . . . . . . . . . . . . 3–6 days
Large . . . . . . . . . . . . . Several weeks
```

Splinter . . . . Immediate relief upon removal

Skin cut (laceration) . . Soreness gone within 24 hours

Headache . . . . Hours to days

Chest pain
Surface soreness . . . . 1–4 days
Angina pectoris
"Heart cramp" . . . . . 1–10 minutes   If it lasts longer and nitroglycerin does not help, suspect a heart attack and get medical help immediately.

Heart attack . . . . Hours to days   Get emergency medical help.

Stomach pain
Indigestion . . . . Minutes to an   If an antacid offers no relief in 15
with nausea,   hour   minutes, there is the possibility of
vomiting, and/or   heart attack or food poisoning.
pain in the lower
part of the
breastbone or pit of
the stomach

Abdominal pain
From overeating . . . . 1–3 hours   If it lasts longer, it may be due to
or constipation   infection or appendicitis (if accompanied by nausea, vomiting, loss of appetite). Get medical help.

See also Arthritis; Backaches; Burns; Chest Pain; Gas Pains; Headaches; Ice; Leg Cramps; Liniment; Shoulder Pain; Sunburn; Throat, Sore; Toothache.

PALMS (*See* SWEATY PALMS.)

PEPTIC ULCER (*See* ULCER, PEPTIC.)

POISONING IN CHILDREN

Seven insights and aids to prevention   Studies by Children's Hospital Medical Center, Boston, and poison control centers reveal facts all parents should keep in mind:

• Most poisonings involve children old enough to walk but not over three years of age.

• The unpleasant taste of a potential poison has little deterrent value. Toddlers will swallow virtually anything.

• The most dangerous time of the day is during the hour just before the evening meal. Some experts call it "the arsenic hour." It's a time when a child is usually hungry, may not have had a snack since lunch, and mother is busy preparing the evening meal. It's the tensest time of day. "We wonder," says one poison control authority, "if it might not be a good idea to put some cookies on the table for a youngster to grab at this particular time."

• Once a child has ingested a nonedible substance, a potential poison, there is a 59 percent chance he or she will ingest another within the next year.

• Most frequently involved products: Medicines make up about 50 percent of the poison control center calls; cleaning agents, about 20 percent; insecticides, about 10 percent; petroleum distillates (gasoline, turpentine, lighter fluid, and so on) about 7 percent. The rest is miscellaneous, with plants rating high in summer, cosmetics in winter when a child is indoors much of the time. Tops among medicines: painkillers such as aspirin and acetaminophen, tranquilizers, sedatives, sleeping pills, and vitamins. Among cleaning agents: detergents, bleaches, strong cleaners. Among plants: mushrooms, poinsettia, jimson weed, pokeweed, wisteria.

• Important in preventing poisoning: Keep all products in their original containers (never place inedibles in food, milk, or beverage containers), and keep all inedibles out of sight, out of reach, with all medicines locked away.

• Never refer to medicine as "candy." Teach children not to take medicine unless it is given by an adult—and, since youngsters tend to mimic parents, don't take medicine in the presence of small children.

Being prepared for poisoning Have two essentials on hand:

- An ounce bottle of syrup of ipecac. Your druggist can provide it without prescription. It is by far the most reliable, safe, effective emetic—vomiting inducer.
- The phone number of the nearest poison control center. There are now about six hundred across the country. You may find the number of the nearest one in the front section of your telephone directory. If not, ask your physician for the number.

What to do in case of poisoning This depends on the nature of the swallowed poison.
- You can safely give one or two glasses of water to dilute the poison.
- Immediately call the poison control center—or a doctor, hospital, or rescue unit. And give as much of this information as you possibly can about what was swallowed: name of product, maker, contents if listed on the container, how much was swallowed. Poison control centers have information about product contents from manufacturers, and, because of this, can give you specific instructions about what to do.
- If you're advised to induce vomiting, give one tablespoonful (one-half-ounce) of syrup of ipecac if your child is one year of age or older, and at least one cup of water. If there is no vomiting within twenty minutes, repeat once. Keep walking the child about, and if there is no vomiting within ten minutes after the second dose, try tickling the back of the throat with a spoon handle or other blunt object.
- When vomiting occurs, place the child over your knee in a spanking position with the head lower than the hips to help avoid inhalation of vomitus.
- If syrup of ipecac is not available, try tickling the back of the throat as above after giving water.
- If vomiting is delayed, get the victim to a hospital emergency room or doctor and if possible bring along the poison's container.

Warning: Don't use saltwater for vomiting Although saltwater has long been considered effective for inducing vomiting and some first-aid manuals still may recommend its use, don't use it. Poison information center experts report that it has led to acute salt intoxication in both adults and children, producing such symptoms as irritability, appetite loss, coma, and convulsions. Several fatalities have been reported.

When an eye is affected Without delay, wash the eye— gently. Use plenty of water with the eyelid held open. Continue for at least 15 minutes. Call a poison control center, doctor, hospital, or rescue unit and take the victim to a medical facility promptly.

When the skin is affected Wash the affected area with a large amount of water. Use soap if available. Remove any poison-contaminated clothing. Call for help.

POISON IVY (*See* ITCHING.)

PORES, ENLARGED

What to do for them Oil is naturally secreted through the pores. When oil secretion is excessive, pore openings may stretch, becoming larger, more visible. Although the pores can't be reduced permanently, astringents may make them appear smaller. You can often make them less visible, too, by keeping the face as free as possible of oil accumulations, which accentuate pore size by reflecting light.

POSTURE

What's good For good posture, according to the President's Council on Physical Fitness and Sports:

- The centers of gravity of many body parts—from the feet to the legs to the hips, trunk, shoulders, and head—must be in a vertical line.

- As viewed from the side when you are standing, the line should run through the earlobe, the tip of the shoulder, the middle of the hip, just back of the kneecap, and just in front of the outer anklebone.

The value Also according to the President's Council, good posture acts to avoid cramping of internal organs, permits better circulation, and prevents undue tensing of some muscles and undue lengthening of others. It thus contributes to fitness.

POTASSIUM

Making it easier to take If your physician has prescribed potassium supplements that you find unpalatable, check with him or her on a way to prepare them in gelatin-dessert form that makes them more tolerable. One physician, writing in the professional journal *Consultant* suggests: Dissolve four twenty-milliequivalent packets of potassium supplement in two cups of boiling water. Add a three-ounce package of gelatin, pour into a mold, and refrigerate. In many cases a quarter portion provides one day's dosage.

See also Blood Pressure: Pressure, Potassium, and the Kitchen.

POTATOES

The not-so-humble tubers Although often scorned in the United States as just stomach fillers, potatoes are second only to eggs as a complete food in terms of nutritional balance—protein, calories, minerals, vitamins. Superior to most other food crops in the quality of its protein, the potato also has a higher ratio of protein to carbohydrate than many cereals and other roots and tubers. And potatoes are not fattening; rather, it's the butter and sour cream or the frying oil that add calories.

POWDER (*See* TALC.)

PREGNANCY

Effects of vigorous exercise   Aerobic exercise appears to have no harmful effects on the majority of pregnant women—and, in fact, one study of sixty-two who exercised for one hour three times a week found a 17.6 percent increase in work capacity compared with a group of nonexercising, nonpregnant women. No significant differences have been found between the birth weight, body length, head circumference, or condition at birth of babies born to exercising mothers and those of babies born to mothers who do not exercise. One difference: Exercising mothers seem to have shorter periods of labor. Exercise, however, may not be advisable for women with preeclampsia, a condition characterized by elevated blood pressure, water retention, and albumin in the urine.

Intercourse and pregnancy   Although having intercourse late in pregnancy has been considered a possible cause of premature membrane rupture, preterm birth, and other complications, that view is challenged now by a United States–Israeli study of 10,981 pregnancies. In the first, second, and third months of pregnancy, 90, 87, and 90 percent, respectively, of the women reported having intercourse. In the fourth, fifth and sixth months, the proportions were 95, 95, and 94 percent. Toward term, 89, 66, and 36 percent reported intercourse in the seventh, eighth, and ninth months. Those having intercourse even late in pregnancy showed no increased risk of premature rupture of membranes, preterm delivery, low birth weight, or perinatal death compared with those who abstained.

Meal skipping—avoid it　During the last three months of pregnancy, even healthy nondiabetic women risk "accelerated starvation" and low blood sugar if they skip a meal. Northwestern University, Evanston, Illinois, physicians recently tested blood-sugar levels during the last six hours of an eighteen-hour overnight fast in twenty-one women in the last trimester of pregnancy and twenty-seven nonpregnant women, all nondiabetic. After twelve hours, the major difference between the groups was lower blood sugar in the pregnant women and, by eighteen hours, their blood sugar was significantly lower. To prevent this, breakfast should not be skipped and a routine bedtime snack is desirable.

Taking a fluoride supplement during pregnancy　You might want to check on this with your physician because of benefits for the baby reported in a recent study published in the *American Journal of Obstetrics and Gynecology*. Investigators evaluated dental development in 492 children of mothers who had been given one milligram of fluoride (2.2 milligrams of sodium fluoride) daily during the last six months of pregnancy. The findings: virtual elimination of decay in the children. At mean ages of 4.7, 6.4, and 7.6 years, they were still 99 percent free of cavities. The investigators recommend a one-milligram fluoride tablet daily from the third through the ninth month, taken on an empty stomach and not followed by milk, antacids, or calcium-containing supplements.

Walking during labor　This can benefit both mother and child, according to a British study. When half of a group of women in labor were asked to walk about while others remained lying down as usual, the women who walked had shorter labors and less need for pain-relieving medication—and their babies' condition at birth was better also. The advantage of walking may be due to the effect of gravity, resulting in a more natural labor process.

Weight gain in pregnancy As a rule, thin or underweight women should gain the most for a healthy pregnancy, and overweight women should keep weight gain to a minimum. These findings came from a study following the course of over 50,000 pregnancies in the United States:

• The lowest infant death rates corresponded with a thirty-pound gain for thin women (those weighing less than 90 percent of the desirable weight), twenty pounds for normally proportioned women (weighing 90 to 135 percent of the desirable weight), and sixteen pounds for overweight women.

• Of all those studied, thin women had the highest infant death rates when their weight gain was low, but had the lowest infant death rates with optimal weight gain.

• Weight gains greater than thirty-two pounds were harmful regardless of the weight of the mother before becoming pregnant.

Where the added weight comes from The average woman produces a 7½ pound baby, 1½ pounds of placenta, 2½ pounds of amniotic fluid in which the baby floats, and gains 2½ pounds in her uterus and 1 pound in each breast. There's also an increase of 4 more pounds in blood volume—for a total gain of 20 pounds. Still more weight gain may come from water retention in the tissues and an increase in fatty deposits.

Working during pregnancy Is the baby harmed? Here's what a study of 7,722 pregnancies by Pennsylvania State University College of Medicine, Hershey, investigators shows:

- For women who worked during the last three months, pregnancy was not shortened.
- Newborns of working women weighed about five to fourteen ounces less than those of mothers who stayed home.
- Growth of the unborn baby was slowed the most when working mothers had been underweight before becoming pregnant and had a low pregnancy weight gain, or had high blood pressure, or when their work required standing.

Does the reduced birth weight mean impairment of long-term growth, survival, and intellectual performance? Not necessarily, say the researchers. They point to a study of the children of Dutch mothers who had almost starved during pregnancy in the 1944–45 Dutch famine. At nineteen years of age, the children had no mental, physical, or health impairments.

The "Drano Test" for baby's sex It has been rumored to be reliable. Just add a little crystal Drano to the mother-to-be's urine and in a minute you can see the results: A green color indicates a boy, yellow to amber a girl. Curious about it, a University of Wyoming, Laramie, doctor repeated the test monthly during the last three months of pregnancy in one hundred women. Of the one hundred, twenty-one failed to show the same color change consistently; for the remaining seventy-nine, the "test" predicted the babies' sex correctly in thirty-seven but incorrectly in forty-two. That makes the "test" about as accurate as flipping a coin.

Maternal age and child abnormalities As maternal age increases, so does the risk of Down's syndrome (mongolism) and other genetic chromosomal abnormalities. A recent medical report (*Obstetrics and Gynecology*) provides these estimated rates of significant abnormalities according to maternal age: 1.9 per 1,000 live births at age 20 rising to 115.0 at age 48, as shown in the table below:

Mother's age	Down's syndrome per 1,000 live births	All cytogenic abnormalities per 1,000 live births
20	0.5– 0.7	1.9
30	0.9– 1.2	2.6
35	2.5– 3.9	5.6
36	3.2– 5.0	6.7
37	4.1– 6.4	8.1
38	5.2– 8.1	9.5
39	6.6– 10.5	12.4
40	8.5– 13.7	15.8
42	13.8– 23.4	25.5
44	22.5– 40.0	41.8
46	36.6– 68.3	68.9
48	59.5–116.8	115.0

See also Allergies: Allergy Shots During Pregnancy; Aspirin: Aspirin Late in Pregnancy—Caution; Exercise: After Childbirth—Four Tips; Heartburn: Heartburn in Pregnancy.

PRESCRIPTIONS

How to read one

• The Rx below your name and address is simply an abbreviation of the Latin word for "prescription."

• The RX is followed by the doctor's orders. For example: Tenormin 50 mg tabs #50. This means that the strength of the drug, Tenormin, is fifty milligrams; it is to be supplied in tablet form (tabs), and the pharmacist is to provide you with fifty tablets.

(If you want to price shop, you can call several pharmacies and ask their charge for fifty tablets of fifty-milligram Tenormin.)

• Following the Rx portion of the prescription, you find the "SiG"—which means instructions the pharmacist is to write on the label. For example: SiG Tq 3-4 h PRN for nervousness. The pharmacist will label the medication: Take (T) one tablet every (q) three to four hours (h) as necessary (PRN) for nervousness.

- If you find an "LAS" on the prescription, it means that the pharmacist should label—identify—the drug for you. A "PPI" means that you are to receive an information packet showing side effects, contraindications (conditions that forbid use of the medicine), and so on.

- In a lower corner, you find the word "Refill." The physician may indicate there if the prescription is to be refilled and how many times.

PROSTATE

A tip for coping with a nightly nuisance Common in older men, nonmalignant prostate enlargement can be a special nuisance at night when it leads to frequent wakings and trips to the bathroom to urinate.

Faced with the problem himself, waking every hour or two, and concerned he might have to have surgery, a retired physician decided to try a simple tactic: He deliberately spent at least a minute and even more voiding each time he felt the urge, carefully not straining, until no more spurts could be obtained.

"Results were immediate and dramatic," he reported in the *New England Journal of Medicine.* "I now sleep three or four hours at a time and occasionally get up only once in eight hours. If I am lazy and fail to take plenty of time to void, there is a prompt return of frequency. Months of this exercise may restore bladder tone so extra effort will not be called for, but even if that does not occur, taking the extra time at each voiding is worthwhile since it improves the night's rest so much."

PROTEINS (*See* EXERCISE; GUIDELINES: PROTEIN CONTENT OF FOODS AND TYPES OF FOODS, and PROTEIN FOODS WITH LOW-FAT CONTENT.)

What prescription terms mean:

ad lib	at pleasure
AC	before meals
bid	twice daily
c̄	with
cap	capsule
cont rem	continue the medicine
d	give
dd in d	from day to day
dexter	the right
div	divide
dos	dose
dur dolor	while pain continues
emp	as directed
febris	fever
garg	gargle
h	an hour
hs	bedtime
ind	daily
liq	liquid
m et n	morning and night
mor dict	in the manner directed
no	number
no rep, nr	not to be repeated
OD	right eye
OL	left eye
pc	after meals
pil	a pill
prn	as necessary
qh	every hour
qid	four times a day
qs	quantity sufficient
qod	every other day
rep	to be repeated
rub	red
sig	write
sing	of each
sol	solution
solv	dissolve
ss	a half
stat	immediately
suppos	suppository
tab	tablet
tere	rub
tid	three times a day
tinct	tincture
ung	ointment
ut dict	as directed

PUBERTY

When it's premature—finally, a treatment   Puberty normally starts around age eleven or twelve, but in some children premature sexual development occurs much earlier, even in infancy, often leading to sexual awakening and emotional upheaval. And while tall for their ages because of a growth spurt triggered by high sex hormone levels, they end up short as adults because they stop growing at an earlier age.

Recently, in more than eighty children with this condition, aged nine months to nine years, physicians at the National Institutes of Health, Bethesda, Maryland, have used a new medication—a synthetic relative of a natural body hormone LHRH. Called LHRH analog, it has produced dramatic results, usually within a year, dropping sex hormone levels to prepubertal levels and halting menstruation, ovulation, and sperm production. In many of the children, pubic and facial hair has disappeared, and premature breast and genital development has regressed. Growth rates have also slowed to normal, allowing the children to reach normal adult heights in due course, after resuming puberty at an appropriate age.

See also Growth in Children.

PUMICE STONE

Use it for many purposes, medical and other   A pumice stone is made of frothlike volcanic glass.

• Because it's unlikely to cause damage when rubbed over wet skin, it can help remove scales, increasing the effectiveness of treatment for scaling skin disorders.

• It's useful for removing dirt and stains from hands. Employed instead of organic solvent cleaners by plumbers, electricians, painters and mechanics, it can remove otherwise stubborn stains without irritation, avoiding occupational skin disorders.

- It can help remove calluses from the feet.
- For women, it is often valuable for smoothing heels to prevent snagging of hose.

PUPPY FAT

Telling if your pet is too fat Of some forty-five million dogs in the country, up to two-thirds are obese, according to a Texas A & M College of Veterinary Medicine, College Station, researcher.

Is yours? This advice from one expert source: "You should not be able to see your dog's ribs, but you should be able to feel them."

RADIATION (*See* TV–COMPUTER HOOKUPS.)

RAYNAUD'S PHENOMENON

Try arm waving Raynaud's phenomenon—blanching and numbness of the fingers, followed by redness and throbbing pain—results from poor blood circulation in the hands brought on by cold or emotional upsets.

Taking a lesson from Vermont skiers who warm their hands by whirling their arms, a Rutland, Vermont, physician asked several of his Raynaud patients to try waving their arms vigorously in the motion of an underhand softball pitcher—downward behind the body and upward in front, in a continuous 360-degree swinging movement, with emphasis on the downward swing—to force blood into the fingers.

The arm waving, he reports, has produced excellent results, reversing Raynaud attacks in as little as one and a half to three minutes.

Keeping warm Most patients with Raynaud's phenomenon, aware of their sensitivity to cold, make efforts to keep their hands warm.

But they often don't recognize that central warming (including the head) is equally important to keep blood from being shunted from the arms and hands to the trunk.

It's also important not to wear constricting garments that can aggravate blood circulation problems.

RECREATION (*See* EXERCISE; GUIDELINES.)

RECTAL ITCHING (*See* ITCHING.)

RELAXATION TECHNIQUES

Two simple methods These are two simple methods of achieving relaxation which can be helpful in combating stress and the health problems associated with it.

1. Developed by Dr. Herbert Benson and his associates at Harvard Medical School, Cambridge, Massachusetts, and useful for many stress-related problems including high blood pressure, the "relaxation response" involves these steps:

- Sit quietly in a comfortable chair with the eyes closed.
- Relax all the muscles of the arms, legs, and torso.
- Breathe through the nose and, on exhaling, say the word "One" silently to yourself as a means of preventing distracting thoughts. ("One" serves just as well, Dr. Benson has found, as the "mantra" of Transcendental Meditation, a word usually derived from Hindu scripture.)
- Continue breathing through the nose, exhaling, and saying "One" for ten to twenty minutes.
- Use the technique once or twice daily—but not within two hours after a meal.

2. Developed by Drs. A. P. French and J. P. Turpin of the University of California, Davis, this "mind-drifting" technique has, in their experience, helped relieve insomnia and has moderated pain, anxiety, and emotional reactions to illness:

- Sit comfortably, feet on the floor, eyes closed.
- Let your breathing become easy and relaxed, with the air flowing gently into and out of the lungs; once breathing is relaxed, allow the muscles to relax.
- Now relax the mind, letting it drift naturally and gently to a pleasant, restful memory. Usually, you can achieve this within a minute.
- Let the memory come to mind without forcing it and let yourself be there and experience the memory. Don't concentrate on it or think about it in the usual sense. If your mind wanders off, simply bring yourself back to the memory gently and naturally.

RUNNING

How long before tests show results Running to promote cardiovascular health does work—but you may have to run at least ten miles a week for almost a year before the benefits become apparent.

Stanford University, Palo Alto, California, researchers studied forty-eight healthy, previously sedentary men, aged thirty to fifty-five, who participated in a fitness program.

- Not until after nine months of running ten miles a week were there higher HDL (high density lipoprotein cholesterol) levels in the blood and lower LDL (low density lipoprotein cholesterol) levels, both measurements associated with reduced risk of heart attack.
- But other desirable results do come sooner: Fitness, measured by treadmill endurance and oxygen uptake tests, improved as early as three months into the running program and at activity levels of even five miles a week or less. De-

creases in body fat also became evident after only three months.

Children's running—some cautions   Youngsters are now running greater distances than ever before. But authorities urge caution.

"The growth tissues in children increase their chances of injury," says Dr. Lyle Micheli, sports medicine director at Children's Hospital, Boston. Although it may be years before long-term studies can establish clearly whether long-distance running is injurious for children, "I think we have enough reason for caution," he adds.

The American Academy of Pediatrics has issued a policy statement that children can be hurt both physically and psychologically if they participate in distance running with unrealistic goals or under parental pressure.

The academy recommends that children not enter competitive long-distance running events designed primarily for adults—and "under no circumstances should a full marathon be attempted" by teens who have not fully matured physically. Among the physical problems children who run long distances may develop are heel cord injuries and chronic joint injuries. Children also do not adapt well to extremes in temperature when they run long distances, says the academy.

Advises Dr. Micheli: Children under fourteen should not be allowed to run distances greater than ten kilometers (about 6.2 miles).

SALT

And high blood pressure—cutting back does help   It helps significantly, according to a recent British study. At Charing Cross Hospital Medical School, London, investigators measured blood pressure—during five days of high salt intake and again during five days of low intake—in 20 men and 21 women with severe hypertension, 18 men and 18 women with mild hypertension and 17 men and 11 women with normal blood pressure. There were no changes in pressure in the normal patients. But the switch from high to low salt intake produced a mean fall in pressure ranging from 6.6 to 9.4 points (millimeters of mercury) in patients with mild elevations and 13.3 to 16.1 in those with severe ones.

The key word for salt—sodium Using less salt at the table is part of the strategy for moderating Americans' excessive salt intake. No less important is reading food labels to spot the word "sodium."

Examples of sodium words are: monosodium glutamate, disodium phosphate, sodium alginate, sodium benzoate, sodium hydroxide, sodium propionate, sodium sulfide, sodium saccharin, and sodium bicarbonate. The order in which label words are listed indicates predominance in prepared products. Avoid foods where sodium is among the first ingredients.

Seven sodium-loaded types of foods In some foods, sodium is hidden by an unsalty taste—such as sweet. Cakes and pies are examples, along with foods produced by fast-food restaurants. But whether your taste buds tell you so or not, sodium-loaded foods include:

• Processed foods, such as some cheeses and instant or other ready-to eat cereals. Especially check labels for the word "sodium."

• Canned and instant soups, and bouillon cubes.

• Ketchup, mustard, prepared horseradish, and salt seasonings, including sea salt and soy, Worcestershire, and barbecue sauces.

• Pickles, olives, and sauerkraut, and other foods prepared in brine.

• Salty or smoked meat—bologna, corned or chipped beef, frankfurters, ham, luncheon meats, salt pork, sausage, and smoked tongue.

- Salty or smoked fish—anchovies, caviar, salted and dried cod, herring, sardines, and smoked salmon.
- Such snack items as potato chips, French fries, pretzels, salted popcorn, salted nuts, and crackers.

Learning to want less salt If you think you can't live without all the salt you're accustomed to though you know you should, take heart. When intake is reduced, the sensitivity to salt taste increases and the craving for it falls over time. This is what University of Pennsylvania, Philadelphia, physicians found in a study with a group of volunteers who selected their own food and were instructed only to avoid salty items. At the end of five months, they had cut back on salt intake by 42 percent and, notably, had learned to enjoy and even prefer such items as low-salt soups and crackers.

See also Baby; Blood Pressure; Lung Disorders; Sleep.

SCALP MASSAGE

Any Value? No. Harmful? Possibly Vigorous massage with or without shampoo, whether the hair is dry, wet, or being toweled dry, and vigorous manipulation by brushing or combing or during shampooing can break hair mechanically. Hair grows slowly—about half an inch a month—and mechanical loss may exacerbate, at least in appearance, the normal loss of twenty-five to one hundred hairs a day. The advice from an American Medical Association expert: Shampoo and dry gently, and avoid scalp massage; neither the scalp nor the hair roots need it.

SCOLIOSIS (TWISTING OF THE SPINE)

A simple seven-part home detection test At least 600,000 American children in the ten-to-fifteen-year age group are affected—and it's important to detect scoliosis early. If progressive and untreated, it can lead to back pain, disability, or deformity. The earlier it's treated, the better the chances of stopping the curvature and avoiding deformity. This test, suggested by the Scoliosis Association for early detection, can be carried out readily at home.

With the child standing straight, view the back:
- Is one shoulder higher than the other?
- Is one shoulder blade more prominent than the other?
- When the arms are hanging loosely at the sides, is the distance between the arm and the body greater on one side than on the other?
- Does one hip seem higher or more prominent than the other?
- Does the child seem to lean to one side?

With the child bending forward, arms hanging down loosely, and palms touching each other at about knee level:
- Do you see a hump in the back in the rib area?
- Is there a hump near the waist?

If the answer to any one of these questions is yes, consult your family physician or pediatrician for further evaluation.

SEBORRHEIC DERMATITIS (*See* DANDRUFF.)

SEIZURES (*See* EPILEPSY.)

SHAVING

Legs or face, the H₂O counts Interestingly, the advice comes from a shaving cream and razor company: No matter what product you use for lathering up, use plenty of water beforehand to set hair up, making it easier for your razor to deliver a close, safe shave.

Note, too: The water will also soften the skin and help keep bumps, cuts, and nicks to a minimum.

And if moisturizer is a must, as it often is on dry, flaky, legs, the advice is to wait several hours after shaving to give the pores a chance to close, then apply.

The right strokes   Most men use the wrong technique. What they do, says a skin specialist, is pull down and stretch the skin with one hand and stroke down hard with the other, using long strokes from the sideburns to neck. They chew up their faces.

The effective way to shave is, first, *with* the grain, using small, light, interrupted strokes. Rinse. Lather again. Then use the same gentle, light strokes to shave *against* the grain. You get a closer shave without chewing up the face.

SHELLFISH

A better bill of health   Shrimp, lobster, and their crusty relatives have long been thought to be bad for you because of their high cholesterol content. Even some physicians still believe that. But the facts are otherwise.

• Shellfish got a bad cholesterol reputation almost fifty years ago when the concern with the relationship between cholesterol and heart disease first began to flourish. At that point, tests for cholesterol content were crude and measured, along with cholesterol, a lot of other compounds. As a result, 100 grams of oysters, for example, were thought to contain 200 milligrams of cholesterol.

• Modern tests now measure only 50 milligrams of cholesterol in 100 grams of oysters.

• You would have to eat more than a dozen oysters or two small lobsters to mach the cholesterol in one egg (250 milligrams).

SHINGLES

Relieving it with a binder Shingles is a nerve inflammation caused by the same virus that produces chicken pox. Also known as herpes zoster, the inflammation most often affects the chest area, producing pain, burning sensations, and itching. A State University of New York, Syracuse, physician who suffered from shingles noticed that slight pressure of his open hand markedly relieved the symptoms. He then decided to apply an elasticized binder, about eight inches wide, with a Velcro closure, to the chest. For the first time in weeks, he was able to sleep uninterruptedly. The slight pressure of the binder necessary to relieve symptoms did not interfere with breathing.

SHOES

The kind to buy for healthier feet
* Make them leather if you possibly can. Podiatrists—foot specialists—increasingly report that widespread use of synthetic shoe materials, often called man-made, are damaging feet and causing fungus infections, such as athlete's foot, and corns, calluses, bunions, deformities, and pain. Because leather is porous, they say, leather shoes breathe and eventually conform to foot contours.
* Also being blamed for increasing foot problems: synthetics in soles, increased use of one-piece molded plastic footwear, and use of running shoes of materials other than leather and rubber.
* Another problem: the narrow lasts often seen on poorly cut, cheap shoes. Blamed for increasing incidence of bunions and deformities of the big toe, especially among women, narrow-lasted shoes, reports one podiatrist, "jam toes together and bend forward the long second toe into a hammer toe. We see inflammation of the bursa, the sacs of fluid in the toes, and this results in bursitis. Spike heels and pointed toes pinch toe

nerves and cause neuroma, a tumor of the third or fourth toe, not to mention puffy ankles."

• Another specialist adds reptile skins to the list of less desirable shoe materials. Alligator does not give or breathe, she reports, and lizard gives but little.

• Advise many podiatrists: For healthy, pain-free feet, wear leather shoes and have them properly fitted.

• And this advice on getting proper fit from one specialist: Buy your shoes, arrange so you'll get your money back if they do not fit—any reputable store will agree provided they're returned in absolutely clean condition—and take the shoes home. Wear them, covered with fabric shoe bags, around the house for two active hours or so. If they're still comfortable after that time, you can be pretty sure your fit is good.

See also Baby.

SHOULDER PAIN

Getting relief at night As victims know, a shoulder injury often leads to sleepless nights. By day, the shoulder can be carried in the least painful manner, but in bed the shoulder position often produces painful tension. Try elevating the head of your bed on twelve-inch blocks, suggests Dr. James A. Nicholas of Cornell University Medical Center, New York City. It often helps.

SINUSES (*See* AIR TRAVEL.)

SITTING HAZARDS—AND AVOIDING THEM (*See* AIR TRAVEL; VEINS.)

SKIN

The dry skin problem Americans spend millions of dollars yearly on lotions, creams, emollients, and special soaps claimed to soften and moisten the skin. Dry skin is common for several reasons: in winter, cold dry outdoor air, still drier heated indoor air; frequent bathing that removes from the skin the natural protective oils that normally help keep it moist; reduced oil gland activity as we get older. Excessively dry skin can feel hard or rough, look cracked or scaly.

Prevention and treatment These suggestions from leading dermatologists should relieve dry skin if it's already present and prevent it in the future unless there are underlying causes needing medical help:

- Use a humidifier in winter.
- For anyone prone to dry skin, a daily shower or bath may be too much, especially in winter. Two or three times a week can be adequate; sponge armpits, groin, and feet. In addition, these areas are the only ones in the body, say some dermatologists, that should be soaped most of the time. Make your shower or bath tepid, not hot; hot water, by opening pores, can increase loss of moisture afterward.
- After a bath or shower, an oil treatment is helpful. Baby oil can be effective—especially for those who dislike greasing up. A neat trick, says one dermatologist, is to pour some baby oil into the hands, and rub it over the entire body after washing and before toweling. Then towel off and the skin will be moisturized without feeling or looking greasy. The baby oil retards moisture evaporation from the skin without closing pores. It may be more effective than moisturizing creams and lotions, which often are mostly water and retard evaporation relatively little.
- This suggestion from an Ann Arbor, Michigan, physician: Adding one cup of salt to a tub of bath water can moisturize the skin at least as well as, if not better than, expensive bath oils. Only rarely is the salt irritating, in which case, it should be discontinued.
- For dry lips, avoid licking, which increases dryness. Use a lip balm or waxy lipstick.
- Emollients leave an oily film on the skin to retard evaporation. As a night emollient, in place of an expensive prepa-

ration, petroleum jelly, mineral oil, or solid vegetable fats such as Crisco can be effective.

- Exercise is a good treatment for dry skin since it helps circulation and brings moisture to the skin—as long as you don't rub off the good with overly energetic bathing and toweling afterward.

Skin rashes from drugs Many drugs can produce rashes. Some hospital studies indicate that 2 to 3 percent of all inpatients get rashes following drug administration.

So if you're taking medication and develop a rash, all drugs being used should be suspected. Because most drug rashes develop within two weeks of beginning treatment, suspicion logically falls on the drug or drugs you've been taking most recently. Check immediately with your physician; he or she may be able to pinpoint the responsible medication and substitute another.

Skin moles—what to watch for Moles can be present for a lifetime without causing trouble. But a change in size, shape, or color can signal a skin cancer. Watch out for shades of blue, red, gray, purple, and black—as contrasted with shades of brown characteristic of most moles. And if a mole has been well defined with clear edges but starts to trail off into the surrounding skin area, see your doctor immediately.

See also Eczema; Feet: Relieving Dry Skin Conditions; Pores, Enlarged.

SLEEP

How much is essential The need for sleep can vary considerably from person to person.

- "Each person has a natural sleep length," says one of the most distinguished sleep researchers, Dr. Wilse Webb of the University of Florida, Gainesville. "Some people are five-hour sleepers, some are seven-hour sleepers, and some are nine-hour sleepers. There's a natural spread, as in any biological system—just like height or weight." And he adds: "To demand that all people sleep seven or eight hours means that something like 60 percent of people are sleeping 'badly' if they get the length of sleep that is natural for them. It's like demanding everyone be a medium-size shirt. The average time that people sleep is seven and a half hours. But statistically, three hours on either side is within the normal range."

• A study in Scotland not long ago found that 8 percent of a large sample of people needed no more than five hours; 15 percent needed five to six hours; the large bulk needed seven to eight. But 13 percent required nine to ten and a few needed even more than ten hours.

• Older people, concerned about shortened sleep, should be reassured. A need for less sleep is normal with aging.

Determining your own needs Here are two methods:
• This one is offered by Dr. Webb. The rule of thumb is simple: If you wake up spontaneously, feeling well rested, and if you don't struggle through periods of intense sleepiness during the day, you're getting adequate sleep. If you're not sure, you can do this: One night the first week, go to bed at five in the morning and get up at seven, note how you feel all day so you'll know the symptoms of not getting enough sleep. One night the next week, go to bed at three, get up at seven, and see how you feel. Let yourself sleep two hours longer one night each week until you find that you wake up spontaneously and aren't tired during the day. That's your natural sleep length.

• Another way: Pick a period when you're relatively free of stress—perhaps a vacation time. Go to bed at the same time each night for two to three weeks and get up in the morning without help from the alarm clock. The average length of nightly sleep during such a period is likely to approximate what is normal for you.

Getting to sleep the night before a "big day" Say Monday is an important day. Do not sleep late Sunday morning, then go to bed early Sunday night; chances are you'll have a difficult time falling asleep. Your best bet: Get up *very early* Sunday morning and stay up a little later Sunday night. The longer the time between waking up from one night's sleep and going to sleep again, the easier it is for most people to get to sleep.

Alcohol and sleep Although a nightcap to serve as a mild sedative at bedtime is often considered useful for assuring a good night's sleep, beware. In fact, reports Dr. Charles E. Becker of San Francisco General Medical Center, alcohol—like other sedatives and sleep-inducing drugs—distorts the normal sleep cycle. It depresses dream sleep, and when the alcohol intake is stopped, there is increased dream-sleep activity that may produce hallucinations. Disruption of the normal sleep cycle may perpetuate underlying sleep difficulties and increase the likelihood of consuming more alcohol or other drugs.

Eighteen medications and other chemical substances that can adversely affect sleep Not uncommonly, sleeping problems can be linked to the following substances and may be solved with a change of dosage or change of medication.
- Nervous system depressants: alcohol, barbiturates, opiates, the tranquilizer meprobamate, and benzodiazepine tranquilizers such as Librium, Valium, Limbitrol, and Tranxene.
- Nervous system stimulants: amphetamines, caffeine, methylphenidate.
- Anti-high-blood-pressure medications: methyldopa, propranolol, reserpine.
- Hormones: cortisone, oral contraceptives, progesterone, thyroxine.
- Ulcer medication: cimetidine.

- Others: antidepressants known as MAO inhibitors, theophylline.

Exercise and sleep   Increased exercise and other physical activity during the day—some hours before sleep—can be valuable. It can increase deepest sleep. But exercise just prior to bedtime has an exciting effect.

Salt and sleep   Although it's well-known that coffee, tea, and other caffeine-containing beverages can lead to insomnia in some people, another cause in some cases—excess salt—gets little attention, according to Dr. Alfred F. Morris of the University of Illinois, Urbana-Champaign. He points to a little-known study done nearly forty years ago in which hospitalized patients being treated for insomnia experienced improvement in both the quantity and quality of sleep when salt intake was reduced, then relapsed when the previous salt intake was restored. Says Morris: "Since most Americans consume seven to fifteen times the salt they need, this may inadvertently lead to widespread insomnia."

Smoking and sleep   Nicotine acts as a stimulant and in some people may affect sleeping patterns, according to recent sleep laboratory studies at Pennsylvania State University, Hershey.
- In one study, fifty subjects who had smoked a mean of 1.25 packs a day for more than three years were paired with fifty nonsmokers of the same sex and age. During four nights in the sleep laboratory, it took smokers an average of fourteen minutes longer to fall asleep than the nonsmokers, and throughout the night they were awake nineteen minutes longer.
- In a second study, eight men who smoked a mean of two packs a day were monitored for nine days. During the first four days, they smoked as usual; on the fifth, they stopped abruptly. Although uncomfortable during the daytime, they

spent an average of 45 percent less time lying awake for the remaining five nights.

To fall asleep, try to stay awake "Paradoxical intention" —doing the opposite of what you want to make happen— sometimes works. *Family Health* reports a study in which five insomnia patients were told they should stay awake as long as possible in order to note their insomniac thoughts so they could be helped. They promptly nodded off. One woman reduced her wakeful period from a mean of ninety minutes a night to only five and a half while a man went from fifty-seven minutes to six. Why does it work? One possibility: Trying to stay awake eliminates anxiety about not being able to fall asleep.

Five steps in learning to fall asleep While there are many possible causes for insomnia, bad sleeping habits are a common one. This is what one sleep researcher, Dr. Richard R. Bootzin of Northwestern University, Evanston, Illinois, who considers misuse of the bed to be an especially bad habit, advises his patients about overcoming it:

- Go to bed only when tired.
- Once in the bedroom, no TV viewing, reading, or worrying.
- If sleep doesn't come in a short time, leave the bed and bedroom and return only when you are ready to try to fall asleep again.
- If you still don't succeed, get out of bed and out of the room again, and keep repeating the process until you do get to sleep quickly after returning to bed.
- Set the alarm for the same time every morning, weekends as well. The body needs rest; a regular schedule will help get it.

One of Bootzin's typical cases: A man who for four years had gone to bed nightly at midnight and had been unable to get to sleep until 3 or 4 A.M., stewing about job, financial, and other problems to the point of turning on the TV to try to stop his ruminating. Typically, when first on the Bootzin program, he had to leave the bedroom four and five times a night. After two months, he was leaving the bedroom no more than once a week.

"Nature's sleeping pill" Some sleep researchers have believed that there might be some natural substance used by the body to regulate sleep. If so, it would have to be available either in food or through natural body processes, and it would have to be shown to produce normal sleep by scientific measurement and do so at doses equivalent to those that might occur naturally.

L-tryptophan, a natural amino acid, one of the building blocks of protein, may be such a substance. It's present in milk, meat, and green vegetables; about half to two grams are consumed in a normal daily diet. In experimental studies, the most common side effect of L-tryptophan in pure form proved to be drowsiness. And in sleep laboratory studies, a dose of one gram was found to halve the time needed to fall asleep, and the sleep was normal.

Tryptophan tablets are available in health-food and other stores. Or you can try the traditional home remedy for sleeplessness: a glass of warm milk. Your belief in it may now be bolstered by the knowledge that it contains L-tryptophan.

See also Baby: When Baby Naps, Don't Tiptoe.

SMOKING

To reduce the harm Cigarette smokers unable to kick the habit but eager to reduce tar and nicotine intake can benefit from a change in smoking habits. Puffing lightly and infrequently can significantly reduce the intake of tar and nicotine, according to a study by the Addiction Research Foundation, Toronto. The average smoker took 9.8 medium-size puffs per cigarette, but some smokers studied took as many as 16 puffs on a king-size cigarette. The latter group's intake of tar and nicotine was approximately two and a half times that of the former group.

See also Cancer: Carotene and Cancer—A Protective Dietary Fiber; Heartburn; Sleep.

SNORING

A medication to help   When snoring is very disturbing, protriptylene, a drug your physician can prescribe, may help. It's commonly used for depression but apparently has other effects, including what appears to be a salutary one on snoring. Writing recently in the *Western Journal of Medicine*, Dr. Jay A. Goldstein of Anaheim Hills, California, reports: "I have been prescribing a small dose of about ten milligrams at bedtime to snoring patients whose spouses or families complained that the noise levels were unbearable.... Most families thus far have reported a diminution or cessation of snoring.... Such a benign intervention appears worthy of further trials."

Three other suggestions for snorers
• Try wearing to bed a cervical collar, the kind used for treating a sprained neck. Snoring is usually at its height when the sleeper lies on his or her back, head sagging on the chest, bending the windpipe, and obstructing breathing. A cervical collar keeps the chin elevated and so prevents windpipe bending and obstruction, according to Dr. E. L. C. Broomes of Lakeside Medical Clinic, East Chicago, Indiana.
• A simpler solution, taught him by his grandmother, says Dr. George D. McGeary of Bend, Oregon, is to sew a small glass marble under a scrap of cloth between the shoulder blades of the snorer's pajama top. As soon as the snorer rolls onto his (or her) back, the marble will make him roll right

back on his side or abdomen to resume sleep without snoring. It's rare for the marble to be forgotten once in place; it can go through the wash and isn't likely to be left behind on trips.

● Along the same lines, Dr. E. F. Schmerl of Oakland, California, favors having snoring patients use a "snore ball" —half of a soft sponge rubber ball about two inches in diameter. Attached to a piece of Velcro, it will cling firmly to the back of a pajama jacket fitted with a corresponding piece of Velcro.

An operation to help　A new and relatively simple surgical procedure apparently can cure snoring when it is very severe, loud enough to be heard in an adjacent room and unresponsive to change in sleep position. It involves removing some of the soft palate in the back of the mouth, any extra tissue on the sides and back wall of the throat, and the tonsils (if present). The surgery, according to Dr. F. Blair Simmons of Stanford University, Palo Alto, California, does cause some throat soreness for several days and costs about the same as a tonsillectomy. Based on reports by spouses, it's effective in 95 percent of cases. Name of the operation: palatopharyngoplasty.

SOUP (*See* COLDS; OBESITY.)

SPICES (*See* LUNG DISORDERS.)

SPINE (*See* SCOLIOSIS.)

SPORTS (*See* EXERCISE; GUIDELINES.)

SPRAIN (*See* ATHLETIC INJURIES; PAIN.)

STOMACH TALK (*See* BOWEL RUMBLING.)

STRESS

Managing it Despite all that has been written about stress, it remains poorly understood. Stress in itself is not necessarily harmful. Life is full of it. It's inescapable. What counts is how one reacts to stress. Poor reactions to stress can be harmful and are thought to be a factor in bringing on heart and other disease.

Cogent tips on effective handling of stress come from Dr. Robert S. Eliot of the University of Nebraska Medical Center, Omaha:

- The bottom line of stress management is not to upset yourself.
- Develop a thick skin. Why hate when a little dislike will do . . . have anxiety when you can be nervous . . . have rage when anger will do the job . . . be depressed when you can be sad?
- Rule number one is, "Don't sweat the small stuff."
- Rule number two is, "It's all small stuff."
- If you can't fight and you can't flee, flow.

See also Exercise: Exercise as an Antidote for Tension and Stress.

STRESS INCONTINENCE (*See* BLADDER TRAINING.)

SUGAR (*See* BURNS: Easing a Burned Tongue with Sugar.)

SUN (*See* HEADACHES; SUNBURN.)

SUNBURN

Preventing it Sunscreen preparations help. So does timing.

• Sunscreens, along with helping to prevent sunburn, may help prevent skin damage and skin cancer. The most potent sunscreens are those labeled as having a sun protection factor of fifteen. For tanning, a sunscreen with a lesser protection factor—in the range of six to ten—may be used.

• Proper timing: The length of your first exposure at the beginning of summer should be limited to about fifteen minutes, with gradual increases of five to 10 minutes a day until the skin has thickened and tanned. Remember that the sun's rays can penetrate clouds, producing a burn even on a cloudy day. Also, from late morning to midafternoon—about 10 A.M. to 4 P.M.—is the period of most intensive burn rays.

Treating it For a severe sunburn, advises Dr. Norman Levine, a University of Arizona, Tucson, dermatologist, apply ice water compresses for the first six to ten hours. Aspirin, too, may help; along with relieving pain, it helps inhibit the formation of prostaglandins, hormonelike substances that lead to inflammation. For the worst cases, you may need a prescription for a potent antiinflammatory drug such as prednisone, which should be taken by mouth for three to five days.

For a mild case of overexposure to the sun, with redness, itching, and mild pain, relief may be obtained by applying cold cream, mineral oil, or talcum powder. Any preparation containing an anesthetic—a "caine"—should be used cautiously if at all.

SUNGLASSES

The right kind Sunglasses should be of gray, green, or brown tints; any other shades can interfere with color perception. They should be dark enough so you can barely see your eyes in a mirror, large enough to cover the area surrounding the eyes while allowing side vision, and they should be impact resistant.

SUPPOSITORIES

Three aids in using them Although valuable for children when oral medication is impractical and for local rectal problems in adults, suppositories are often used improperly. Proper insertion can make them more effective and can ease apprehension and discomfort.

• For most people, advises Dr. George E. Downs of Hahnemann Medical College and Hospital, Philadelphia, the best position is in bed, on one side, with the uppermost leg bent. The buttocks can then be spread apart with one hand and the suppository easily inserted with the other.

• Cocoa butter suppositories need no lubrication. Water-soluble kinds can be lubricated by moistening them with water.

• Keep suppositories in the refrigerator to keep them from melting. But they'll be less irritating if they are warmed to room temperature before use.

SURGERY

A helpful beforehand measure—fiber in the diet A common discomfiting problem after surgery is interruption of normal bowel activity and abdominal distention with gas. But a high-fiber diet beforehand may help.

In a study reported in Britain, twenty-one of forty-two women undergoing cesarean section, hysterectomy, or elective surgery used a bran-enriched diet starting ten days before their operations. They passed both gas and stools much earlier than the twenty-one others who remained on their usual diet —often within the first or second postoperative day rather than the fourth day or even later.

SWEATY PALMS

An effective aid If you're troubled with persistent excessive sweating of the palms without evident cause, you can ask your doctor for a prescription for Drysol—a 20 percent solution of aluminum chloride (hexahydrate) in anhydrous ethyl alcohol. It's often notably effective, according to Dr. Walter Shelley of the University of Pennsylvania Department of Dermatology, Philadelphia.

The preparation, recommends Dr. Shelley, should be applied nightly to dry palms, just before retiring, with the hands *not* washed before application. The palms then should be covered with clear plastic wrap and gloves to hold the wrap in place. In the morning, the coverings should be removed and the hands washed in the usual fashion.

The procedure should be repeated nightly for three weeks, suggests Dr. Shelley, and if it is effective should be continued about once a week.

SWIMMING

Water to avoid Avoid any water with a greenish color indicating a high concentration of algae, which may foster the breeding of infectious organisms.

Relief for eye irritation   When chlorine in a pool irritates the eyes, a simple treatment is to hold a cold wet towel over closed eyes.

See also Cystic Fibrosis; Ears; Eyes; Headaches.

TALC

A caution for women   Many women apply talc to sanitary napkins and to genitals. This may be risky. A possible link between use of talc and the development of ovarian cancer was uncovered in a study of 215 women diagnosed as having the cancer at Boston hospitals. While researchers say that more study is needed, they did find that of the 215, 43 percent had dusted talc on genitals *or* sanitary napkins, as compared with 28.4 percent of a group of cancer-free women of similar age, background, and marital status. Women who dusted both napkins *and* genitals were three times as likely to develop ovarian cancer as those who did not use talc at all.

TAPING INJURIES

For better adhesion   To make adhesive tape stick better and increase its durability, rub a moistened bar of soap across the edges of the tape, suggests Dr. Harold B. Henig of Tucson, Arizona. As the soap dries, it will harden and seal the tape, preventing premature loosening.

TEA (*See* CONSTIPATION.)

TEETH

Cheese to combat decay   Surprisingly, eating certain cheeses can help prevent tooth decay. University of Minnesota, Minneapolis, studies have found that aged Cheddar, Swiss, and Monterey Jack apparently work to prevent sugar from forming an acid layer on teeth. Studies elsewhere indicate as well that such cheeses may work by triggering an increase in the production of saliva, which contains many substances useful in combating decay—enzymes that can kill decay organisms, minerals that strengthen the teeth, and buffering compounds.

Other new insights about decay

• Not only refined sugar but also honey, molasses, and dried fruit can cause decay; along with high sugar content, these foods are sticky, making them harder to remove from teeth.

• It's the frequency of eating sweets, not the amount eaten, that's most important in causing decay. Studying rats dining exclusively on chocolate cookies, researchers found that the animals fed once an hour had 50 percent fewer cavities than those fed every ten minutes. It appears that the amount of acid produced is about the same no matter how much sugar is consumed at one time—but decay increases when the mouth doesn't have time enough to neutralize the acid. So if you must eat sweets, it's better to eat them in one sitting.

• Here's an index—with some surprises—ranking snacks according to their decay-causing potential, with ordinary sugar rated at 1.0 for comparison:

Filled chocolate cookie	1.4
Cereal (14% sugar)	1.1
Cereal (8% sugar)	1.0
Coated chocolate candy	0.9
Potato chips	0.8
Caramel	0.7
Chocolate bar	0.7
Cereal (2% sugar)	0.5
Starch	0.5

Replacing a knocked-out tooth If a child accidentally knocks out a permanent tooth, the best bet is to replace it in the socket if you can—and, next best, put it in milk—and get to a dentist quickly. University of Florida, Gainesville, researchers have found that milk is 80 percent better than air drying, 75 percent better than water, 50 percent better than saliva for keeping the tooth alive. Milk enables ligament cells on the outside of the tooth to continue to function; it is also relatively free of bacteria.

Tooth gnashing Gnashing or grinding teeth during sleep (bruxism), which affects about 10 percent of all people, can seriously damage teeth, gums, and supporting structures. Although the cause is not known, a link to alcohol has been found in a Boston study of a group of men and women with bruxism histories of many years who were moderate social drinkers, averaging one to four drinks a day. The study found that bruxism was mild or absent on nights after no alcohol consumption, loud and disturbing to spouses after two or more drinks. In a sleep laboratory study, one woman was found to have twenty-two episodes of gnashing and grinding after alcohol consumption, only six on an alcohol-free night.

See also Toothache.

TENNIS ELBOW

A test for proneness Tennis does not necessarily cause tennis elbow; the trouble can lie with a weak wrist. Players free of the problem have this in common, according to Dr. Willibald Nagler of New York Hospital–Cornell Medical Center, New York City: They can grip a weight of eight to ten pounds, bend the wrist backward against the weight resistance, hold it bent for five seconds, and repeat this fifteen times without difficulty. Most of those with tennis elbow histories, Dr. Nagler finds, are unable to carry out the maneuver, even when free of pain, with a weight of more than three pounds, and many can't get beyond one pound.

One exercise to help　For the weak wristed, a progressive exercise program has cut tennis elbow recurrences sharply, advises Dr. Nagler. This is the program:

- Place the playing arm on a table, palm down. With a firm tennis grip on a three-pound dumbbell, bend the wrist upward and hold for five seconds. Return to the starting position and rest for three seconds.
- Work up to fifteen repetitions, then increase the weight by one pound. But never increase it at this or any other level if you feel pain or strain during or after the exercise. You're not ready to go on. Keep practicing.
- As you can, increase the weight pound by pound until you can manage eight to ten pounds without difficulty.

An alternative exercise　This one is suggested by Dr. James Puscas of Anaheim, California:

- Cut an eighteen-inch length from a broom handle or round pole, tie a twenty-four-inch-long cord or heavy string to the middle of the handle or pole, and nail it in place. Then tie the end of the string or cord to a weight.
- For the exercise, hold the stick ends with your palms down and arms outstretched. Roll the stick toward you, winding the weighted string.
- An average man may begin with a two-pound weight, winding and unwinding the string ten times, three times a day. Weight and repetitions can be increased every few days by one to two pounds and two to four windings.

Six other aids
- Stroke properly. Use the power of the shoulder muscles as well as body weight in swinging a racket, reducing strain on the elbow. Don't rely on power force of the forearm; it transmits too much strain to the elbow, especially in backhand strokes.

- Eliminate excessive bending of the wrist in backhand stroking. Meet the force of the ball by rotating the whole arm from the shoulder rather than by suddenly extending the elbow or wrist.
- Better yet, train for a two-handed backhand stroke.
- Backhand or forehand, try to hit the ball with the center ("sweet spot") of the racket to lessen muscular stress.
- Wear an elbow band to help distribute stress on the muscles.
- Use the right racket. Some experts recommend a flexible steel racket with gut or nylon stringing at a tension not greater than fifty pounds.

TENSION

How to ease it when it's excessive Excessive muscle tension can cause problems. Any time a muscle is used—which means it is tensed—blood flow in that area is briefly constricted. With the constriction, nutrients can't reach cells and cell-produced wastes can't be carried away. All that is entirely tolerable for short periods. But continued muscle tension can lead to fatigue, weakness, and aches and pains. Here are ways to detect excessive tension and relax it, suggested by Richard Grossman of Montefiore Hospital and Medical Center, Bronx, New York:

- Every time you have occasion to look in a mirror— morning and night, while washing and so on—note if you're frowning deeply, wrinkling your forehead, or tightly compressing your lips. Feel if you're holding your facial muscles too tight. If you are, exaggerate the feeling: Make a deliberate effort to tense your face, raising your eyebrows as far as possible, squeezing your eyes shut tightly, frowning as much as you can. Then completely relax the muscles you've used. Repeat this until you're very much aware of the difference between tension and relaxation.

• Check your shoulders. A slow rise in the position of the shoulders is common as a reaction to daily stress. The large muscle extending from the top of the shoulders into the neck and head can become constricted. Moreover, breathing may become restricted. If you find you're holding your shoulders high, suggests Grossman writing in *Family Health,* just let them drop, take four or five deep breaths, and feel your head and neck muscles relax at the same time. It's a good idea to check your shoulder position half a dozen times a day.

• Similarly check the feet and hands. There is a common tendency under stress to hold the fingers or toes tight. If you find such finger or toe tension, squeeze harder to exaggerate the tension, then let the muscles go limp.

Observes Grossman: "Though our bodies may appear to go about their business automatically, we can still exert some control over them. And one way to do that is to tell the body when to let go—to give the muscle structure a chance to restore itself right in the midst of our daily activity."

See also Exercise: Exercise as Antidote for Tension and Stress.

THROAT, SORE

Five relief aids A sore throat can result from a variety of causes—allergy, low humidity, toxic fumes, yelling, an unusual amount of talking or singing, or bacterial or viral infection. These suggestions can often ease discomfort:

• Use a saltwater gargle—about half a teaspoon of salt to a cup of warm water.

• Dissolve throat lozenges slowly in your mouth.

• Use aspirin or acetaminophen (nonaspirin pain reliever).

• Drink lots of fluids to moisten the throat.

• Get as much rest as you possibly can until you feel well.

When to call the doctor If bacterial infection is the cause, a prescribed antibiotic is often needed. And that's especially important if the infection is caused by strep bacteria —which can be determined through a culture of a small amount of mucus taken from the back of the throat. In any case, check with your doctor if any of the following holds true:

- Pain is severe enough to affect swallowing.
- A fever or a skin rash accompanies the sore throat.
- In a child, the sore throat is accompanied by fever, headache, vomiting, stomach pain, or swollen glands.
- A mild sore throat lasts for more than 48 hours.
- A sore throat develops after exposure to someone with a strep throat.
- A sore throat occurs in anyone with a history of rheumatic fever or kidney disease.

The family pet as a strep throat source If a child has repeated streptococcal sore throats and there's a pet in the home, it may be wise to have the pet checked. A State University of New York College of Medicine, Stony Brook, physician has reported that on one hundred occasions when he thought it worth checking on pets, forty cultures of the dogs or cats were positive for strep bacteria. When the infected pets were treated for their infections by veterinarians, all the families were freed of the recurrent strep throat problem.

TOOTHACHE

Five ways to deal with a middle-of-the-night episode You can't call the dentist. What can you do?

- First, try flossing between the aching tooth and its neighbors; sometimes impacted food can set up the pain.
- If impaction is not the problem and you can see no obvious cavity, apply an ice bag or cold compress against the jaw on the affected side.

- If cold doesn't help, try heat, which sometimes does. Apply a hot-water bottle or warm compress.
- If you see a cavity, clean it out gently, using sterile cotton on the end of a toothpick; then saturate another bit of cotton with oil of cloves and pack it gently into the cavity with a toothpick.
- Still another alternative: Apply ice to the web of skin between the thumb and index finger on the same side of the body as the toothache. How this works is unknown, but it often does, respected Canadian investigators at McGill University, Montreal, report. Interestingly, the web site is where the Chinese insert acupuncture needles to relieve tooth pain.

Aspirin and toothache Although aspirin may provide some relief for toothache when taken internally, don't try placing a tablet on or near an aching tooth. That can lead to burning, ulcerated sores, and may even damage the tooth nerve or pulp, according to the American Dental Association.

TOXIC SHOCK SYNDROME (*See* DIAPHRAGM CONTRACEPTION.)

TOY BOX ACCIDENTS (*See* CHILDREN.)

TRAVEL (*See* AIR TRAVEL; WATER.)

TRAVELER'S DIARRHEA (*See* DIARRHEA.)

TRYPTOPHAN (*See* SLEEP.)

TV–COMPUTER HOOKUPS

A possible hazard If you're hooking up a microcomputer to an old color TV set for recreational or other activities, there could be a radiation hazard. Twenty-five million sets were produced before 1970, when radiation emission standards for color TVs were adopted. Many of these older sets are still in use.

● Surveys indicate that as many as 16.2 percent of these older sets may exceed emissions set by the standards. For general viewing at average viewing distances, the radiation dose appears safe. But radiation intensity depends upon distance from the source and computer users tend to position themselves close to the screen, increasing radiation exposure.

● Youngsters especially who use older color TVs for display screens may be at risk for radiation exposure far in excess of radiation standards.

● Suggest researchers: Only color TV receivers made after January 15, 1970, should be used as display elements for computers in the home.

TYPE A BEHAVIOR

What it is   There is a type of personality given to a kind of behavior now commonly called Type A and so named in the 1950s by its discoverers, Drs. Meyer Friedman and Ray Rosenman of Mt. Zion Hospital and Medical Center, San Francisco. That behavior has been described as amounting to "an unremitting battle against time and other persons" (who are suspected of threatening the security of the individual). It can have any of many manifestations: tense body posture, fist clenching, hostile laugh, hurrying or interrupting the speech of others, facial tension, thinking or doing two or more things simultaneously, difficulty in sitting and doing nothing, and easily aroused irritability with others.

What it can do   Especially in the extreme, Type A behavior is considered a significant risk factor for coronary heart disease and heart attack—perhaps as important as high blood cholesterol, high blood pressure, and excessive cigarette smoking.

Nine helpful steps to modify it   It's not easy to modify this behavior, but these may be helpful steps:

- Keep a week-long log of circumstances in which you find yourself becoming irritated, impatient, or frustrated—when and why you have a sense of great time urgency and your biggest battles with the clock.
- Make contracts with your self—not to try to change overnight but rather to focus on one occasion or event that irritates you and makes you impatient and to change your handling of it. Then, move on to another.
- Evaluate yourself realistically. Whatever success you've achieved—is it really due to hurry, hurry, or to other characteristics and talents you have?
- Cut down on needless clutter in your calendar—appointments and obligations that really don't matter and are not essential.
- Try to relax more. Use music for that. Also, take exercise breaks, even very brief ones, to release tension.
- Get up fifteen or twenty minutes earlier so you can begin the day more calmly, less rushed.
- Facing a deadline, work—but take an occasional break for a chat with someone, a walk around the room, anything to periodically break the tension.
- Make a determined effort to stop interrupting others.
- Pick a model—some non–Type A person you know whom you respect for his or her achievements and calm, efficient approach. Study how he or she copes with daily work and stress. Try to do the same.

ULCER, PEPTIC

Milk—does it help?   Milk, once considered almost essential in ulcer treatment, no longer is. Yet, while there have been studies suggesting it does little or no good, some ulcer patients find it comforting, capable of bringing quick relief. And while there is no accepted medical explanation for milk-induced relief, it should not be held up to derision, suggests Dr. H. M. Spiro of Yale University, New Haven, professor of medicine and chief of gastroenterology. "Can anything," he says, "which really makes you feel so much better be so bad for you?" And, he points out, recent studies indicate that the mixture of milk with an acid-pepsin combination like that found in the stomach leads to formation of pain-relieving substances much like the body's natural opioid pain-relieving agents. Thus the legendary relief attributed to milk may turn out, in the end, to have a scientific basis.

A combination to avoid At the same time that many ulcer patients take a prescription drug, Tagamet, they may also take antacids to ease the gnawing stomach pain. But the two should not be taken together. When they are, the antacids decrease Tagamet's ability to reduce acid secretions, George Washington University Medical Center, Washington, D.C., studies have shown recently.

• Usually patients are instructed to take Tagamet with meals and at bedtime, antacids between meals and at bedtime. Commonly they take the two together at night and, for convenience, many take them together during the day.

• The new recommendation: Take antacids one hour before Tagamet at bedtime, one hour after Tagamet at mealtimes.

Another possible error Once you take your nightly dose of an antiulcer agent such as Tagamet, avoid further cigarette smoking for the night. The medication is intended to reduce acid secretion during sleep—but smoking can interfere. In a British study, investigators found that smoking following nightly medication led to a 91.5 percent increase in acid secretion compared to no smoking after medication. The increase is highly undesirable because control of acid secretion at night may be critical in promoting ulcer healing.

Fiber to help prevent recurrence   After a duodenal ulcer has healed, a high-fiber diet may reduce the risk of relapse. Norwegian physicians in a study of seventy-three patients with healed ulcers randomly assigned some to a diet high in fiber (including fiber-rich bread, whole-grain cereals, and vegetables) and others to one low in fiber (omitting unrefined bread and cereal products and other fibrous foods). Over a six-month period, twenty-eight of the thirty-five (80 percent) of those on low-fiber intake experienced ulcer recurrence as against seventeen of the thirty-eight (45 percent) on high-fiber diets.

URINARY INFECTIONS

Urinate promptly   Failure to do so may be a reason for repeated urinary tract infections in some women. Studying eighty-four women with recurrent infections and others without them, State University of New York, Stony Brook, researchers recently found that the most striking difference between the two groups was in voiding behavior.

• Only 11 percent of the noninfected women held their urine for more than an hour after experiencing the urge to urinate as against 61 percent of the troubled women.

• When the patients were then asked to follow a preventive plan, only 15 percent experienced reinfection within six months as against their usual 80 percent reinfection rate in the past.

• The preventive plan: Regular complete bladder emptying without delay; drinking at least six glasses of fluid daily; voiding within ten minutes after coitus; adequate lubrication during intercourse; wiping the perineum from front to back rather than back to front after voiding.

See also Bladder Infections.

VACCINATION (*See* IMMUNIZATION.)

VAGINAL DISCHARGE

Some discharge is normal   Many women get the impression from commercial advertising that no moisture should ever emerge from the vagina. They may worry needlessly over normal secretions. Actually, vaginal secretions contain antimicrobial substances and help prevent infection. They also remove cell and bacterial debris.

Vaginal hygiene—what's necessary, what's not   Just keeping the external genitalia clean by washing the labia with a mild soap or by soaking in warm water periodically is all that is usually needed.

- Here's what a recent medical review of the whole subject in *Modern Medicine* has to say: "There is no evidence that the vaginal mucosa needs cleansing any more often than would the nasal or rectal mucosa. Nor is there evidence that acidifying agents, such as acetic acid (vinegar), promote vaginal health in any way. . . . In general, chemical irritants, including douches of all kinds, feminine hygiene sprays, bubble baths, and scented napkins or tampons, are best avoided."
- Note, too: In some women, tight clothing, including synthetic underwear, tight jeans, and bathing suits, may interfere with normal vaginal drainage. There may then be overgrowth of vaginal yeast and excessive discharge. Many women with the problem respond well to hot soaks and the change to cotton fabrics and looser clothing.

VEINS

A help when they're "poor"   Repeated administration of medication by vein (intravenous) is needed for some problems. In some people, a suitable vein is difficult to find. For them, when there is time between administrations, a helpful measure may be to squeeze a small rubber ball repeatedly, as often as possible, whenever possible. The exercise, one physician reports, can make "poor" veins visible and more readily accessible.

Three helps for preventing vein clots   Vein clots are common, especially in the legs, affecting hundreds of thousands of people yearly. They can produce inflammation—thrombophlebitis—with leg swelling, heaviness, and aching pain. Sometimes a leg vein clot can break loose, travel to a lung, and produce a pulmonary embolism, a potentially serious problem affecting an estimated 700,000 Americans yearly.

Vein clots can result from accidental injury or infection—and when blood pools, or accumulates, in the legs as the result of inactivity. To help prevent them:

• Understand that blood must return from the legs to the heart against the force of gravity, and this is usually achieved through contraction of the leg muscles, with the contraction pushing against the veins and producing a pumping action. If you sit or stand still for long periods, there may be little or no pumping action.

• If your job requires much standing, move about as often as you can, giving the leg muscles a chance to contract. Short of that, at least get up on your toes often while standing.

• If you must sit for long periods—at work or while traveling—make it a point to contract your calf muscles and move your feet about frequently. It helps, too, to elevate your legs horizontally to the thighs every once in a while—and to get up and walk around, even if just briefly, from time to time.

VITAMINS (*See* BREAST DISEASE, FIBROCYSTIC; CANCER; CANKER SORES; COLDS; INSECT BITES AND STINGS; GUIDELINES: GUIDE TO VITAMINS AND MINERALS.)

WALKERS, INFANT

Can they do more harm than good? Infant walkers—seats on wheels—provide no proven benefit and can be dangerous.

• A survey of parents of 150 children aged 5 to 15 months, all users of walkers, found that 47 youngsters had suffered mishaps. Most had bruises and abrasions, but some had serious injuries when the walkers either tipped over or fell down stairs.

• Report Drs. Carol A. Kavanagh of the Joseph C. Wilson Health Center, Rochester, New York, and Leonard Banco of Hartford (Connecticut) Hospital, the two pediatricians who made the survey: Infants certainly learn to walk without the practice they get in infant walkers and some research even indicates that infants not using walkers may walk slightly earlier than users.

WALKING

The many benefits for older people A healthy activity at all ages, walking can be especially valuable for many older people. Investigators at the Veterans Administration Hospital, Madison, Wisconsin, conducted a special study that included ten men, median age seventy-six years, all with numerous chronic medical problems, restlessness, malaise, and social isolation. To determine what useful effects walking might have, the men participated in a program for thirty weeks, walking forty-five to sixty minutes twice a week. A comparison of the results of physical and psychologic examinations before and after the program showed striking effects:

- Blood pressure declined by an average of thirteen points.
- Heart rate was reduced by ten beats a minute, also a healthy effect.
- Leg muscle strength increased and walking endurance went up by at least 90 percent in all ten men.
- In addition, report the researchers who supervised the study, feelings of hopelessness, depression, and anxiety were relieved by the walking program.

WATER

Tap water when you travel In areas with low sanitary standards, tap water—if hot enough—can be used fairly safely after cooling for brushing teeth, washing glasses and dishes, washing fruits, and even for diluting drinks.

Testing hot and cold tap water in hotels, private homes, and restaurant washrooms in six West African countries, Dr. Hans H. Neumann of the New Haven, Connecticut, Department of Health found cold tap water samples generally unsafe, but hot water satisfactory.

Most intestinal disease organisms are heat sensitive. As a rule of thumb, suggests Dr. Neumann, if the unmixed stream from the hot water tap is too hot to be tolerated by the hand, it's hot enough to have killed the organisms.

See also Burns: Reset That Water Heater.

WEANING (*See* BABY.)

WEIGHT

Successful dieters What characterizes people who are able to take off excess weight and keep it off? To find out,

Case Western University School of Medicine, Cleveland, researchers studied three groups of people: successful reducers who had kept off twenty pounds or more for at least two years; others who had tried unsuccessfully to lose and keep off weight; and still others who had always been thin. These are the findings:

• Successful reducers tended to lose weight at a much slower pace than the unsuccessful.

• The unsuccessful group showed a higher rate of high blood pressure and cardiovascular illness.

• For most Americans about 42 percent of daily calories come from fats. The always-thin group reported about 35 percent of calories coming from fats. The successful dieters also reported 34 to 35 percent of calories coming from fats.

• Many of the successful dieters exercised regularly as an adjunct to losing weight and maintaining the weight loss.

• The successful group reported greater support and encouragement from family in their weight-control efforts. Some of the unsuccessful said family members actually tried to sabotage their efforts. "My husband brought home cream-filled doughnuts," said one participant.

• Both groups with weight problems said they ate more in response to emotions such as anger, anxiety, and frustration. The lean group reported eating less.

• Successful dieters reported they had eaten 4,200 calories per day during their overweight period. The unsuccessful group reported only a 2,600-calorie intake. "This," report the investigators, "might indicate that those who do not have much success losing weight underestimate what they actually eat. It takes a lot of calories to maintain someone at a higher body weight and in other instances where overweight people have provided accurate food intake records, their average calorie intake was between 3,500 and 4,000 calories daily."

• The successful weight reducers cut back to 1,200 calories when dieting and, during maintenance, consumed about

1,800 calories daily. The lean group averaged about 1,900 calories per day. In effect, the successful started to eat like people who had never been fat and did not revert to old eating habits.

Other tips for successful weight loss   Based on the findings of the study noted above, and findings from other studies, the Case Western investigators have this advice if you're trying to lose weight and keep it off:

- Start with the knowledge you are going to have to change your eating habits permanently. You can't give up doughnuts today and go back to them tomorrow. It just doesn't work.
- Eat three meals a day. Eat smaller portions.
- Cut back on fats, but do not remove all fats from your diet. Fats do provide some satiety, helping to prevent or ease any hunger pangs.
- Eat more vegetables and other complex carbohydrates, using whole-grain products such as whole-wheat bread and brown rice.
- Do not decrease carbohydrates. If you do, you decrease bulky foods that are fairly low in calories yet make you feel full. It's not carbohydrates that are fattening, but fats like butter and sauces that you put on them.
- Trim fat off meat or prepare it so fat drips away. Broil, bake, or stir-fry.

Weight loss and blood pressure drugs   If you have mild high blood pressure—in the range of 90 to 104 diastolic—weight reduction could be a worthwhile first approach. It may eliminate the need for drug treatment. St. Louis University School of Medicine researchers followed 709 men who had mild pressure elevations and exceeded desirable weights by 15 percent or more and who chose to try losing weight rather than take drugs. Of the 709, 174—25 percent—were able to bring their diastolic pressure down below 90, the normal level, and keep it there over the first four years of a continuing study.

See also Calories; Exercise; Fat; Obesity; Pregnancy; Guidelines.

WINE (*See* DIABETES.)

ZINC (*See* EARS: Ear Noises and Hearing Problems—Zinc to Help.)

·II·
GUIDELINES

THE CURRENT AMERICAN DIET AND GOALS FOR IMPROVEMENT

Ten Present Food Constituent Intakes and Ten to Be Desired

The first public statement by a federal agency on the relationship between diet and disease risk factors was produced by the U.S. Senate Select Committee on Nutrition and Human Needs in 1977 in a report called "Dietary Goals for the United States."

The report identifies the proportion of total intake derived from protein, fats, and carbohydrates in the current American diet and offers specific goals for altering these proportions to achieve better health.

The following chart comes from that report:

	Current	Goals
Carbohydrates (total percentage)	46%	58%
Complex carbohydrates and naturally occurring sugars	28	48
Sugars, refined and processed	18	10
Protein (total percentage)	12%	12%
Fats (total percentage)	42%	30%
Saturated	16	10
Monounsaturated	19	10
Polyunsaturated	7	10
Cholesterol (milligrams per day)	600	300
Salt (grams per day)	6–18	5

You can see that presently the proportions of fats and carbohydrates in the American diet are almost equivalent; the Dietary Goals propose a large increase in the proportion of calories from food starches and a corresponding reduction in fats.

This may surprise those who have always thought of starches as fattening and bad for you. In fact, starches are relatively low in calories (unless buttered or sugared) and are high in nutrient concentration.

To follow these goals would require eating more fruits, vegetables and whole-grain cereals; eating less sugar, fats, and salt; and selecting lean meats and low-fat dairy products. The result would be an increase in the nutrient concentration, but not calories, of our diet.

The Dietary Goals were designed to improve the diets of healthy people, but its recommendations were actually quite similar to those proposed for some years by organizations such as the American Heart Association (which has been mainly concerned with reducing the potential of the American diet to favor heart disease) and the National Cancer Institute (concerned with reducing risk of malignancy).

Moreover, because of increasing evidence that diets high in starch and fiber control levels of blood sugar and insulin as well as blood fats, the American Diabetes Association now recommends that patients with diabetes consume a high-carbohydrate, low-fat diet in proportions nearly identical to those of the Dietary Goals.

Interestingly, too, these recommendations are also supported by exercise physiologists who advise athletes. They advocate high-carbohydrate diets to increase athletic endurance.

SPECIFIC FOOD SUBSTANCES AND SPECIFIC DISEASES

Nine Major Illnesses and Eleven Suspected Dietary Causes

Of the ten leading causes of death in the United States, six have been linked with overconsumption of certain foods: coronary heart disease, cancers of the bowel and breast, cerebrovascular disease (stroke), diabetes, arteriosclerosis, and cirrhosis of the liver.

The following table lists these diseases and others believed associated with "overnutrition," along with the specific dietary substances suspected to be at fault when eaten in unbalanced amounts (usually in excess).

Most of the evidence that associates these dietary factors with disease incidence comes from epidemiologic, or population, studies. They show, for example, that populations with a high intake of cholesterol or saturated fats have a greater frequency of coronary heart disease than do groups with a low fat intake. Similar studies relate excessive salt intake to high blood pressure, and low fiber intake to bowel cancer and other intestinal diseases.

Disease	Suspected dietary cause	
	Too little	*Too much*
Coronary heart disease, cerebrovascular disease, arteriosclerosis		Saturated fat, cholesterol
Cancer	Fiber	Fat, cholesterol
High blood pressure		Salt, calories
Obesity		Calories
Diabetes		Calories
Cirrhosis of the liver		Alcohol
Dental decay		Sucrose (table sugar)

MEETING THE GOALS FOR AN ADEQUATE, HEALTHY, SAFE DIET

Nine Essential Components

The following table offers simple, flexible guidelines for meeting the Dietary Goals. Since fruits, vegetables, and grains are relatively inexpensive, these are affordable guidelines requiring no special purchases, adaptable to all food preferences and ethnic traditions

Components of an adequate, healthy, safe diet
A wide variety of foods, not always the same
Unprocessed foods
Fresh fruits and vegetables
Whole-grain cereals

Legumes (peas and beans)
Lean meats
Low-fat dairy products
Herbs and spices as salt substitutes
Moderate amounts of all foods

THE BASIC FOUR FOOD GROUPS

The Groups, the Foods Composing Them, the Essential Nutrients Supplied

Group	Nutrients supplied	Daily adult servings	One serving equals
Meat and meat substitutes	Protein, fat, iron, niacin, thiamine, vitamins B_{12} and E, copper, phosphorus	2	2 oz. cooked lean meat, fish, or poultry; 2 eggs; 1 cup cooked dry beans, peas, or lentils; ½ cup nuts or 4 tbsp. peanut butter; 2 oz. hard cheese; ½ cup cottage cheese
Dairy products	Protein, fat, calcium, riboflavin, vitamins A and D, zinc, magnesium	2	1 cup milk or yogurt; 1 oz. cheese; ½ cup cottage cheese; ½ cup ice cream; 1 cup milk-based pudding, soup, or beverage
Fruits and vegetables	Carbohydrates, water, vitamins A and C, iron, magnesium	4	1 cup cut-up raw fruit or vegetables; 1 medium apple, banana, orange, tomato, or potato; ½ melon or grapefruit; ½ cup cooked vegetable or fruit; ½ cup fruit or vegetable juice
Grains	Carbohydrates, fat, protein, thiamine, niacin, vitamin E, calcium, iron, phosphorus, magnesium, zinc, copper	4	1 slice bread; 1 oz. dry cereal; 1 roll or muffin; 1 pancake or waffle; ½ cup rice, pasta, or cooked cereal

PROTEIN CONTENT OF FOODS AND TYPES OF FOODS

Fifteen Foods/Food Types and Grams of Protein per Serving

Food/food type	Portion	Protein (grams)
Bread, wheat	1 slice	2–3
Cereals	½ cup	1–3
Cheese		
Cheddar	1 oz.	7
Cottage	2 oz.	10
Dried peas or beans	1 cup, cooked	7–8
Egg	1 med.	6
Fish	3 oz.	15–25
Fruits	1 cup	1–2
Meat	3 oz.	15–25
Milk, whole	1 cup	9
Pasta	1 cup	2
Peanut butter	2 tbsp.	8
Poultry	3 oz.	15–25
Rice	½ cup	2
Vegetables	½ cup	1–3

PROTEIN FOODS WITH LOW-FAT CONTENT

Nine Foods Especially Low in Fat

Food	Portion	Fat (grams)
Skimmed milk	9 oz.	0.1
Cottage cheese, uncreamed	2 oz.	0.17
Shrimp, cooked	1½ oz.	0.5
Chicken, without skin	1½ oz.	1.5
Pink salmon, canned	1¾ oz.	3.0
Haddock	1¾ oz.	3.3
Veal, trimmed	1½ oz.	4.5
Yogurt, low fat	10 oz.	5.0
Hamburger, lean	1½ oz.	5.0

CARBOHYDRATE CONTENT OF SOME FOODS

Eighteen Foods and Grams of Carbohydrate per Serving

Food	Portion	Carbohydrate (grams)
Bread, white or whole grain	1 slice	13
Cereals		
Bran flakes	1 cup	28
Cornflakes, sugared	1 cup	36
Oatmeal	1 cup	23
Chocolate	1 oz.	14
Dried beans, cooked	½ cup	17–26
Dried peas, cooked	½ cup	17–26
Fruits		
Orange	1	16
Prunes, dried	4	18
Milk	1 cup	12
Nuts	¼ cup	4–10
Pasta, cooked	½ cup	16
Potato, 2¼-inch diameter	1	17
Rice, cooked	½ cup	25
Soft drinks	8 oz.	21–33
Sugar	1 tbsp.	11
Vegetables, cooked		
Green beans	½ cup	4
Green peas	½ cup	10

DIETARY FIBER CONTENT OF SOME FOODS

Seventeen Foods and Their Grams of Fiber per Serving

Food	Fiber per 3½ oz. serving (grams)
Breads and cereals	
White bread	2.72
Whole-wheat bread	8.50
All-bran cereal	26.70
Cornflakes	11.00
Puffed wheat	15.41
Puffed wheat, sugar coated	6.08
Vegetables	
Broccoli tops, boiled	4.10
Lettuce	1.53
Carrots, boiled	3.70
Peas, canned	6.28
Corn, cooked	4.74
Fruits	
Apple, without skin	1.42
Peach, with skin	2.28
Strawberries	2.12
Nuts	
Brazil nuts	7.73
Peanuts	9.30
Peanut butter	7.55

FOODS RICH IN CALCIUM

Sixteen Varied Foods with High Calcium Content

Food	Portion	Calcium (milligrams)
Sardines, with bones	3 oz.	372
Skim milk	1 cup	296
Whole milk	1 cup	288
Yogurt	1 cup	272
Cheese		
Cheddar	1 oz.	213
Cottage, creamed	½ cup	116
Oysters	¾ cup	170
Salmon, canned, with bones	3 oz.	167
Collard greens	½ cup	145
Spinach	½ cup	106
Mustard greens, cooked	½ cup	97
Kale, cooked	½ cup	74
Broccoli stalks, cooked	½ cup	68
Orange	1 med.	54
Corn muffin	1	96
Ice cream	½ cup	97

CAFFEINE IN BEVERAGES, FOODS, AND DRUGS (in milligrams)

Amounts in Twenty-six of the Most Commonly Used

Beverage/food/drug		Caffeine (milligrams)
Coffee (6 oz.)		
Automatic drip		181
Automatic perk		125
Instant		54
Tea (6 oz.)		
Iced		69
Red Rose	weak	45
	medium	62
	strong	90
Tetley	weak	18
	medium	48
	strong	70
English	weak	26
breakfast	medium	78
	strong	107
Soft drinks (12 oz.)		
Dr Pepper		38
Pepsi-Cola		38
Coca-Cola		33
Tab		32
RC Cola		26
Cocoa		
Chocolate candy (2 oz.)		45
Baking chocolate (1 oz.)		45
Milk chocolate candy (2 oz.)		12
Drugs (per tablet)		
Dexatrim		200
No Doz		100
Anacin		32.5
Midol		32.4
Coricidin		30

CHOLESTEROL CONTENT OF COMMON FOODS

Twenty-four Meats, Cheeses, and Other Foods

The table below shows the number of milligrams of cholesterol contained in 3½ ounce (100 gram) portions:

Food	Cholesterol (milligrams)
Beef, raw	70
Brains, raw	2000+
Butter	250
Caviar or fish roe	300+
Cheddar cheese	100
Creamed cottage cheese	15
Cream cheese	120
Cheese spread	65
Chicken, raw	60
Egg, whole	550
Egg white	0
Ice cream	45
Kidney, raw	375
Lamb, raw	70
Lard and animal fat	95
Liver, raw	300
Margarine, vegetable fat	0
Margarine, ⅔ animal fat	65
Milk, whole	11
Milk, skim	3
Mutton	65
Pork	70
Sweetbreads	250
Veal	90

SALT CONTENT OF FOODS

Sixty-three Foods and Condiments

The table below shows salt content in milligrams per 100 grams (3½ ounces):

Food	Salt (milligrams)	Food	Salt (milligrams)
Grapes	0.4	Pie, apple	301
Corn	0.7	Gelatin, dessert powder	318
Apples	1	Soup, chicken	382
Apricots	1	Doughnuts	401
Bananas	1	Pancakes	425
Blueberries	1	Bread	200–600
Grapefruit	1	Salad dressing	500–1300
Asparagus	1	Peanut butter	607
Wheat	3	Chocolate	615
Potatoes	4	Pizza	702
Peanuts	5	Tuna, canned in oil	800
Lettuce	9	Bran flakes	925
Onions	10	Margarine	987
Jams, preserves	12	Crabmeat, canned	1000
Broccoli	15	Cornflakes	1005
Cashew nuts	15	Bacon	1021
Mushrooms	15	Waffles, prepared mix	1029
Beans	19	Frankfurters	1100
Cream, light	43	Cheese, American	1136
Carp	50	Biscuit, prepared mix	1300
Chicken	50	Pickles, dill	1428
Milk	50	Pretzels	1680
Beets	60	Corned beef	1740
Pork	70	Popcorn	1940
Bluefish	74	Caviar	2200
Herring, fresh	74	Olives	2400
Lamb	75	Bacon, Canadian	2555
Eggs	122	Olives, Greek	3288
Asparagus, canned	236	Beef, chipped, dried	4300
Beans, canned	236	Herring, salt	6235
Peas, canned	236	Soy sauce	7325
		Bouillon cubes	24,000

CALORIE CONTENT OF FOODS

Calories per Serving in 150 Commonly Used Foods

Food	Portion	Calories
SOUP		
Bouillon or consomme	1 cup	30
Cream soups	1 cup	150
Split pea	1 cup	200
Vegetable-beef or chicken	1 cup	70
Tomato	1 cup	90
Chicken noodle	1 cup	65
Clam chowder	1 cup	85
MEAT AND FISH		
Beefsteak	3 oz.	300
Roast beef	3 oz.	300
Ground beef	3 oz.	245
Roast leg of lamb	3 oz.	250
Rib lamb chop	1 med.	130
Loin pork chop	1 med.	235
Ham, smoked or boiled	2 slices	240
Bacon	2 strips	100
Frankfurter	5½″ x ¾″	125
Tongue or kidney	average portion	150
Chicken	6 oz.	190
Turkey	3½ oz.	200
Salami	2 oz.	260
Bologna	4 oz.	260
Veal cutlet, unbreaded	3 oz.	185
Hamburger patty	3 oz.	245
Beef liver, fried	2 oz.	130
Bluefish, baked	3 oz.	135
Fish sticks, breaded (with fat for frying)	4 oz.	200
Tuna fish, canned, drained	⅔ cup	170
Salmon, drained	⅔ cup	140
Sardines, drained	4 oz.	260
Shrimp, canned	4 to 6	65
Trout	average portion	250
Fish (cod, haddock, mackerel, halibut, white—broiled or baked)	average portion	190
Whole lobster	1 lb.	145

Food	Portion	Calories
VEGETABLES		
Asparagus	6–7 stalks	20
Beans, green	½ cup	15
kidney	½ cup	335
lima	½ cup	80
Beets	½ cup	30
Broccoli	1 large stalk	30
Cabbage, raw	½ cup	12
cooked	½ cup	20
Carrots	½ cup or 1 med.	25
Cauliflower	½ cup	15
Celery	1 large stalk	5
Corn	½ cup or 5″ ear	70
Cucumber	½ med.	5
Eggplant	½ cup or 2 slices	25
Green pepper	1	20
Lettuce	3 small leaves	3
Peas	½ cup	55
Potato, sweet	1 med.	200
white	1 med.	100
Potato chips	10	100
Radishes	2 small	4
Spinach	½ cup	25
Squash, summer	½ cup	15
winter	¼ cup	45
Tomato, raw	1 med.	30
canned or cooked	½ cup	25
FRUITS		
Apple	med.	75
Applesauce, unsweetened	½ cup	50
sweetened	½ cup	95
Apricots, raw	2–3	50
canned or dried	4–6 halves	85
Avocado	½ small	250

CALORIE CONTENT OF FOODS (*cont.*)

Calories per Serving in 150 Commonly Used Foods

Food	Portion	Calories
FRUITS (*cont.*)		
Banana	med.	85
Cantaloupe	½ med.	63
Cherries, fresh	15 large	60
canned in syrup	½ cup	100
Cranberry sauce	½ cup	250
Fruit cocktail, canned	½ cup	90
Grapefruit	½ med.	55
Olive	1 large	8
Orange	1 med.	70
Peach, fresh	1 med.	45
canned in syrup	2 halves, 1 tbsp. juice	70
Pineapple, canned in syrup	1 slice	90
Prunes, cooked with sugar	5 large	135
Raisins, dried	½ cup	200
Tangerine	1 large	45
CEREALS, BREADS, CRACKERS		
Puffed wheat	1 cup	45
Other dry cereal	average portion	100
Farina, cooked	¾ cup	100
Oatmeal, cooked	1 cup	135
Rice, cooked	1 cup	200
Macaroni or spaghetti, cooked	1 cup	200
Egg noodles, cooked	1 cup	100
Flour	1 cup	400
Bread, white, rye, or whole wheat	1 slice	77
Ry-Krisp	1 double square	20
Saltine	1 (2″ square)	15
Ritz cracker	1	15
Biscuit	1 (2″ diameter)	110
Hard roll	1 average	95
Pancakes	2 med.	130
Waffles	1 med.	230
Bun, cinnamon with raisins	1 average	185
Danish pastry	1 small	140
Muffin	1 med.	130

Food	Portion	Calories
DAIRY PRODUCTS		
Whole milk	1 cup	160
Evaporated milk	½ cup	170
Skim milk	1 cup	90
Buttermilk (from skim milk)	1 cup	90
Light cream, sweet or sour	1 tbsp.	30
Heavy cream	1 tbsp.	50
Yogurt	1 cup	120
Whipped cream	1 tbsp.	50
Ice cream	⅙ quart	200
Cottage cheese	½ cup	100
Cheese	1 oz. or slice	100
Butter	1 pat	60
Egg, plain		80
fried or scrambled		110
DESSERTS		
Chocolate layer cake	1/12 cake	350
Angel food cake	1/12 cake	115
Spongecake	2″ x 2–¾″ x ½″	100
Fruit pie	⅙ pie	375
Cream pie	⅙ pie	200
Lemon meringue pie	⅙ pie	280
Chocolate pudding	½ cup	220
Jell-O	1 serving	65
Fruit ice	½ cup	145
Doughnut, plain	1	130
Brownie	2″ square	140
Cookie, plain	3″ diameter	75

CALORIE CONTENT OF FOODS (*cont.*)

Calories per Serving in 150 Commonly Used Foods

Food	Portion	Calories
MISCELLANEOUS		
Sugar, white	1 tbsp.	50
Peanut butter	1 tbsp.	100
Jam or jelly	1 tbsp.	60
Ketchup or chili sauce	2 tbsp.	35
White sauce, med.	¼ cup	100
Brown gravy	½ cup	80
Boiled dressing (cooked)	1 tbsp.	30
Mayonnaise	1 tbsp.	100
French dressing	1 tbsp.	60
Salad oil, olive oil, etc.	1 tbsp.	125
Margarine	1 tbsp.	100
Herbs and spices		0
Chocolate sauce	2 tbsp.	90
Cheese sauce	2 tbsp.	65
Butterscotch sauce	2 tbsp.	200
SNACKS		
Chocolate bar	1 small	155
Chocolate creams	1 average size	50
Popcorn	1 cup popped	55
Potato chips	10 or ½ cup	100
Peanut or pistachio nut	1	5
Walnuts, pecans, filberts, or cashews	4 whole	40
Brazil nut	1	50
Butternut	1	25
Pickles, sour	1 large	10
sweet	1 average	15
Chocolate nut sundae		270

CALORIES IN ALCOHOLIC AND CARBONATED BEVERAGES

Twenty-six Drinks

Beverage	Portion	Calories
Beer	12 oz.	144
Gin, rum, vodka, Scotch, rye, bourbon		
86 proof	1½ oz.	107
100 proof	1½ oz.	127
Mixed drinks		
Creme de menthe	⅔ oz.	67
Daiquiri	3½ oz.	122
Manhattan	3½ oz.	164
Martini	3½ oz.	140
Old-fashioned	4 oz.	179
Tom Collins	10 oz.	180
Highball	8 oz.	166
Wines		
Dessert (18.8% alcohol by volume)	3½ oz.	137
Table (12.2% alcohol by vol.)	3½ oz.	85
Champagne	4 oz.	84
Sherry	2 oz.	84
Carbonated beverages		
Quinine sodas, sweetened	10 oz.	88
Club soda	10 oz.	0
Tom Collins mixer	10 oz.	130
Ginger ale	7 oz.	62
Root beer	10 oz.	117
Cola type	10 oz.	111
Fruit-flavored pop sodas	10 oz.	130
Diet cola and pop	10 oz.	60

GUIDE TO VITAMINS AND MINERALS

Specific Usefulness, Daily Requirements, Good Sources, Latest Research Findings

Vitamin/mineral	Usefulness/daily requirements	Good sources	Notes
A (retinol)	Acts to form and maintain skin, mucous membranes, eye pigments. Needs: children, 400–700 retinol equivalents; men, 1000; women, 800 except 1000 during pregnancy, 1200 while lactating.	Meat, poultry, eggs, milk, hard cheeses, butter, A-fortified margarine, green leafy and yellow vegetables.	Some evidence now that risk of many cancers—lung, breast, bladder, skin—decreases with greater consumption of foods rich in vitamin A or beta-carotene, which the body forms into vitamin A. Foods high in carotene include dark-green, leafy vegetables and deep-yellow fruits and vegetables such as carrots, spinach, broccoli.
B₁ (thiamine)	Helps utilize carbohydrates, promotes normal appetite, nervous system and heart functioning. Needs: children, 0.3 to 1.2 milligrams; men, 1.4; women to age 22, 1.1; thereafter 1.0 except 1.5 during pregnancy, 1.6 during lactation.	Whole grains, enriched breads/cereals, liver, pork, legumes, potatoes, nuts, wheat germ.	Recent findings indicate deficiency may occur not just late but early in alcoholism and may be involved in alcohol-related nervous system and psychiatric problems; thiamine supplementation may help.
B₂ (riboflavin)	Aids body use of protein, fat, carbohydrates; contributes to energy production in cells, mucous membrane integrity, healthy skin. Needs: children, 0.4 to 1.4 milligrams; men, 1.7; women, 1.3 except 1.6 during pregnancy, 1.8 during lactation.	Milk, cheese, eggs, meat, liver, enriched breads/cereals, leafy green vegetables.	Recent finding: Women who exercise regularly may need twice as much riboflavin as others; may also hold true for men who exercise.

Vitamin/mineral	Usefulness/daily requirements	Good sources	Notes
B₃ (niacin)	Promotes normal appetite, digestion, nervous system functioning. Needs: infants, 6–8 milligrams; children, 9–18; men, 18; women, 13 except 15 during pregnancy and lactation.	Whole grains, enriched bread/cereal products, liver, meat, fish, legumes, dried yeast.	Sometimes prescribed in massive doses for schizophrenia, a controversial use. Helps lower high cholesterol levels in familial hypercholesterolemia, a disorder that runs in families, quintuples heart disease risk, and often resists dietary changes.
B₆ (pyridoxine)	Aids regeneration of red blood cells, use of protein, fat, carbohydrates. Needs: infants, 0.3–0.6 milligrams; children, 0.9–1.8; men, 2.2; women, 2.0 except 2.6 in pregnancy, 2.5 during lactation.	Pork, organ meats, fish, whole-grain cereals, legumes.	Helpful for some women with infertility, premenstrual acne or depression; combats fatigue, depression associated with the pill. Sometimes effective (used with magnesium oxide) in preventing chronic kidney stone formation.
Folic acid (folacin)	Aids blood formation, functioning of many body chemical systems. Needs: infants, 30–45 micrograms; children, 100–400; men, 400; women, 400 except 800 during pregnancy, 500 during lactation.	Fresh green leafy vegetables, fruits, milk, eggs, organ meats, liver, dried yeast.	Ninety percent destroyed by cooking, especially boiling. A daily 100-microgram supplement now recommended for pill users to combat anemia. Some evidence 10 milligrams daily may reduce risk of cervical cancer in women on the pill who show cervical cell abnormalities.
B₁₂ (cobalamin)	Aids red blood cell formation, nervous system functioning. Needs: infants, 0.5–1.5 micrograms; children, 2–3; men, 3; women 3 except 4 during pregnancy, lactation.	Liver, milk, eggs, beef, pork, organ meats.	Deficiency mostly in older people because of inadequate amounts of intrinsic factor, a stomach material needed for cobalamin absorption. Treatment to overcome deficiency requires injection of the vitamin.

GUIDE TO VITAMINS AND MINERALS (cont.)

Specific Usefulness, Daily Requirements, Good Sources, Latest Research Findings

Vitamin/mineral	Usefulness/daily requirements	Good sources	Notes
C (ascorbic acid)	Forms cement that holds body cells together, strengthens blood vessels, aids wound healing, increases resistance to infection. Needs: infants, children, 35–50 milligrams; men, 60; women, 60 except 80 during pregnancy, 100 during lactation.	Citrus fruits, tomatoes, potatoes, cabbage, green peppers, strawberries, cantaloupe.	May reduce common cold severity, help lower blood cholesterol. Recent studies suggest possible action against gum disease. May reduce risk of stomach and esophagus cancer.
D	Helps absorb calcium and phosphorus for bone growth/maintenance. Needs: infants, children, 10 micrograms; ages 19–22, 7.5; men, 5; women, 5 except 10 during pregnancy and lactation.	Fortified milk, fish liver oils, butter, egg yolk, liver, fish, sunlight.	Vitamin D was recently found to break down in body into compounds that act as hormones. One, 1,25-D_1 is under study for preventing osteoporosis (bone thinning). Recently approved, too, by FDA to promote bone growth/health in 200,000 Americans with bone disease due to kidney failure.
E	Aids red blood cell formation, helps protect vitamin A and unsaturated fatty acids from destruction by oxygen. Needs: infants, children, 3–10 milligrams; men, 10, women, 8 except 10 during pregnancy.	Vegetable oils, wheat germ, cereals, legumes, egg yolk, green leafy vegetables, margarine.	Reported to relieve a breast disease, chronic cystic mastitis, in about 70% of cases. May help relieve intermittent claudication (leg cramps on walking). May protect against formation in body of cancer-causing nitrosamines.

Vitamin/mineral	Usefulness/daily requirements	Good sources	Notes
K	Promotes normal blood clotting to prevent hemorrhaging. No special needs.	Leafy vegetables, pork, liver, vegetable oils. As well as being plentiful in foods, K is also produced by bacteria normally present in intestinal system.	
Calcium	Helps form/maintain bones, teeth; aids blood clotting, nerve, muscle, heart function. Needs: infants, 360–540 milligrams; children to 10, 800; ages 11–18, 1200; men, 800; women, 800 except 1200 during pregnancy and lactation.	Milk, milk products, meat, fish, eggs, cereal products, beans, fruits, vegetables	Adequate lifelong intake can help prevent osteoporosis, the bone loss that affects some men and 25% of postmenopausal women. Recent studies indicate need at menopause increases to about 1500 milligrams daily.
Phosphorus	Works with calcium to form/maintain bones, teeth. Also participates in energy production. Needs: infants, 240–360 milligrams; children, 1–10 years, 800; ages 11–18, 1200; men, 800; women, 800 except 1200 during pregnancy and lactation.	Milk, cheese, meat, fish, poultry, cereals, legumes, nuts.	Usually, more than adequate amounts are obtained from Americans' ample intake of meats, also from phosphates used in processed foods. Chronic antacid use may cause phosphorus loss.
Potassium	Involved in heart and muscle activity, nerve impulse transmission, energy release from carbohydrates, fat, protein. Needs: adults, 1875–5625 milligrams.	Meat, milk, fruits, vegetables. Oranges, tomatoes, bananas are especially rich sources.	Deficiency—with muscle weakness, cramps, apathy—may follow severe diarrhea or use of some diuretics ("water pills") for high blood pressure or other purposes. Deficiency can be overcome with foods high in the mineral.

GUIDE TO VITAMINS AND MINERALS (*cont.*)

Specific Usefulness, Daily Requirements, Good Sources, Latest Research Findings

Vitamin/mineral	Usefulness/daily requirements	Good sources	Notes
Iron	Forms hemoglobin, the red cell pigment that transports oxygen. Needs: infants, children to age 10, 10 milligrams; boys, 11–18, 18; men, 10; girls and women to age 50, 18—thereafter, 10.	Beef, kidney, liver, beans, clams, peaches.	An estimated 60% of menstruating women are iron deficient because of blood loss and inadequate dietary intake. Foods rich in iron can avoid much deficiency. If necessary, iron supplements can be used. Note: Vitamin C helps increase iron absorption from food.
Magnesium	Enters into bone/tooth formation, nervous system and muscle functioning. Needs: infants, 50–70 milligrams; children, 150–250; men, 350; women, 300 except 450 during pregnancy and lactation.	Meat, fish, seafood, whole grains, wheat bran, leafy green vegetables, nuts.	Deficiency may occur with chronic alcoholism, also with use of some diuretic medications for high blood pressure, other purposes. Sometimes helpful, along with vitamin B_6, in stopping chronic kidney stone formation.
Zinc	Aids growth, sexual maturation, enzyme formation. Needs: infants, 3–5 milligrams; children to 10, 10; older children, men, 15; women, 15 except 20 in pregnancy, 25 while lactating.	Green leafy vegetables, seafood, nuts, meat, eggs.	Zinc supplementation helps some cases of impaired growth, slow-healing wounds, infant skin disorders, taste/smell disturbances. A very high-fiber diet may reduce zinc absorption, so that zinc supplements may be needed.

Vitamin/mineral	Usefulness/daily requirements	Good sources	Notes
Selenium	May protect membranes, other fragile body structures from damage by oxygen.	Meats, seafood, whole grains.	
Chromium	Promotes normal use of blood sugar.	Whole grains, meats.	
Copper	Aids body storage of iron, forms enzymes. May be needed for bone, muscle development, nervous system functioning.	Organ meats, seafood, whole-grain cereals, nuts, raisins, legumes.	
Manganese	For normal bone structure, enzyme systems.	Whole-grain cereals, tea, green leafy vegetables, fruits, nuts.	

SPORTS AND ACTIVITIES BEST LIKED BY AMERICANS

Forty, Ranked by Numbers of Participants

They rank in the following order based on a nationwide survey of Americans over age seventeen that suggested total numbers participating on a regular basis.

Sport	No. participants (in millions)	Sport	No. participants (in millions)
Walking	34.5	Waterskiing	4.5
Swimming	27.0	Weight lifting	4.5
Bowling	21.0	Badminton	3.0
Bicycling	19.5	Ice skating	3.0
Jogging	16.5	Racquetball	3.0
Camping	15.0	Sailing	3.0
Tennis	13.5	Skiing (cross country)	3.0
Calisthenics	12.0	Yoga	3.0
Basketball	10.5	Archery	1.5
Hiking	10.5	Boxing	1.5
Softball	10.5	Gymnastics	1.5
Baseball	9.0	Handball	1.5
Golf	7.5	Hockey	1.5
Volleyball	7.5	Karate	1.5
Dancercize	6.0	Mountain climbing	1.5
Football	6.0	Soccer	1.5
Frisbee	6.0	Squash	1.5
Table tennis	6.0	Track and field	1.5
Slimnastics	4.5	Wrestling	1.5
Skiing (downhill)	4.5	Judo	1.5

JOGGING AND RUNNING: THE DIFFERENCES

Half a Dozen Authoritative Opinions

Jogging is commonly thought to mean running at slow speeds—and running as jogging at high speeds. But there's no unanimity of opinion among experts about the differences between the two. Some opinions:

- ". . . If you feel that you're running, no matter how slow you're going, no one can say you're not"—James F. Fixx, *The Complete Book of Running*.

- "When you cover a mile in less than seven minutes you're running . . . a 'runner' is one who competes against others. A 'jogger' only competes against herself"—*Guidelines for Successful Jogging*, American Running and Fitness Association.

- "Anything faster than a nine-minute mile, I call running. Anything slower I call jogging"—Kenneth H. Cooper, M.D., *The Aerobics Way*.

- "Jogging is once or twice around the block in your baggy high school sweats. Running is when you measure time or distance and strive for goals"—Frank Shorter, Olympic gold medalist.

- "Jogging is running, but it's generally thought to be running long, slow distances. Its goal is elevation of the pulse rate to a level that is consistent with your level of fitness, age and capability"—Bernard L. Gladieux, Jr., former editor of *Running & Fitness*, quoted in *Executive Fitness*.

- "Jogging is the stage between walking and running . . . a slow, easy form of running. It starts for most people at 4.5 to 5 miles per hour. Just where jogging ends and running begins is not defined. It may be a psychological point where you decide you will move along to get where you want to go as fast as you can"—Alan J. Ryan, M.D., editor *The Physician and Sportsmedicine*.

CALORIES EXPENDED PER MILE OF RUNNING/JOGGING CONSIDERING WEIGHT AND SPEED

For Weights Between 120 and 220

Weight	Minutes to complete 1 mile		
	6	8	10
120	83	79	76
130	89	85	82
140	95	92	88
150	102	98	94
160	109	104	100
170	115	111	106
180	121	117	112
190	128	123	118
200	135	129	124
210	141	136	130
220	148	142	136

LATEST HEIGHT–WEIGHT TABLES

Height Feet	Inches	Women Small frame	Medium frame	Large frame		Height Feet	Inches	Men Small frame	Medium frame	Large frame
4	10	102–111	109–121	118–131		5	2	128–134	131–141	138–150
4	11	103–113	111–123	120–134		5	3	130–136	133–143	140–153
5	0	104–115	113–126	122–137		5	4	132–138	135–145	142–156
5	1	106–118	115–129	125–140		5	5	134–140	137–148	144–160
5	2	108–121	118–132	128–143		5	6	136–142	139–151	146–164
5	3	111–124	121–135	131–147		5	7	138–145	142–154	149–168
5	4	114–127	124–138	134–151		5	8	140–148	145–157	152–172
5	5	117–130	127–141	137–155		5	9	142–151	148–160	155–176
5	6	120–133	130–144	140–159		5	10	144–154	151–163	158–180
5	7	123–136	133–147	143–163		5	11	146–157	154–166	161–184
5	8	128–139	136–150	146–167		6	0	149–160	157–170	164–188
5	9	129–142	139–153	149–170		6	1	152–164	160–174	168–192
5	10	132–145	142–156	152–173		6	2	155–168	164–178	172–197
5	11	135–148	145–159	155–176		6	3	158–172	167–182	176–202
6	0	138–151	148–162	158–179		6	4	162–176	171–187	181–207

Weights at ages 25–59 based on lowest mortality rates according to weight. Weight in pounds according to frame—in indoor clothing weighing 3 pounds for women, 5 pounds for men, shoes in both cases with one-inch heels.

GUIDE TO METRIC WEIGHTS, MEASURES, AND EQUIVALENTS

Including Household Measures

Metric System

Weight

1 kilogram (kg)	= 1000 grams
1 gram (gm)	= 1000 milligrams (mg)
1 milligram (mg)	= 1000 micrograms

Volume

1 liter (L) = 1000 milliliters (ml) = 1000 cubic centimeters (cc)

Household Measures

1 teaspoon (tsp)	= 4 ml
1 dessert spoon	= 8 ml
1 tablespoon (tbsp)	= 15 ml = ½ fluid ounce
1 teacup	= 120 ml = 4 fluid ounces

CONVERSIONS FROM METRIC TO U.S. MEASURES AND VICE VERSA

Thirty Formulas

LENGTH

To convert from	To	Multiply by
centimeters	inches	.394
meters	yards	1.094
meters	feet	3.281
kilometers	miles	.622
inches	centimeters	2.54
yards	meters	.914
feet	meters	.305
miles	kilometers	1.609

AREA

To convert from	To	Multiply by
square centimeters	square inches	.155
square meters	square yards	1.196
square kilometers	square miles	.386
square kilometers	acres	247.16
square inches	square centimeters	6.452
square yards	square meters	.836
square miles	square kilometers	2.59
acres	square kilometers	.004

VOLUME

To convert from	To	Multiply by
liters	fluid ounces	33.81
liters	quarts	1.057
liters	gallons	.264
fluid ounces	liters	.0296
quarts	liters	.946
gallons	liters	3.785

MASS

To convert from	To	Multiply by
grams	ounces	.035
grams	pounds	.0022
kilograms	ounces	35.27
kilograms	pounds	2.205
ounces	grams	28.35
pounds	grams	453.6
ounces	kilograms	.0284
pounds	kilograms	.4536

MEDICAL DICTIONARY

A Concise Guide to Often-Used Medical Terms

Addison's disease. Underfunctioning of the adrenal glands atop the kidneys, leading to skin darkening, weakness, weight loss, diarrhea, and vomiting.

Allergy. Sensitivity to one or more substances—eaten, inhaled, or touched—usually harmless to most people. Among common allergies: hay fever, asthma, hives, eczema (itchy rash), and contact dermatitis.

Anaphylactic shock. A serious, potentially lethal allergic reaction, with a drop in blood pressure, weak pulse, difficulty breathing, blueness, convulsions, and unconsciousness.

Anemia. A deficiency in red blood cells or their pigment, hemoglobin. May cause fatigue, pallor, shortness of breath, and other symptoms.

Angina pectoris. Chest pain, usually with exertion, resulting from inadequate blood supply to the heart muscle because of coronary artery disease.

Ankylosing spondylitis. Arthritis of the small joints of the spine, producing stiffness, pain, and difficult movement—most often in men aged ten to thirty.

Appendicitis. An inflammation of the two-and-a-half- to three-inch appendix located at the junction of large and small intestines. Typically, pain starts in navel area, shifts to the right lower quadrant of abdomen, often accompanied by nausea and sometimes by fever, constipation, or diarrhea.

Arrhythmia. Heartbeat rhythm variation. Among the many forms: a slowdown to under sixty beats a minute, an increase to over one hundred, or premature or "skipped" beats.

Arteriosclerosis/atherosclerosis. In arteriosclerosis, arteries thicken and lose elasticity. Atherosclerosis, a much more common and serious form of arteriosclerosis—and usually what is meant when hardening of the arteries is referred to—involves accumulations of fatty deposits on the inner wall of an artery, impeding normal blood flow. Most often affected are the heart, brain, and leg arteries.

Arthritis. Joint inflammation. Osteoarthritis, the most common form, usually occurs in middle age and affects weight-bearing joints such as the hips, spine, knees, ankles; its cause is not clear, though aging, obesity and joint injury predispose one to it. Rheumatoid arthritis, cause unknown, is really a systemic illness manifesting itself primarily by joint pain and inflammation but in some cases affecting other organs such as the lungs. Juvenile rheumatoid arthritis is mostly similar to adult form; often fever may precede joint pain, and spleen and lymph nodes may enlarge. Psoriatic arthritis is similar to rheumatoid except that joint flare-ups coincide with flare-ups of the skin disease. *Note:* Rheumatism, a term often used for arthritis, really refers to muscle pain, inflamed muscle tissues, or inflamed connective tissue components of muscles, joints, tendons, and ligaments.

Asthma. A chronic disease with periodic attacks of wheezing and breathing difficulty due to the obstruction of air flow in smaller air passages. May be caused by allergy, sensitivity to the bacteria producing respiratory infections, or nervous tension.

Bell's palsy. An inflammation of the facial nerve controlling expression. Of unknown cause, often fleeting.

Bronchiectasis. A chronic dilation of air passages, with a cough, breathing difficulty on exertion, and repeated respiratory infections. May be congenital or result from chronic sinusitis, allergy, emphysema, pneumonia, a lung abscess, or a tumor.

Bronchitis. An inflammation of air passages which may follow a common cold or other upper respiratory infection. May produce a sore throat, nasal discharge, slight fever, cough, and back and muscle pain. Chronic form, believed mostly due to smoking and air pollution, can lead to breathing difficulty, wheezing, blueness, paroxysms of coughing, and sputum production.

Bursitis. An inflammation of a bursa, one of the small,

fluid-filled sacs that facilitate joint movement. Usually results from excessive use of a joint, or a chilling or draft. Causes severe pain and limitation of movement.

Carcinoma. A form of cancer affecting connective tissue and coverings of internal and external surfaces. Includes most gland malignancies and cancers of the breast, stomach, uterus, skin, and tongue.

Cataract. A clouding of the lens of an eye, usually occurring with age, sometimes from injury. Leads to blurring and dimming of vision.

Cerebral palsy. Partial paralysis and lack of muscle coordination from a defect, injury, or a disease of nerve tissue in the brain. Believed caused at or near birth by a lack of oxygen, premature delivery, head injury, or infection. The three major forms: athetoid, with muscle tension and uncontrollable movements; atactic, with poor balance and coordination and a staggering gait; and spastic, with muscle spasm.

Cholecystitis. A gallbladder inflammation, usually from a gallstone, producing pain about the stomach or right upper quadrant of the abdomen extending to the right shoulder.

Cirrhosis of the liver. Chronic liver cell degeneration and thickening of the surrounding tissue. May result from severe malnutrition accompanying alcoholism, viral hepatitis, or other disease. May lead to fatigue, weight loss, reduced resistance to infections, gastrointestinal disturbances, vomiting of blood, and jaundice.

Colitis. An inflammation of the large bowel (colon). Most common form, also called irritable bowel, can result from anxiety and stress or from lack of adequate fiber in the diet and may produce cramplike pain, mucus in stools, and constipation sometimes alternating with diarrhea. Ulcerative colitis, less common but more serious, mostly affects young adults, produces bloody diarrhea attacks.

Concussion. A violent jarring of the brain from head injury, with nausea, vertigo, unconsciousness, weak pulse, and rapid or slow breathing.

Conjunctivitis. An inflammation of the thin membrane

(conjunctiva) covering the eyeball and lining the eyelid, from allergy or infection. Pink eye, one form, is highly contagious.

Coronary occlusion. The closing of a coronary artery feeding the heart muscle by fatty deposits or a blood clot. Commonly called a heart attack.

Croup. See Laryngitis, Acute Obstructive.

Cushing's syndrome. Excessive adrenal gland activity, producing obesity, rounding of the face, fat accumulation in the back, muscle wasting, weakness, excessive hairiness, and menstrual irregularities.

Cystic fibrosis. An inherited disorder of the pancreas, sweat glands, and respiratory system. May produce a cough, protuberant abdomen, persistent respiratory infection, barrel chest, and other symptoms.

Cystitis. A bladder inflammation caused by an infection ascending from the exterior or descending from the kidney, with urinary frequency and urgency, sometimes blood in the urine.

Diabetes insipidus. Deficiency of a pituitary gland hormone, vasopressin, marked by excessive thirst and urination.

Diabetes mellitus. The common form of diabetes caused by inadequate insulin production by the pancreas or by disturbance in the body's use of insulin. Marked by excessive thirst, urination, itching, hunger, weakness, and weight loss.

Diverticulitis. An inflammation of small pouches (diverticula) formed in colon wall and lining because of high pressure associated with chronic constipation. Inflammation develops when bacteria or other irritants are trapped in the pouches, causing spasm and pain in lower left side of the abdomen, distention, nausea, vomiting, constipation or diarrhea, and fever.

Down's syndrome. Congenital physical malformation and mental retardation. Also called mongolism because its facial characteristics resemble those of persons of the Mongolian race.

Eclampsia. A pregnancy complication marked by high

blood pressure, sometimes convulsions, and coma. Preventable by proper early pregnancy care.

Eczema. Itching, blistering, oozing, and scaling skin rash.

Emphysema. Distention and destructive changes in the air spaces in the lungs caused by smoking and pollution. May produce wheezing, chronic cough.

Empyema. A complication of respiratory disease, with pus developing between the membranes encasing a lung. May cause one-sided chest pain, cough, fever, and breathing difficulty.

Encephalitis. Viral infection of the brain, producing headache, fever, a stiff neck, and vomiting and sometimes tremors, confusion, and convulsions.

Endocarditis. Bacterial infection of the membrane lining the chambers of the heart. May produce fever, chills, joint pains, and lassitude.

Epilepsy. A nervous system disorder. Petit mal form produces a few seconds loss of consciousness; psychomotor, a very brief clouding of consciousness, with purposeless movements such as hand clapping; grand mal, unconsciousness with foaming at the mouth, and violent limb thrashing.

Gallstones. Stonelike masses, formed in the gallbladder, cause unknown. Their presence, known as cholelithiasis, may produce no symptoms in some cases; in others, bloating, belching, nausea, and upper abdominal discomfort.

Gastroenteritis. An inflammation of the lining of the stomach and intestines. May be caused by alcohol, food allergy, food poisoning, intestinal virus, or cathartics or other drugs. Produces malaise, nausea, vomiting, gas sounds in the intestines, diarrhea, and sometimes fever and prostration.

Gingivitis. Gum inflammation with redness, swelling, and bleeding—the result of tartar, food impaction, malocclusion, and other causes.

Glaucoma. An increase of pressure within the eye. Symptomless to begin with, it later may lead to loss of side vision, blurring or fogging of vision, and the appearance of colored rings or halos around bright objects. If untreated, it can damage retina and optic nerve.

Glomerulonephritis. Kidney inflammation, usually related to previous strep throat, sinus or tonsil infection, producing blood in the urine, urine color change, reduced urine volume, and face and eyelid puffiness.

Goiter. Enlargement of the thyroid gland with swelling in front of neck, from iodine deficiency due to inadequate dietary intake or drug effects.

Gout. A recurring arthritis, mostly in men, usually affecting one joint; sometimes, later, two or more simultaneously. Produces throbbing, crushing pain, most often in a big toe.

Gynecomastia. Breast enlargement in the male, often of unknown cause, sometimes related to hormone secretions, liver or other disease, or the side effect of medication.

Hansen's disease. Leprosy. Chronic, communicable (but not easily), caused by a bacterium. Produces skin swellings, open sores, loss of sensation, loss of body hair.

Heart failure, congestive. Reduced pumping efficiency of the heart, resulting in less circulation of blood to body tissues, congestion in the lungs, ankle swelling, breathing difficulty. May stem from coronary or other heart disease, lung disease, severe anemia, or low thyroid function.

Hematoma. Mass of clotted blood in a tissue. A black eye is a familiar form.

Hemiplegia. Paralysis of one side of body from a brain tumor or stroke.

Hemophilia. Inherited male disorder, transmitted through the female. Involves impaired blood-clotting ability and excessive bleeding from minor cuts and wounds.

Hemorrhage. Bleeding from a ruptured blood vessel. The bleeding, which can be external, internal, or into the skin or other tissue, is bright red and in spurts when an artery is affected, dark red and in a steady flow when from a vein. Can cause many disturbances when massive, including rapid, shallow breathing, thirst, visual disturbances, and extreme weakness.

Hepatitis. An inflammation of the liver. May produce nausea, fever, liver tenderness and enlargement, and jaundice. Can be caused by infectious mononucleosis, cirrhosis, toxic materials such as carbon tetrachloride, or viral infection transmitted via foods, liquids, or blood transfusions.

Hernia, hiatal. A protrusion of the stomach above the diaphragm (the dome-shaped muscle that separates the chest from abdomen) through the enlargement of the diaphragm opening which the esophagus passes through to join the stomach. May produce no symptoms or, in some cases, heartburn, swallowing difficulty, and the vomiting of blood.

Herpes simplex. The virus of fever blisters and painful genital blisters.

Herpes zoster. Nerve inflammation caused by the same virus that produces chicken pox. May cause chills, fever, the eruption of blisters, and pain along course of affected nerve.

Hodgkin's disease. A malignancy arising in lymph gland system, causing gland enlargement, severe itching, sweating, fever, weakness, and weight loss.

Huntington's chorea. A rare hereditary disease with brain changes, personality disturbances, memory and judgment impairment, shuffling gait, jerky movements, and speech disturbance.

Hydatidiform mole. A degeneration of pregnancy consisting of mass of cysts, usually benign, causing rapid uterus size increase shortly after conception, with vaginal bleeding.

Hyperparathyroidism. Overactivity of parathyroid glands near the thyroid, with urinary calcium stones, excessive urination, and abdominal pain.

Hypertension. Elevated blood pressure, silent in the beginning, later producing headaches, nervousness, dizziness, and palpitation. Considered a major risk factor for heart attack and stroke.

Hyperthyroidism. Overactivity of the thyroid gland, producing weakness, sweating, heat sensitivity, restlessness, weight loss despite increased appetite, palpitation, tremor, stare, and eye protrusion.

Hypoglycemia. Low blood sugar, often without physical cause, producing hunger, trembling, headache, dizziness, and weakness several hours after meals.

Hypoparathyroidism. Underfunctioning of parathyroid glands, with severe muscle spasm and neurotic symptoms.

Hypothyroidism. Thyroid gland underfunctioning. May produce one or more such symptoms as dry cold skin, hand and face puffiness, weight gain, slow speech, mental apathy, constipation, hearing loss, and memory impairment.

Impetigo. Highly contagious skin disease mostly of infants and young children, with pus-filled lesions that rupture or crust.

Inflammation. A body response to infection or injury, in which more blood flows to the affected area and protective white cells and body fluids collect there. Symptoms from these activities are redness, swelling, heat, and pain.

Jaundice. The yellowing of skin and eyes from excess bile pigment. Not a disease, jaundice is a symptom of disorders of the liver, gallbladder, and blood that can interfere with normal bile flow.

Laryngitis. An inflammation of the larynx (voice box) with hoarseness or loss of voice, throat tickling, and rawness.

Laryngitis, acute obstructive (Croup). An obstruction of the larynx (voice box) from an infection, allergy or foreign body, producing a barking cough, croaking sounds during breathing, and spasms of choking.

Laryngotracheobronchitis. An inflammation of mucous membranes of the voice box, windpipe, and lung passages, with severe breathing difficulty, high fever, an almost constant nonproductive cough, and hoarseness.

Leprosy. See Hansen's disease.

Leukemia. Malignant disease of the bone marrow, spleen, and lymph nodes, with uncontrolled multiplication of white blood cells and reduced red cells and platelets, leading to anemia, increased susceptibility to infection, and hemorrhage.

Leukoplakia. Thickened white patches on the gums, lips, and tongue from repeated injury, poor dentures, sharp tooth surfaces, tobacco, or highly seasoned food. In time, they may become malignant.

Leukorrhea. Excessive vaginal discharge, usually white or yellow, indicating an infection or other disorder.

Lupus erythematosus. A disorder of unknown cause, most often in young women, which may be limited to the skin, producing a butterfly-shaped red eruption on the nose and cheek—or, in more serious form, may affect joints, lungs or kidneys, producing fever, and muscle/joint pain.

Lumbago. Popular term for low-back pain, caused by injury, arthritis, abuse of back muscles, poor posture, sagging mattress, or ill-fitting shoes.

Malaria. Mosquito-transmitted disease, mostly tropical and subtropical, with attacks of chills, fever, headache, nausea, and body pains.

Mastitis, chronic cystic. The most common breast disease, benign, with cysts, usually in both breasts, producing a cobblestone feel.

Mastoiditis. A complication of middle ear infection, with spread to the mastoid bone behind the ear, pain, and discharge from the ear.

Meniere's disease. An inner ear disturbance, often without apparent cause, producing episodes of hearing impairment, ringing in the ears, dizziness, nausea and vomiting, and sometimes eyeball oscillation.

Meningitis. An inflammation of the membranes (meninges) covering the brain and spinal cord—the result of bacterial, viral or fungal infection with a stiff neck, persistent headache, fever, and convulsions.

Metastasis. The transfer of disease from one organ to other tissues not directly connected to it, especially the spread of cancer cells.

Migraine. A severe, usually one-sided headache, with nausea/vomiting, sometimes visual disturbances such as light flashes before the eyes.

Mononucleosis, infectious. An acute infectious disease, believed viral, causing gland swellings in the neck and elsewhere (giving it its other name, glandular fever) with fatigue, headache, chilliness, sometimes a sore throat, fever, abdominal pain, jaundice, a stiff neck, chest pain, a cough, and breathing difficulty.

Multiple sclerosis. A disease of unknown cause producing hardened patches in the brain and spinal cord, which interfere with nerve activity and may produce vision disturbances, weakness, tremor, impaired balance, a stiff gait, loss of bladder/bowel control, and paralysis.

Muscular dystrophies. Several related muscular disorders, involving loss of protein in the affected muscles and replacement by fat and connective tissue, with muscle wasting and weakness.

Myasthenia gravis. Muscular weakness thought to be due to a chemical defect at sites where nerves and muscles interact. May produce eyelid drooping and swallowing and speaking difficulty.

Myeloma, multiple. A malignant disease originating in bone marrow, causing persistent bone pain, weight loss, and repeated infections.

Narcolepsy. A disorder of unknown cause producing brief, recurrent sleep attacks, sometimes also with momentary limb paralysis during emotional reactions and hallucinations at the beginning of sleep.

Neuralgia. Paroxysms of severe, throbbing, or stabbing pain along the course of a nerve, for which no cause can usually be found.

Neuritis. Nerve inflammation from injury, pressure, infection, or toxic substances, with pain or numbness and tingling.

Osteomyelitis. Bone inflammation from bacteria that invade through a compound fracture or other injury from a nearby infection or via the blood. May produce sudden bone pain, fever, painful movement, and swelling.

Osteoporosis. Porousness and brittleness of bones, most common in women after menopause, with pain in vertebrae, rounding of shoulders, height loss, and proneness to fractures.

Otitis media. Middle ear inflammation caused by disease organisms spreading from the nose and throat or as a result of eardrum injury. With earache, fever, chills, and hearing impairment.

Otosclerosis. Spongy bone formation in the internal ear, fixing the stapes bone so it cannot conduct sound, with progressive hearing loss.

Paget's disease. A bone disorder of unknown cause that may lead to pain and thickening, enlargement, and deformity of bone.

Pancreatitis. Inflammation of the pancreas from alcoholism, infectious disease, or drugs, with abdominal pain (often relieved by sitting up), fever, nausea, and vomiting.

Periodontitis (pyorrhea). Gum inflammation with gum recession, bleeding on brushing of the teeth; if unchecked, loosening of teeth.

Peritonitis. An inflammation of the membrane (peritoneum) lining the abdominal cavity and abdominal organs, caused by organisms escaping from a burst appendix, perforated ulcer, ruptured gallbladder or ruptured spleen, producing severe constant abdominal pain, fever, chills, and nausea/vomiting.

Pharyngitis. Inflammation of the five-inch-long cavity (pharynx) behind the nose, mouth, and larynx, because of common cold or other infection, producing dryness or a lump in the throat, chills, fever, swallowing difficulty, hoarseness, and neck gland swelling.

Pleurisy. An inflammation of the membrane around the lungs, often a complication of pneumonia, influenza, and other lung disease, producing a sticking chest pain, fever, cough, chills, and rapid shallow breathing.

Pneumonia. Lung inflammation caused by bacteria or viruses, producing chill followed by fever, headache, chest pain, breathing difficulty, and rusty sputum. Lobar pneumonia involves one lobe of a lung; double pneumonia, both lungs; bronchial pneumonia is localized in or around the air passages (bronchi).

Polyps.   Growths extending from mucous membranes in the nose, ears, mouth, lungs, or gastrointestinal tract, usually benign but sometimes becoming malignant.

Prolapse of uterus.   Protrusion of the uterus through the vaginal orifice from the weakening of holding muscles and ligaments, caused by many pregnancies, inherited weakness, age, or excessive coughing or straining at stool, with lower abdominal cramps, vaginal discharge and pain, frequent and urgent urination, and painful intercourse.

Prostatic hypertrophy, benign.   Enlargement of the prostate gland from unknown cause, usually after age fifty, with increased urinary frequency, urgency, and difficulty.

Prostatitis.   Inflammation of the prostate from infection, with frequent, painful urination, fever, swelling, and tenderness of the prostate.

Psoriasis.   Chronic recurrent skin disease of unknown cause producing red patches with silvery scales, most often on the knees, elbows, scalp, chest, abdomen, backs of arms and legs, palms of hands, and soles of feet.

Pulmonary embolism.   A traveling blood clot, usually from a leg vein, which lodges in a lung artery producing chest pain, a cough, and labored breathing.

Pyelonephritis.   Kidney inflammation from infection, producing painful, frequent, urgent urination, sometimes with chills, fever, and low back pain.

Raynaud's disease.   A blood vessel disorder of unknown cause, mostly in women, with attacks of finger pallor and blueness.

Rheumatic fever.   A complication of strep infection of the tonsil, throat or ears, producing fever and joint pains.

Rheumatism.   See Arthritis.

Rhinitis, allergic.   A sensitivity disorder (to pollens, dust, dander, feathers, or other substances) called hay fever when seasonal, perennial allergic rhinitis when year-round, producing itching of the nose, mouth, throat, and eyes, sneezing, and nasal discharge.

Ringworm. Fungal infection of the scalp, body, genital area, nails, or areas between the toes, with reddish, scaly or blistered ring-shaped patches.

Rocky Mountain spotted fever. A tick-spread infection, with chills, fever, headache, pain behind eyes, joint and muscle pain, and sore throat.

Scabies ("The Itch"). A mite-caused skin disorder that produces intense itching, usually worse at night.

Sciatica. An inflammation of sciatic nerve, extending from the base of the spine to foot, from osteoarthritis or rupture of an intervertebral disk, with pain beginning in the buttock and extending to the ankle.

Serum sickness. An allergic reaction developing one to two weeks after administration of a drug or serum to a sensitive person, with mild fever, hives, or skin rash, gland swelling, itching, and joint pains.

Shock. Disruption of blood circulation caused by a steep fall in blood pressure from a severe injury, major surgery, hemorrhage, dehydration, heart attack, overwhelming infection, poisoning, or drug reaction, with a racing pulse, pallor, moist and cool skin, apathy, or agitation.

Sinusitis. An inflammation of one or more of the hollow skull cavities (sinuses) that connect with the nasal cavity, from irritation, infection, colds, or allergies, with headache, nasal and postnasal discharge, fever, eye puffiness, and toothache.

Stroke. Damage to a portion of brain from loss of blood supply as a result of blood vessel spasm, rupture, or blocking by a clot, with unconsciousness, paralysis, or other symptoms depending on the site and extent of brain damage.

Sty. An infection of an eyelid sebaceous gland, with a foreign body sensation in the eye, tearing, pain, redness, and a pimplelike lesion.

Tonsillitis. An inflammation of the two lymph tissue

masses (tonsils) in the sides of the throat, from infection, with sore throat, pain during swallowing, fever, headache, and sometimes a stiff neck.

Trichinosis. An infection by a roundworm usually acquired by eating poorly cooked pork, with eye pain, eyelid swelling, sensitivity to light, muscle pain, chills, profuse sweating, and hives.

Uremia. Accumulation in the blood of waste substances ordinarily eliminated in urine. Occurs when kidneys lose filtering ability because of temporary poisoning or severe kidney disease, with a drop in urine volume, urine smell on breath and sweat, itching, vomiting, convulsions, and a yellowish-brown skin discoloration.

Urethritis, nongonococcal. Common inflammation of urethra, the canal from bladder to outside, from unknown organisms, with a slight watery, whitish secretion, sometimes mild pain on urination, and lower abdominal pain.

Uterus, myoma of. Also called a fibroid tumor, a benign growth of smooth muscle fibers of the uterus that may press on nearby organs causing painful menstruation, abnormal menstrual bleeding, vaginal discharge, and urinary frequency.

Venous thrombosis. Clot in a vein. Also called phlebothrombosis when little or no inflammation is present with the clot; thrombophlebitis or phlebitis when inflammation is present. Symptoms may include leg swelling and pain. Clot may form because of injury to vein lining, infection, or a standstill of blood in the vein as the result of inactivity or bed rest.

Vulvitis. An inflammation of the external parts of the female reproductive system surrounding the opening of the vagina. May result from infection, allergy, or irritation. Symptoms can include burning, itching, and pain.

THE BEGINNINGS AND ENDINGS OF COMMONLY USED MEDICAL TERMS

What They Mean

Beginnings	Meanings	As in
a-	lack of	arrhythmia
cardi-	heart	cardiogram
derm-	skin	dermatitis
dys-	abnormal	dystrophy
endo-	inside	endocarditis
epi-	upon	epidermis
gastr-	stomach	gastritis
hem-	blood	hemorrhage
hyper-	increased, excessive	hyperthyroid
hypo-	decreased, deficient	hypothyroid
myel-	spinal cord or bone marrow	myeloma
mal-	bad, abnormal	malnutrition
micro-	small	microscopic
myo-	muscle	myoma
nephr-	kidney	nephritis
neur-	nerve	neuritis
os-	bone	osteomyelitis
pneum-	air or gas	pneumonia
psych-	mind	psychiatry
pulmo-	lung	pulmonary
py-	pus	empyema

THE BEGINNINGS AND ENDINGS OF COMMONLY USED MEDICAL TERMS (*cont.*)

What They Mean

Endings	Meanings	As in
-algia	pain in	neuralgia
-ectomy	cutting out	tonsillectomy
-ia or -osis	disease	anemia, neurosis
-itis	inflammation	appendicitis
-oid	similar to	viroid
-ology	study of	neurology
-oma	tumor	carcinoma
-ostomy	making an opening	colostomy
-otomy	cutting into	phlebotomy
-rrhage or -rrhea	flow	hemorrhage, dysmenorrhea

DRUG SIDE EFFECTS

Guide to the Reaction Symptoms and the Drugs That May Produce Them

In working against a problem for which it is prescribed, a drug may produce undesirable effects. These occur in only a small minority of patients—often well under 1 percent. In some cases, the side effects are temporary and disappear as the body adjusts to continued use; in other cases, they may be alleviated by a change in dosage of the drug; in still others, the drug may need to be discontinued and another substituted.

Here, listed alphabetically, are side effect symptoms and, in each case, the drugs that may sometimes be responsible.

If you're taking medication and develop one or more

symptoms, you can check to see whether the medication could be responsible, then consult with your physician about what to do.

Abdominal bloating. Aristocort, Butazolidin, Decadron, Demulen, Medrol, Norlestrin preparations, Ortho-Novum preparations, Ovral, Ovulen-21, Tandearil.

Abdominal cramps. Aldactazide, Aldactone, Aldoril, Coumadin, Demulen, Diuril, Drixoral, E-Mycin, Erythrocin, Erythromycin, Esidrix, HydroDIURIL, Hygroton, Inderal, Norlestrin preparations, Ortho-Novum preparations, Ovral, Ovulen-21, Pediamycin, Premarin, Rauzide, Salutensin.

Abdominal discomfort or pain. Ambenyl Expectorant, Atromid-S, Azo Gantrisin, Benadryl, Cleocin, Cyclospasmol, Darvon preparations, Dimetapp, Gantanol, Gantrisin, Indocin, Kaon, Keflex, Lomotil, Macrodantin, Marax, Ornade, Pavabid, penicillin G potassium, Penicillin VK, Pentids, Pen-Vee K, Periactin, Ritalin, Sumycin, Talwin, Tenuate, Terramycin, tetracycline, Tetrex, Tofranil, Tuss-Ornade, V-Cillin K, Zyloprim.

Agitation. Butazolidin, Compazine, Demerol, Mellaril, Stelazine, Tandearil, Tofranil, Triavil.

Anaphylaxis. Amcill, ampicillin, Declomycin, Dimetane, Diupres, Dyazide, E-Mycin, Equanil, erythromycin, Erythrocin, Etrafon, Macrodantin, Mellaril, Minocin, Omnipen, Parafon Forte, Pediamycin, penicillin G potassium, Pentids, Penicillin VK, Pen-Vee K, Periactin, Polycillin, Principen, Stelazine, Sumycin, Terramycin, tetracycline, Tetrex, V-Cillin K, Vibramycin.

Anemia. Achromycin V, Aldactazide, Ambenyl Expectorant, Amcill, ampicillin, Atromid-S, Azo Gantrisin, Benadryl, Butazolidin, Declomycin, Dimetane, Diupres, Diuril, Equanil, Esidrix, Gantanol, Gantrisin, Garamycin, Hygroton, Indocin, Lasix, Macrodantin, Mellaril, Minocin, Mysteclin-F, Omnipen, Orinase, penicillin G potassium, Penicillin VK, Pentids, Pen-Vee K, Periactin, Polycillin, Principen, Rauzide, Regroton, Ritalin, Salutensin, Ser-Ap-Es, Sumycin, Tandearil,

Terramycin, tetracycline, Tetrex, Tolinase, V-Cillin K, Vibramycin.

Angina aggravation. Aldomet, Aldoril.

Angioneurotic edema (Giant hives). Declomycin, Equanil, Etrafon, Lomotil, Macrodantin, Mellaril, Minocin, Mysteclin-F, Parafon Forte, Sumycin, Terramycin, tetracycline, Tetrex, Tuinal, Vibramycin.

Anogenital irritation/itching. Minocin, Sumycin, Terramycin, tetracycline, Tetrex, Valium, Vibramycin.

Anxiety. Apresoline, Drixoral, Elavil, Etrafon, Hydropres, Rauzide, reserpine, Salutensin, Ser-Ap-Es, Tenuate, Tofranil, Triavil, Valium.

Appetite loss. Achromycin V, Aldactazide, Aldomet, Aldoril, Apresoline, Azo Gantrisin, Bendectin, Chlor-Trimeton, Dalmane, Dimetane, Dimetapp, Diupres, Diuril, Drixoral, Esidrix, Etrafon, Gantanol, Gantrisin, Garamycin, HydroDIURIL, Hydropres, Hygroton, Indocin, Lanoxin, Lomotil, Macrodantin, Mellaril, Minocin, Mysteclin-F, Ornade, Pavabid, Periactin, Polaramine, Premarin, Rauzide, Regroton, reserpine, Ritalin, Salutensin, Ser-Ap-Es, Sinequan, Stelazine, Sumycin, Terramycin, tetracycline, Tetrex, Triavil, Tuss-Ornade, Vibramycin.

Asthma. Combid, Etrafon.

Backache. Norlestrin preparations, Ortho-Novum preparations, Ovral, Ovulin-21.

Bleeding, gastrointestinal. Butazolidin, Indocin, Parafon Forte, Tandearil.

Bloated feeling. Bentyl, Combid.

Blood disturbances. Aldactazide, Aldomet, Aldoril, Amcill, ampicillin, Apresoline, Azo Gantrisin, Butazolidin, Cleocin, Combid, Compazine, Declomycin, Diabinese, Dilantin, Dimetane, Dimetapp, Diuril, Doriden, Elavil, Equanil, Esidrix, Gantanol, Gantrisin, HydroDIURIL, Inderal, Indocin, Lasix, Librax, Librium, Macrondantin, Mellaril, Minocin, Mysteclin-F, Omnipen, Orinase, Ornade, penicillin G potassium, Penicillin VK, Pentids, Pen-Vee K, Periactin, Phenergan preparations, Placidyl, Polycillin, Principen, Rauzide,

Regroton, Salutensin, Ser-Ap-Es, Serax, Sinequan, Stelazine, Sumycin, Tandearil, Tenuate, Terramycin, tetracycline, Tetrex, Thorazine, Tigan, Tofranil, Tolinase, Triavil, Tuss-Ornade, Valium, V-Cillin K, Vibramycin, Zyloprim.

Bone fractures. Aristocort, Decadron, prednisone.

Breast engorgement. Hydropres, Mellaril, Ser-Ap-Es, Thorazine.

Breast enlargement. Aldomet, Aldoril, Demulen, Elavil, Norlestrin preparations, Ortho-Novum preparations, Ovral, Ovulin-21, Premarin, Sinequan, Tofranil, Triavil.

Breast secretion. Norlestrin preparations, Ortho-Novum preparations, Ovral, Ovulen-21.

Breast tenderness. Norlestrin preparations, Ortho-Novum preparations, Ovral, Ovulen-21, Premarin.

Breath, shortness of. Dalmane.

Breathing difficulty. Aldoril, Apresoline, Diupres, Hydro-DIURIL, Hydropres, Inderal, Indocin, Macrodantin, quinidine sulfate, Rauzide, reserpine, Salutensin, Ser-Ap-Es.

Bronchospasm. Equanil, meprobamate.

Bruising. Aldactazide, Aldoril, HydroDIURIL, Medrol.

Burning. Afrin, Aldactazide, Aldomet, Aldoril, Cordran, HydroDIURIL, Hygroton, Kenalog, Mycolog, Sinequan, Synalar, Valisone, Vioform-Hydrocortisone.

Cataracts. Aristocort, Decadron, Medrol, prednisone, Zyloprim.

Chest pain. Apresoline, Dalmane, Diupres, Drixoral, Hydropres, Macrodantin, Marax, Ornade, Proloid, Rauzide, Regroton, reserpine, Ritalin, Salutensin, Ser-Ap-Es, Tenuate, thyroid, Tuss-Ornade.

Chest tightness. Ambenyl Expectorant, Benadryl, Dimetane, Dimetapp, Ornade, Periactin, Tuss-Ornade.

Chills. Apresoline, Azo Gantrisin, Equanil, Gantanol, Gantrisin, Macrodantin, meprobamate, penicillin G potassium, Penicillin VK, Pentids, Pen-Vee K, Sinequan, Talwin, V-Cillin K.

Concentration, disturbed. Elavil, Triavil.

Confusion. Aldactazide, Aldactone, Ambenyl Expectorant, Benadryl, Butazolidin, Dalmane, Dilantin, Dimetane, Drixoral, Elavil, Etrafon, Indocin, Kaon, Librax, Librium, Mellaril, Norgesic, Periactin, quinidine sulfate, Sinequan, Tandearil, Tofranil, Tranxene, Triavil, Valium.

Constipation. Aldomet, Aldoril, Ambenyl Expectorant, Apresoline, Artane, Benadryl, Bendectin, Bentyl, Combid, Dalmane, Darvon, Demerol, Dilantin, Dimetane, Dimetapp, Diupres, Diuril, Dyazide, Elavil, Esidrix, Etrafon, Feosol, Fiorinal, HydroDIURIL, Hygroton, Inderal, Ionamin, Librax, Librium, Mellaril, Norgesic, Ornade, Pavabid, Percodan, Phenaphen with Codeine, Pro-Banthine, Rauzide, Regroton, Salutensin, Ser-Ap-Es, Sinequan, Stelazine, Talwin, Tenuate, Thorazine, Tofranil, Triavil, Valium.

Cough. Macrodantin.

Delusions. Etrafon, Tofranil, Triavil.

Depression. Aldomet, Aldoril, Apresoline, Azo Gantrisin, Demulen, Diupres, Gantanol, Gantrisin, Hydropres, Inderal, Indocin, Lomotil, Norlestrin preparations, Ortho-Novum preparations, Ovral, Ovulen-21, Rauzide, Regroton, reserpine, Ser-Ap-Es, Tenuate, Valium.

Diarrhea. Aldactazide, Aldactone, Aldomet, Aldoril, Ambenyl Expectorant, Amcill, ampicillin, Apresoline, Atromid-S, Azo Gantrisin, Benadryl, Bendectin, Butazolidin, Cleocin, Coumadin, Dalmane, Declomycin, Diabinese, Dimetane, Dimetapp, Diupres, Diuril, Dyazide, Elavil, E-Mycin, Equanil, erythromycin, Erythrocin, Feosol, Gantanol, Gantrisin, HydroDIURIL, Hydropres, Hygroton, Inderal, Indocin, Ionamin, Kaon, Keflex, Lanoxin, Lasix, Macrodantin, Mellaril, meprobamate, Minocin, Mycostatin, Mysteclin-F, Noludar, Omnipen, Ornade, Pavabid, Pediamycin, penicillin G potassium, Penicillin VK, Pentids, Pen-Vee K, Polycillin, Principen, Rauzide, Regroton, reserpine, Salutensin, Ser-Ap-Es, Sinequan, Talwin, Tandearil, Terramycin, tetracycline, Tetrex, Tigan, Tofranil, Triavil, Tuss-Ornade, V-Cillin K, Vibramycin, Zyloprim.

Dizziness/vertigo. Aldactazide, Aldomet, Aldoril, Ambenyl Expectorant, Apresoline, Aristocort, Artane, Artomid-S,

Azo Gantrisin, Benadryl, Bendectin, Bentyl, Butazolidin, Chlor-Trimeton, Combid, Compazine, Dalamane, Darvon, Decadron, Demerol, Dilantin, Dimetane, Dimetapp, Diupres, Diuril, Drixoral, Dyazide, Elavil, Equanil, Esidrix, Etrafon, Fiorinal, Gantanol, Gantrisin, Garamycin, Hydropres, Hygroton, Indocin, Ionamin, Isordil, Keflex, Lasix, Lomotil, Macrodantin, Marax, Medrol, meprobamate, nitroglycerin, Noludar, Norgesic, Norlestrin preparations, Ornade, Ortho-Novum preparations, Ovral, Ovulen-21, Parafon Forte, Pavabid, Percodan, Periactin, Peritrate, Phenergan preparations, Placidyl, Polaramine, prednisone, Pro-Banthine, quinidine sulfate, Rauzide, Regroton, reserpine, Ritalin, Salutensin, Ser-Ap-Es, Serax, Sinequan, Stelazine, Sumycin, Talwin, Teldrin, Tenuate, Terramycin, tetracycline, Tetrex, Thorazine, Tofranil, Tolinase, Tranxene, Triaminic, Triavil, Tuss-Ornade, Valium, Vasodilan.

Drowsiness. Aldactazide, Aldactone, Ambenyl Expectorant, Antivert, Artane, Atarax, Atromid-S, Bellergal, Benadryl, Bendectin, Bentyl, Benylin Cough Syrup, Butisol Sodium, Chlor-Trimeton, Combid, Compazine, Dalmane, Dimetane, Dimetapp, Dramamine, Drixoral, Elavil, Equanil, Etrafon, Fiorinal, Hydropres, Librax, Librium, Lomotil, Macrodantin, Marax, Mellaril, meprobamate, Naldecon, Nembutal, Noludar, Norgesic, Novahistine DH, Novahistine Expectorant, Ornade, Parafon Forte, Pavabid, Phenergan with Codeine, Pro-Banthine, Rauzide, Regroton, reserpine, Ritalin, Ser-Ap-Es, Serax, Sinequan, Stelazine, Teldrin, Tenuate, Tigan, Tranxene, Triaminic, Triavil, Tuss-Ornade, Valium, Vistaril.

Ear ringing. Azo Gantrisin, Dimetane, Dimetapp, Elavil, Gantanol, Gantrisin, Garamycin, Lasix, Periactin, Sinequan, Talwin, Triavil.

Edema (Fluid accumulation). Aldomet, Aldoril, Apresoline, Aristocort, Butazolidin, Combid, Decadron, Demulen, Diabinese, Diupres, Etrafon, Librax, Librium, Medrol, Norlestrin preparations, Ortho-Novum preparations, Ovral, Ovulen-21, penicillin G potassium, Penicillin VK, Pentids, Pen-Vee K, prednisone, Premarin, quinidine sulfate, Salutensin, Serax, Sinequan, Stelazine, Tandearil, Tofranil, Triavil, V-Cillin K.

Ejaculation inhibition. Combid, Mellaril.

Esophagitis. Aristocort, Medrol, Noludar, prednisone.

Euphoria. Demerol, Dimetane, Equanil, Ionamin, Lomotil, meprobamate, Percodan, Periactin, Serax, Talwin, Tenuate.

Excitement. Dimetane, Doriden, Elavil, Equanil, Etrafon, Marax, Mellaril, meprobamate, Nembutal, Noludar, Periactin, phenobarbital, quinidine sulfate, Seconal, Triavil, Tuinal.

Eye disturbances. Aristocort, Azo Gantrisin, Dalmane, Decadron, Gantanol, Gantrisin, Indocin, Medrol, Norlestrin preparations, Ortho-Novum preparations, Ovral, Ovulen-21, Thorazine.

Facial redness. Aristocort, Decadron, Medrol, prednisone.

Faintness. Dalmane, Demerol, Dimetapp, Diupres, Equanil, Hydropres, Indocin, Librax, Librium, meprobamate, nitroglycerin, Periactin, Salutensin, Ser-Ap-Es, Serax, Talwin, Thorazine.

Fatigue. Atromid-S, Bendectin, Dimetane, Elavil, Inderal, Keflex, Lasix, Norlestrin preparations, Ortho-Novum preparations, Ovral, Ovulen-21, Periactin, Sinequan, Stelazine, Tofranil, Tolinase, Tranxene, Triavil, Valium.

Fever. Aldactazide, Aldactone, Aldoril, Apresoline, Azo Gantrisin, Butazolidin, Combid, Coumadin, Diabinese, Diuril, Equanil, Gantanol, Gantrisin, Garamycin, Hydro-DIURIL, Inderal, Macrodantin, Mellaril, meprobamate, Mysteclin-F, penicillin G potassium, Penicillin VK, Pentids, Pen-Vee K, quinidine sulfate, Ritalin, Serax, Stelazine, Sumycin, Tandearil, Terramycin, tetracycline, Tetrex, Thorazine, thyroid, Tofranil, V-Cillin K, Zyloprim.

Flushing. Apresoline, Bellergal, Cyclospasmol, Dalmane, Demerol, Donnagel-PG, Donnatal, Diupres, Isordil, nicotinic acid, Peritrate, Regroton, Salutensin, Ser-Ap-Es, Sinequan, Talwin, Tofranil, Triaminic.

● 279

Gastrointestinal upset. Mycostatin, nicotinic acid, Parafon Forte, Pyridium, quinidine sulfate, Tranxene, Triaminic.

Gynecomastia (Breast enlargement in a male). Aldactazide, Aldactone, Aldomet, Aldoril, Hydropres, Lanoxin, Mellaril, Premarin, Ser-Ap-Es, Sinequan, Tenuate, Tofranil.

Hair, abnormal growth of. Aldactazide, Aldactone, Cordran, Kenalog, Mycolog, Norlestrin preparations, Ortho-Novum preparations, Ovral, Ovulen-21, Synalar, Valisone.

Hair loss. Coumadin, Inderal, Indocin, Macrodantin, Norlestrin preparations, Ortho-Novum preparations, Ovral, Ovulen-21, Ritalin, Sinequan, Tenuate, Tofranil, Zyloprim.

Hallucinations. Azo Gantrisin, Dalmane, Demerol, Elavil, Gantanol, Gantrisin, Inderal, Periactin, Serax, Sinequan, Talwin, Triavil.

Hangover. Butisol Sodium, Doriden, Nembutal, Placidyl, Seconal, Tuinal.

Headache. Afrin, Aldactazide, Aldomet, Aldoril, Ambenyl Expectorant, Apresoline, Aristocort, Artane, Atromid-S, Azo Gantrisin, Benadryl, Bendectin, Bentyl, Butazolidin, Butisol Sodium, Chlor-Trimeton, Combid, Cyclospasmol, Dalmane, Darvon, Decadron, Demerol, Demulen, Dilantin, Dimetane, Dimetapp, Diupres, Diuril, Drixoral, Dyazide, Equanil, Esidrix, Etrafon, Gantanol, Gantrisin, Garamycin, HydroDIURIL, Hydropres, Hygroton, Indocin, Ionamin, Isordil, Keflex, Lanoxin, Lasix, Lomotil, Macrodantin, Marax, Medrol, Mellaril, meprobamate, nicotinic acid, nitroglycerin, Noludar, Norgesic, Orinase, Ornade, Pavabid, Periactin, Polaramine, prednisone, Premarin, Pro-Banthine, quinidine sulfate, Rauzide, Regroton, reserpine, Ritalin, Salutensin, Ser-Ap-Es, Serax, Stelazine, Sumycin, Talwin, Tandearil, Tenuate, Terramycin, tetracycline, Tetrex, thyroid, Tofranil, Tolinase, Tranxene, Tuss-Ornade, Valium.

Hearing loss. Butazolidin, Diupres, Hydropres, Indocin, Lasix, quinidine sulfate, Regroton, reserpine, Salutensin, Ser-Ap-Es, Tandearil.

Heartbeat, fast. Apresoline, Bentyl, Cyclospasmol, Demerol, Dimetane, Teldrin, Tenuate, Thorazine, thyroid, Tofranil.

Heartbeat, slow. Aldomet, Aldoril, Demerol.

Heartburn. Chlor-Trimeton, Cyclospasmol, Dalmane, Etrafon, Orinase, Polaramine.

Heart rhythm disturbances. Elavil, Hydropres, Kaon, Lanoxin, Marax, Proloid, Rauzide, reserpine, Ritalin, Ser-Ap-Es, Tenuate, Tofranil, Triavil.

Hives. Achromycin V, Aldactazide, Aldactone, Aldoril, Ambenyl Expectorant, Amcill, ampicillin, Apresoline, Atromid-S, Azo Gantrisin, Benadryl, Bentyl, Butazolidin, Cleocin, Coumadin, Declomycin, Demerol, Dimetane, Dimetapp, Diuril, Dyazide, Elavil, E-Mycin, erythromycin, Erythrocin, Esidrix, Etrafon, Gantanol, Gantrisin, Garamycin, HydroDIURIL, Hygroton, Indocin, Ionamin, Keflex, Lasix, Lomotil, Macrodantin, Minocin, Mysteclin-F, Norgesic, Omnipen, Orinase, Pediamycin, penicillin G potassium, Penicillin VK, Pentids, Pen-Vee K, Periactin, Placidyl, Polycillin, Principen, Rauzide, Regroton, Ritalin, Salutensin, Ser-Ap-Es, Stelazine, Sumycin, Talwin, Tandearil, Terramycin, tetracycline, Tetrex, Thorazine, Tofranil, Tolinase, Triavil, Tuinal, Vibramycin, Zyloprim.

Hoarseness. Sumycin, Terramycin, tetracycline, Tetrex.

Hypertension (High blood pressure). Aristocort, Decadron, Demulen, Drixoral, Elavil, Etrafon, Ionamin, Medrol, Norlestrin preparations, Ornade, Ortho-Novum preparations, Ovral, Ovulen-21, prednisone, thyroid, Tofranil, Triavil.

Hypotension (Low blood pressure). Ambenyl Expectorant, Apresoline, Benadryl, Elavil, Etrafon, Inderal, Kaon, nicotinic acid, Ornade, Periactin, Placidyl, Rauzide, Tigan, Tofranil, Triavil, Valium.

Impotence. Aldactazide, Aldactone, Aldomet, Aldoril, Atromid-S, Bentyl, Diupres, Hydropres, Hygroton, Ionamin, Pro-Banthine, Rauzide, Regroton, reserpine, Salutensin, Ser-Ap-Es, Tenuate, Tofranil.

Insomnia. Afrin, Ambenyl Expectorant, Azo Gantrisin, Benadryl, Bentyl, Butazolidin, Compazine, Dilantin, Dimetane, Drixoral, Elavil, Etrafon, Gantanol, Gantrisin, Ionamin, Marax, Ornade, Periactin, Pro-Banthine, Ritalin, Stelazine,

Talwin, Tedral, Tenuate, thyroid, Tofranil, Tranxene, Triavil, Tuss-Ornade, Valium.

Irritability. Bendectin, Dalmane, Ornade, Tranxene, Tuss-Ornade.

Itching. Aldactazide, Apresoline, Atromid-S, Azo Gantrisin, Combid, Cordran, Dalmane, Demerol, Diupres, Etrafon, Gantanol, Gantrisin, Garamycin, Indocin, Keflex, Kenalog, Lomotil, Lasix, Macrodantin, Mycolog, Mysteclin-F, nicotinic acid, Norlestrin preparations, Orinase, Ortho-Novum preparations, Ovral, Ovulen-21, Percodan, Regroton, reserpine, Salutensin, Ser-Ap-Es, Sinequan, Stelazine, Synalar, Valisone, Vioform-Hydrocortisone, Zyloprim.

Jaundice. Aldactazide, Aldoril, Cleocin, Combid, Compazine, Demulen, Diabinese, Diupres, Diuril, Elavil, Esidrix, Etrafon, HydroDIURIL, Hygroton, Indocin, Lasix, Macrodantin, Mellaril, nicotinic acid, Norlestrin preparations, Orinase, Ortho-Novum preparations, Ovral, Ovulen-21, Parafon Forte, Placidyl, Rauzide, Regroton, Salutensin, Ser-Ap-Es, Serax, Sinequan, Stelazine, Thorazine, Tigan, Tofranil, Tolinase, Triavil, Valium.

Joint pain. Aldomet, Aldoril, Apresoline, Atromid-S, Azo Gantrisin, Butazolidin, Dalmane, Gantanol, Gantrisin, Macrodantin, Mysteclin-F, penicillin G potassium, Penicillin VK, Pentids, Pen-Vee K, Ritalin, Ser-Ap-Es, Sumycin, Tandearil, Terramycin, tetracycline, Tetrex, Valium, V-Cillin K, Zyloprim.

Kidney disturbances. Butazolidin, Tandearil.

Lactation suppression. Bentyl, Bentyl with Phenobarbital.

Leg swelling. Combid, Mellaril.

Lethargy. Aldactazide, Aldactone, Butisol Sodium, Butazolidin, Dalmane, Lomotil, Mellaril, Nembutal, Serax, Tandearil.

Libido alteration. Aldomet, Aldoril, Atromid-S, Mellaril, Norlestrin preparations, Ortho-Novum preparations, Ovral, Ovulen-21, Premarin, reserpine, Salutensin, Serax, Sinequan, Valium.

Lightheadedness. Afrin, Aldomet, Aldoril, Dalmane, Darvon, Demerol, Indocin, Lasix, Parafon Forte, Percodan, Talwin.

Light sensitivity. Achromycin V, Aldactazide, Aldoril, Ambenyl Expectorant, Azo Gantrisin, Benadryl, Diuril, Dyazide, HydroDIURIL, Orinase, Periactin, Phenergan preparations, Rauzide, Regroton, Sinequan, Tofranil, Tolinase, Vibramycin.

Menstrual irregularities. Aldactazide, Aldactone, Aristocort, Combid, Decadron, Demulen, Etrafon, Librax, Librium, Medrol, Mellaril, prednisone, Serax, Stelazine, Tenuate.

Migraine. Norlestrin preparations, Ortho-Novum preparations, Ovral, Ovulen-21, Premarin.

Mouth dryness. Aldomet, Aldoril, Ambenyl Expectorant, Antivert, Artane, Atarax, Bellergal, Benadryl, Bendectin, Bentyl, Chlor-Trimeton, Combid, Dalmane, Demerol, Dimetane, Donnagel-PG, Donnatal, Diupres, Dyazide, Etrafon, Hydropres, Ionamin, Librax, Librium, Mellaril, Norgesic, Ornade, Phenergan preparations, Polaramine, Pro-Banthine, Rauzide, Regroton, reserpine, Salutensin, Ser-Ap-Es, Sinequan, Stelazine, Teldrin, Tenuate, Thorazine, Tofranil, Tranxene, Tuss-Ornade, Vistaril.

Mouth inflammation. Amcill, ampicillin, Azo Gantrisin, Indocin, Mysteclin-F, Omnipen, Polycillin, Principen, Sumycin, Terramycin, tetracycline, Tetrex, Tofranil, Vibramycin.

Movements, involuntary. Aldomet, Aldoril, Combid, Compazine, Triavil.

Muscle ache. Atromid-S, Diupres, Hydropres, Rauzide, Regroton, reserpine, Salutensin, Ser-Ap-Es.

Muscle cramps. Apresoline, Atromid-S, Dyazine, Lasix, Regroton, Ser-Ap-Es, Tigan.

Muscle pain. Aldomet, Aldoril, phenobarbital, Tenuate.

Muscle spasm. Aldoril, Compazine, Diupres, Diuril, Esidrix, HydroDIURIL, Hygroton, Rauzide, Salutensin, Stelazine, Triavil.

Muscle weakness. Aristocort, Atromid-S, Decadron, Medrol, Marax, prednisone, Stelazine.

Nail discoloration. Mysteclin-F, Sumycin, Terramycin, tetracycline, Tetrex.

Nasal congestion. Afrin, Apresoline, Combid, Diupres, Etrafon, Hydropres, Regroton, reserpine, Salutensin, Ser-Ap-Es, Stelazine, Thorazine.

Nasal dryness. Afrin, Ambenyl Expectorant, Benadryl, Dimetane, Marax, Ornade, Tuss-Ornade.

Nasal stuffiness. Aldomet, Aldoril, Ambenyl Expectorant, Benadryl, Dimetane, Mellaril.

Nausea/vomiting. Achromycin V, Aldactazide, Aldomet, Aldoril, Ambenyl Expectorant, Amcill, ampicillin, Apresoline, Artane, Atromid-S, Azo Gantrisin, Benadryl, Bendectin, Bentyl, Butisol Sodium, Butazolidin, Cleocin, Coumadin, Dalmane, Darvon, Declomycin, Demerol, Demulen, Dilantin, Dimetapp, Diabinese, Diupres, Diuril, Doriden, Drixoral, Dyazide, Elavil, E-Mycin, Equanil, Erythrocin, erythromycin, Esidrix, Etrafon, Feosol, Fiorinal, Gantanol, Gantrisin, Garamycin, Hydergine, HydroDIURIL, Hydropres, Hygroton, Inderal, Indocin, Isordil, Kaon, Keflex, Lanoxin, Lasix, Librax, Librium, Lomotil, Macrodantin, Marax, meprobamate, Mellaril, Minocin, Mycostatin, Mysteclin-F, Nembutal, Noludar, Norgesic, Pavabid, Pediamycin, penicillin G potassium, Penicillin VK, Pentids, Pen-Vee K, Percodan, Periactin, Peritrate, Phenergan preparations, Placidyl, Polaramine, Polycillin, Premarin, Pro-Banthine, quinidine sulfate, Rauzide, Regroton, Salutensin, Ser-Ap-Es, Serax, Sinequan, Stelazine, Sumycin, Talwin, Tandearil, Tenuate, Terramycin, tetracycline, Tetrex, thyroid, Tofranil, Tolinase, Triavil, Tuss-Ornade, Valium, V-Cillin K, Vibramycin, Zyloprim.

Nervousness. Ambenyl Expectorant, Artane, Bentyl, Dalmane, Dilantin, Dimetane, Diupres, Hydropres, Marax, Norlestrin preparations, Ornade, Ortho-Novum preparations, Ovral, Ovulen-21, Periactin, Polaramine, Pro-Banthine, Rauzide, Ritalin, Salutensin, Ser-Ap-Es, Tenuate, Tranxene, Triaminic, Tuss-Ornade.

Nightmares. Aldomet, Aldoril, Diupres, Elavil, Hydropres, Regroton, reserpine, Salutensin, Ser-Ap-Es, Tofranil, Triavil.

Nosebleed. Indocin, Salutensin, Ser-Ap-Es.

Numbness. Apresoline, Elavil, Etrafon, Garamycin, Lomotil, Ser-Ap-Es, Talwin, Tofranil, Triavil.

Pallor. Isordil, Mellaril, Peritrate.

Palpitations. Afrin, Ambenyl Expectorant, Apresoline, Benadryl, Bendectin, Bentyl, Dalmane, Demerol, Dimetane, Dimetapp, Drixoral, Elavil, Equanil, Etrafon, Ionamin, Marax, meprobamate, nitroglycerin, Norgesic, Ornade, Periactin, Ritalin, Ser-Ap-Es, Tedral, Tenuate, Tofranil, Triaminic, Triavil, Tuss-Ornade, Vasodilan.

Proctitis. Equanil, meprobamate, Mysteclin-F, Sumycin, Terramycin, tetracycline, Tetrex.

Pulse, fast. Elavil, Equanil, Ionamin, meprobamate, nitroglycerin, Norgesic, Triavil.

Restlessness. Aldactazide, Aldoril, Ambenyl Expectorant, Benadryl, Chlor-Trimeton, Dalmane, Darvon, Demerol, Dimetane, Diupres, Diuril, Drixoral, Elavil, Esidrix, HydroDIURIL, Hygroton, Ionamin, Isordil, Lomotil, Mellaril, Percodan, Periactin, Peritrate, Polaramine, Regroton, Salutensin, Ser-Ap-Es, Tenuate, Tofranil, Triavil.

Salivary gland inflammation. Aldoril, Diupres, Diuril, HydroDIURIL, Tofranil.

Sedation. Actifed, Actifed-C Expectorant, Aldomet, Aldoril, Bendectin, Darvon, Demerol, Dimetane, Diupres, Lomotil, Naldecon, Percodan, Periactin, Salutensin, Talwin.

Seizures. Elavil, Etrafon, Tofranil, Triavil.

Skin dryness. Donnagel-PG, Donnatal, Kenalog, Mycolog, nicotinic acid, Synalar, Valisone.

Skin rash or eruption. Achromycin V, Aldactazide, Aldactone, Aldomet, Aldoril, Ambenyl Expectorant, Amcill, ampicillin, Apresoline, Atromid-S, Azo Gantrisin, Benadryl, Bendectin, Butisol Sodium, Butazolidin, Cleocin, Coumadin, Dalmane, Darvon, Declomycin, Demerol, Demulen, Drixoral, Dyazide, Elavil, E-Mycin, Equanil, Erythrocin, erythromycin, Esidrix, Etrafon, Fiorinal, Gantrisin, Garamycin, HydroDIURIL, Hygroton, Inderal, Indocin, Isordil, Keflex, Kenalog, Lasix, Librax, Librium, Macrodantin, Mellaril, meprobamate, Minocin, Mysteclin-F, Mycolog, Nembutal, Norgesic, Norlestrin preparations, Omnipen, Orinase, Ornade, Ortho-Novum preparations, Ovral, Ovulen-21, Parafon Forte, Pavabid, Pediamycin, penicillin G potassium, Penicillin VK, Pentids, Pen-Vee K, Periactin, Peritrate, phenobarbital, Polaramine, Polycillin, Premarin, Principen, Pro-Banthine, quinidine sulfate, Rauzide, Regroton, reserpine, Ritalin, Salutensin, Ser-Ap-Es, Serax, Sinequan, Stelazine, Sumycin, Synalar, Talwin, Tandearil, Tenuate, Terramycin, tetracycline, Tetrex, Thorazine, Tigan, Tofranil, Tolinase, Tranxene, Triavil, Tuss-Ornade, Valisone, Valium, Vasodilan, V-Cillin K, Vibramycin, Vioform-Hydrocortisone, Zyloprim.

Speech slurring. Dalmane, Dilantin, Equanil, meprobamate, Serax, Tranxene, Valium.

Stimulation. Actifed, Actifed-C Expectorant, Empirin with Codeine, Equanil, Ionamin, meprobamate, Parafon Forte, Sudafed, Tenuate, Tedral.

Stomach irritation, pain or upset. Aldoril, Bendectin, Butazolidin, Dalmane, Dimetane, Diupres, Diuril, Drixoral, Esidrix, Hydergine, HydroDIURIL, Hygroton, Indocin, Lasix, Placidyl, Rauzide, Regroton, Salutensin, Ser-Ap-Es, Tandearil, Teldrin.

Swallowing difficulty. Combid, Compazine, Declomycin, Minocin, Mysteclin-F, Stelazine, Sumycin, Terramycin, tetracycline, Tetrex, Triavil, Vibramycin.

Sweat, cold. Quinidine sulfate.

Sweating. Aristocort, Dalmane, Decadron, Demerol, Drixoral, Isordil, Lasix, Marax, Medrol, Pavabid, Peritrate, Polaramine, prednisone, Talwin, thyroid, Tofranil.

Taste disturbance. Bentyl, Pro-Banthine, Sinequan.

Testicular swelling. Sinequan, Tofranil.

Thirst. Bendectin, Lasix.

Throat dryness. Ambenyl Expectorant, Benadryl, Dimetane, Marax, Ornade, Tuss-Ornade.

Throat, sore. Inderal, Mysteclin-F, Tofranil.

Tingling. Aldactazide, Aldomet, Aldoril, Ambenyl Expectorant, Apresoline, Elavil, Equanil, Esidrix, Etrafon, Garamycin, HydroDIURIL, Hygroton, Inderal, Kaon, Lasix, meprobamate, Ser-Ap-Es, Sinequan, Talwin, Tofranil, Triavil.

Tongue, black/hairy. Amcill, ampicillin, Elavil, Mysteclin-F, Omnipen, penicillin G potassium, Penicillin VK, Pentids, Pen-Vee K, Polycillin, Principen, Sumycin, Terramycin, tetracycline, Tetrex, Tofranil, Triavil, V-Cillin K.

Tongue inflammation. Amcill, ampicillin, Declomycin, Mysteclin-F, Minocin, Omnipen, Polycillin, Principen.

Tongue, sore. Aldomet, Aldoril, Amcill, ampicillin, Omnipen, Polycillin.

Tremor. Aldomet, Aldoril, Apresoline, Atarax, Compazine, Demerol, Elavil, Etrafon, Hydropres, Ionamin, Mellaril, Ornade, Rauzide, Regroton, reserpine, Salutensin, Ser-Ap-Es, Serax, Sinequan, Stelazine, Talwin, Tenuate, Thorazine, thyroid, Tigan, Tofranil, Triavil, Tuss-Ornade, Valium, Vistaril.

Ulcer, gastrointestinal (Esophagus, stomach or duodenum). Aristocort, Butazolidin, Decadron, Indocin, Medrol, nicotinic acid, prednisone, Tandearil.

Urinary incontinence. Etrafon, Mellaril, Valium.

Urination, difficult. Apresoline, Benadryl, Dimetane, Donnagel–PG, Donnatal, Ornade, Periactin, Ser-Ap-Es, Tedral, Tuss-Ornade.

Urination, diminished. Azo Gantrisin, Equanil, Gantanol, Gantrisin, Garamycin, meprobamate.

Urination, excessive. Chlor-Trimeton, Polaramine, Tenuate.

Urination, frequent. Dimetane, Dimetapp, Elavil, Etrafon, Periactin, Triavil.

Urination hesitancy. Bentyl, Combid, Librax, Librium, Marax, Norgesic.

Urination, painful. Bendectin, Chlor-Trimeton, Dimetapp, Drixoral, Ornade, Polaramine, Rauzide, Regroton, Salutensin, Ser-Ap-Es, Tenuate, Tuss-Ornade.

Urine, discoloration. Parafon Forte.

Urine retention. Bentyl, Combid, Demerol, Dimetane, Elavil, Etrafon, Marax, Mellaril, Norgesic, Periactin, Sinequan, Talwin, Thorazine, Tofranil, Triavil, Valium.

Vaginal bleeding. Indocin.

Vaginal discharge. Keflex.

Vision blurring. Aldoril, Ambenyl Expectorant, Antivert,

Artane, Bellergal, Benadryl, Bendectin, Bentyl, Butazolidin, Combid, Compazine, Dalmane, Dimetane, Donnagel-PG, Donnatal, Diupres, Diuril, Doriden, Elavil, Etrafon, HydroDIURIL, Indocin, Lanoxin, Lasix, Librax, Librium, Mellaril, Norgesic, Periactin, Phenergan preparations, Placidyl, Pro-Banthine, Regroton, reserpine, Salutensin, Serax, Sinequan, Stelazine, Talwin, Tandearil, Tigan, Tofranil, Tranxene, Triaminic, Triavil.

Vision, color disturbance of. Aldoril, Esidrix, Hydro-DIURIL, Hygroton, Rauzide, Regroton, Salutensin.

Vision, double. Ambenyl Expectorant, Benadryl, Dimetane, Periactin, Polaramine, Serax.

Voice deepening. Aldactazide, Aldactone.

Vomiting blood. Butazolidin, Tandearil.

Weakness. Aldactazide, Aldomet, Aldoril, Artane, Bentyl, Cyclospasmol, Dalmane, Darvon, Diabinese, Diupres, Diuril, Drixoral, Dyazide, Elavil, Endrix, Equanil, Etrafon, HydroDIURIL, Hygroton, Inderal, Isordil, Lanoxin, Lasix, meprobamate, nitroglycerin, Norgesic, Ornade, Peritrate, Polaramine, Rauzide, Regroton, Salutensin, Ser-Ap-Es, Sinequan, Talwin, Tofranil, Tolinase, Triavil, Tuss-Ornade.

Weight gain/loss. Aldomet, Aldoril, Atromid-S, Demulen, Diupres, Hydropres, Mellaril, Norlestrin preparations, Ortho-Novum preparations, Ovral, Ovulen-21, Rauzide, Regroton, reserpine, Ritalin, Salutensin, Serp-Ap-Es, Thorazine.

Wheezing. Ambenyl Expectorant, Dimetane, Periactin.

THE DRUGS THAT MAY SOMETIMES CAUSE SYMPTOMS AS SIDE EFFECTS

Trade Names, Generic Names, and Uses

Achromycin V (tetracycline). For infection.

Actifed (tripolidine, pseudoephedrine). For nasal congestion.

Actifed-C Expectorant (Actifed, codeine). For cough.

Afrin (oxymetazoline hydrochloride). For nasal congestion.

Aldactazide (spironolactone, hydrochlorothiazide). For high blood pressure, fluid retention.

Aldactone (spironolactone). For high blood pressure, fluid retention.

Aldomet (methyldopa). For high blood pressure.

Aldoril (methyldopa, hydrochlorothiazide). For high blood pressure.

Ambenyl Expectorant (codeine sulfate, bromodiphenhydramine hydrochloride, diphenhydramine hydrochloride, ammonium chloride, potassium guiaiacolsulfonate, menthol). For cough.

Amcill (ampicillin). For infection.

Ampicillin (ampicillin). For infection.

Antivert (meclizine hydrochloride). For motion sickness, vertigo.

Apresoline (hydralazine hydrochloride). For high blood pressure.

Aristocort (triamcinolone). For allergy, skin disorders, arthritis.

Artane (trihexyphenidyl). For parkinsonism.

Atarax (hydroxyzine hydrochloride). For anxiety, tension.

Atromid-S (clofibrate). For high blood fat levels.

Azo Gantrisin (sulfisoxazole, phenazopyridine hydrochloride). For urinary infections.

Bellergal (phenobarbital, belladonna, ergotamine tartrate). For menopausal symptoms, premenstrual tension, throbbing headaches, nervous stomach, uterine cramps, some heart conditions.

Benadryl (diphenhydramine hydrochloride). For allergy, motion sickness, insomnia.

Bendectin (doxylamine succinate, pyridoxine hydrochloride). For the nausea and vomiting of pregnancy.

Bentyl (dicyclomine hydrochloride). For irritable bowel, intestinal inflammation.

Bentyl with Phenobarbital (dicyclomine hydrochloride, phenobarbital). For irritable bowel, intestinal inflammation.

Benylin Cough Syrup (diphenhydramine hydrochloride, alcohol). For cough.

Butazolidin and Butazolidin Alka (phenylbutazone). For arthritic conditions, gout, painful shoulder.

Butisol Sodium (sodium butabarbital). For sedation, sleep.

Chlor-Trimeton (chlorpheniramine maleate). For allergy.

Cleocin (clindamycin). For infection.

Combid (prochlorperazine, isopropamide iodide). For peptic ulcer, irritable bowel, diarrhea.

Compazine (prochlorperazine). For severe nausea, anxiety, tension, agitation.

Cordran (flurandrenolide). For inflammatory skin conditions.

Cortisporin (polymyxin B sulfate, neomycin sulfate, gramicidin, hydrocortisone). For infected and inflammatory skin conditions.

Coumadin (warfarin sodium). For vein clots, pulmonary embolism, abnormal heart rhythm, coronary occlusion.

Cyclospasmol (cyclandelate). For intermittent claudication (leg cramps on walking), thrombophlebitis, Raynaud's disease, nocturnal leg cramps, some other blood vessel disorders.

Dalmane (flurazepam hydrochloride). For insomnia.

Darvon (propoxyphene hydrochloride); Darvon Compound-65 (with aspirin, phenacetin, caffeine); Darvon with N/ A.S.A. (with aspirin); Darvocet-N (with acetaminophen). For mild to moderate pain.

Decadron (dexamethasone). For endocrine gland disorders, arthritis, bursitis, severe allergic, skin, eye, intestinal, respiratory, blood, and malignant diseases.

Declomycin (demeclocycline). For infection.

Demerol (meperidine hydrochloride). Narcotic pain reliever.

Demulen (ethynodiol diacetate, ethinyl estradiol). Oral contraceptive.

Dilantin (phenytoin). For epilepsy.

Dimetane (brompheniramine maleate). For allergy.

Dimetapp (brompheniramine maleate, phenylephrine hydrochloride, phenylpropanolamine hydrochloride). Decongestant for allergy.

Diabinese (chlorpropamide). For diabetes.

Diupres (chlorothiazide, reserpine). For high blood pressure.

Diuril (chlorothiazide). For fluid retention, high blood pressure, toxemia of pregnancy.

Donnagel-PG (kaolin, pectin, hyoscyamine sulfate, atropine sulfate, scopolamine hydrobromide). For diarrhea.

Donnatal (hyoscyamine sulfate, atropine suflate, scopolamine hydrobromide, phenobarbital). For digestive disorders, gallbladder inflammation, urinary frequency, painful menstruation, premenstrual tension, motion sickness.

Doriden (glutethimide). Nonbarbiturate for insomnia.

Dramamine (dimenhydrinate). For motion sickness.

Drixoral (dexbrompheniramine maleate, pseudoephedrine). For nasal congestion.

Dyazide (triamterene, hydrochlorothiazide). For fluid retention, high blood pressure.

Elavil (amitriptyline hydrochloride). For mental depression.

Empirin with Codeine (aspirin, codeine). For pain.

E-Mycin (erythromycin). For infection.

Equanil (meprobamate). For anxiety, tension.

Erythrocin (erythromycin). For infections.

Erythyromycin (erythromycin). For infections.

Esidrix (hydrochlorothiazide). For high blood pressure, fluid retention, toxemia of pregnancy.

Etrafon (perphenazine, amitriptyline). For anxiety, agitation, depressed mood.

Feosol (ferrous sulfate). For iron deficiency.

Fiorinal (butalbitol, caffeine, aspirin, phenacetin). For headache, other pain.

Fiorinal with Codeine (Fiorinal, codeine). For pain, cough.

Gantanol (sulfamethoxazole). For infections.

Gantrisin (sulfisoxazole). For infections.

Garamycin (gentamicin). For infections.

Hydergine (dihydroergocornine mesylate, dihydroergocristine mesylate, dihydroergocryptine mesylate). For mood depression, confusion, unsociability, dizziness in the elderly.

HydroDIURIL (hydrochlorothiazide). For fluid retention.

Hydropres (hydrochlorothiazide, reserpine). For high blood pressure.

Hygroton (chlorthalidone). For high blood pressure, fluid retention.

Inderal (propranolol hydrochloride). For high blood pressure, angina pectoris, heart rhythm abnormality.

Indocin (indomethacin). For arthritic conditions, painful shoulder, acute gout.

Ionamin (phentermine resin). For weight reduction.

Isordil (isosorbide dinitrate). For angina pectoris.

Kaon (potassium gluconate). For correcting low blood potassium levels.

Keflex (cephalexin). For infections.

Kenalog (triamcinolone acetonide). For inflammatory skin conditions.

Lanoxin (digoxin). For congestive heart failure, other heart conditions.

Lasix (furosemide). For fluid retention.

Librax (chlordiazepoxide hydrochloride, clidinium bromide). For gastrointestinal disturbances.

Librium (chlordiazepoxide hydrochloride). For anxiety, tension.

Lomotil (diphenoxylate hydrochloride, atropine sulfate). For diarrhea.

Macrodantin (nitrofurantoin). For urinary tract infections.

Marax (ephedrine sulfate, theophylline, hydroxyzine hydrochloride). For asthma.

Medrol (methylprednisolone). For endocrine and rheumatic disorders, serious skin diseases, allergic states, other conditions.

Mellaril (thioridazine). For psychiatric disorders.

Meprobamate (meprobamate). For anxiety, tension.

Minocin (minocycline hydrochloride). For infections.

Mycolog (nystatin, neomycin sulfate, triamcinolone acetonide, gramicidin). For some skin disorders.

Mycostatin (nystatin). For fungal infections.

Mylanta (aluminum and magnesium hydroxides, simethicone). For relief of gas and stomach hyperacidity.

Mysteclin-F (tetracycline, amphotericin B). For infections.

Naldecon (phenylpropanolamine hydrochloride, phenylephrine hydrochloride, phenyltoloxamine citrate, chlorpheniramine maleate). For symptoms of colds, sinusitis, hay fever, other pollen allergies.

Nembutal (sodium pentobarbital). For sedation, insomnia.

Neosporin (polymixin B, neomycin, gramicidin). For skin infections.

Nicotinic Acid (nicotinic acid.). For lowering high blood fat levels.

Nitroglycerin (nitroglycerin). For preventing/treating anginal attacks.

Noludar (methyprylon). For insomnia.

Norgesic (orphenadrine citrate, aspirin, caffeine). For pain.

Norlestrin (norethindrone acetate, ethinyl estradiol). Oral contraceptive.

Novahistine DH (codeine phosphate, phenylpropanolamine hydrochloride, chlorpheniramine maleate, alcohol). For cough, nasal congestion.

Omnipen (ampicillin). For infections.

Orinase (tolbutamide). For diabetes.

Ornade (phenylpropanolamine hydrochloride, chlorphen-iramine maleate). For nasal congestion.

Ortho-Novum (norethindrone, mestranol). Oral contra-ceptive.

Ovral (norgestrel, ethinyl estradiol). Oral contraceptive.

Ovulen (ethynodiol diacetate, mestranol). Oral contra-ceptive.

Parafon Forte (chlorzoxazone, acetaminophen). For acute, painful musculoskeletal conditions.

Paregoric (powdered opium, anise oil, benzoic acid, cam-phor, glycerin, in diluted alcohol). For diarrhea.

Pavabid (papaverine hydrochloride). For reduced blood flow in heart, brain.

Pediamycin (erythromycin). For infection.

Penicillin G Potassium (penicillin G potassium). For in-fection.

Penicillin VK (penicillin V potassium). For infection.

Pentids (penicillin G potassium). For infection.

Pen-Vee K (penicillin V potassium). For infection.

Percodan (oxycodone hydrochloride, oxycodone tere-phthalate, aspirin). For pain.

Periactin (cyproheptadine hydrochloride). For allergies.

Peritrate (pentaerythritol). For angina pectoris.

Phenaphen with Codeine (codeine phosphate, acetamin-ophen). For pain and anxiety.

Phenergan (promethazine hydrochloride). For allergies, motion sickness, nausea/vomiting.

Phenobarbital (phenobarbital). For sedation.

Placidyl (ethclorvynol). For insomnia.

Polaramine (dexchlorpheniramine maleate). For aller-gies.

Polycillin (ampicillin). For infection.

Prednisone (prednisone). For severe skin and other dis-eases, hypersensitivity, malignancy.

Premarin (conjugated estrogens). For amenorrhea, estro-gen deficiency states, some abnormal uterine bleeding con-ditions, prostate cancer.

Principen (ampicillin). For infection.

Pro-Banthine (propantheline bromide). For peptic ulcer.

Proloid (thyroglobulin). For low thyroid function.

Pyridium (phenazopyridine hydrochloride). For urinary pain, burning, urgency, frequency.

Quinidine Sulfate (quinidine sulfate). For heart rhythm abnormalities.

Rauzide (rauwolfia serpentina, bendroflumethiazide). For high blood pressure.

Regroton (chlorthalidone, reserpine). For high blood pressure.

Reserpine (reserpine). For high blood pressure.

Ritalin (methylphenidate hydrocholoride). For mild depression, apathetic or withdrawn senile behavior, minimal brain dysfunction in children.

Salutensin (hydroflumethiazide, reserpine). For high blood pressure.

Seconal (secobarbital sodium). For insomnia.

Ser-Ap-Es (reserpine, hydralazine hydrochloride, hydrochlorothiazide). For high blood pressure.

Serax (oxazepam). For anxiety, tension, agitation, irritability.

Sinequan (doxepin hydrochloride). For anxiety, depression.

Sudafed (pseudoephedrine). For colds, ear infections, asthma, acute tracheobronchitis, other upper respiratory infections.

Sumycin (tetracycline). For infections.

Synalar (fluocinolone acetonide). For inflammatory skin conditions.

Talwin (pentazocine). For moderate to severe pain.

Tandearil (oxyphenbutazone). For arthritis, gout, painful shoulder, some other inflammatory conditions.

Tedral (theophylline, ephedrine hydrochloride, phenobarbital). For asthma, bronchitis.

Teldrin (chlorpheniramine maleate). For allergies.

Tenuate (diethylpropion hydrochloride). For weight reduction.

Terramycin (oxytetracycline). For infections.

Tetracycline (tetracycline). For infections.

Tetrex (tetracycline phosphate complex). For infections.

Thorazine (chlorpromazine). For psychiatric disorders, nausea/vomiting, tetanus, agitation, excessive anxiety, tension.

Thyroid (thyroid). For thyroid deficiency.

Tigan (trimethobenzamide hydrochloride). For nausea/vomiting.

Tofranil (imipramine). For depression, childhood bedwetting.

Tolinase (tolazamide). For diabetes.

Tranxene (clorazepate dipotassium). For anxiety.

Triaminic (phenylpropanolamine hydrochloride, pheniramine maleate, pyrilamine maleate). For nasal congestion, postnasal drip.

Triavil (perphenazine, amitriptyline hydrochloride). For anxiety and/or depression.

Tuinal (secobarbital sodium, amobarbital sodium). For insomnia.

Tuss-Ornade (caramiphen edisylate, phenylpropanolamine hydrochloride). For cough, upper respiratory congestion, excessive nasal secretion.

Tylenol (acetaminophen). For pain.

Tylenol with Codeine (acetaminophen, codeine). For pain.

Valisone (betamethasone valerate). For inflammatory skin conditions.

Valium (diazepam). For tension, anxiety, muscle spasm.

Vasodilan (isoxsuprine hydrochloride). For blood vessel disorders, threatened abortion.

V-Cillin K (penicillin V potassium). For infections.

Vibramycin (doxycycline). For infections.

Vioform-Hydrocortisone (iodochlorhydroxyquin, hydrocortisone). For some skin disorders.

Vistaril (hydroxyzine hydrochloride). For anxiety, tension, agitation.

Zyloprim (allopurinol). For gout.

GUIDE TO MEDICAL SPECIALISTS

And the Diseases and Disorders Treated by Each

Allergist: Concerned with diagnosing and treating allergic problems such as asthma, hay fever, year-round nasal stuffiness (perennial allergic rhinitis), hives, nausea, vomiting, abdominal pain, and other gastrointestinal symptoms possibly related to food sensitivity.

Cardiologist: Specializes in diagnosis and treatment of heart problems.

Dermatologist: Diagnoses and treats skin disorders, including acne, psoriasis, eczema, skin cancer, pigmentation problems, light sensitivities, and birthmarks.

Emergency physician: Trained in quick recognition, evaluation, stabilization, and care of accidental injuries, illness, and emotional crises. One of the newest specialties, with some nine thousand members in the American College of Emergency Physicians. Usual practice is in hospital and other emergency facilities.

Endrocrinologist: An expert in glandular and metabolic disturbances.

Family practitioner: A physician in general practice trained to provide comprehensive health maintenance and medical care for the whole family regardless of sex, age, or type of problem, using a core of knowledge derived from internal medicine, pediatrics, psychiatry, and other disciplines.

Gastroenterologist: Diagnoses and treats digestive tract diseases, including peptic ulcer, hiatal hernia, esophagus disorders, gallbladder disease, inflammatory bowel disorders, pancreatitis, liver troubles, and malignancies of the stomach, pancreas, and colon.

Gynecologist: Treats disorders of the female reproductive system, including the ovaries, fallopian tubes, uterus, vagina, and vulva. Performs operations such as dilatation and curettage, myomectomy (removal of a fibroid tumor), hysterectomy (removal of the uterus), oophorectomy (removal of one or both ovaries).

Hematologist: Specializes in blood disorders such as sickle cell and other types of anemia, hemophilia, blood cell disorders, and leukemias.

Internist: Trained in the diagnosis and treatment of diseases and injuries of the internal organ systems. Internal medicine includes cardiology, endocrinology, gastroenterology, and nephrology; many internists specialize in one of these areas.

Nephrologist: An expert in the diagnosis and treatment of kidney diseases and in maintaining patients with kidney failure who are on dialysis.

Neurologist: Treats nervous system diseases. Some neurologists are also neurosurgeons, operating on brain tumors, brain aneurysms (ballooning brain blood vessels), blocked arteries carrying blood to the brain, damaged arm and leg nerves, and herniated spinal discs.

Obstetrician: Concerned with pregnancy from prenatal care to delivery and the period immediately afterward. Also trained as a gynecologist (see earlier entry).

Oncologist: a specialist in the diagnosis and treatment of cancer by drugs and other measures.

Ophthalmologist: A specialist in the diagnosis and treatment—by medical or surgical measures—of injuries, diseases, and other disorders of the eyes. Refracts and measures vision loss and prescribes corrective eyeglasses or contact lenses.

Orthopedist: Deals with musculoskeletal injuries, skeletal deformities, and chronic diseases of the joints and spine, using medical and surgical measures.

Otolaryngologist: Specializes in ear, nose, and throat problems. Tonsillectomies, operations to restore hearing, and treatments for sinus conditions are a few examples of work in this specialty.

Pathologist: Rarely seen by patients, the pathologist is an expert in disease processes, tissue specimen evaluation, blood and other testing, aiding other physicians in diagnosis and evaluating the results of treatment.

Pediatrician: Specializes in the practice of medicine as it relates to children from infancy to adolescence.

Physiatrist: Specializes in physical medicine and rehabilitation, helping injured or deformed patients to walk, work, and live more normal lives. May prescribe special exercises, heat, light, cold, medication, occupational therapy, or speech therapy.

Plastic surgeon: Specializes in cosmetic surgery such as face lifting, nose reshaping, and breast reduction and augmentation. Also performs reconstructive surgery to correct cleft lips and other congenital defects, and restorative surgery to correct damage after injury, burns, or cancer surgery.

Proctologist: Specializes in diagnosis and treatment of colon and rectal disorders.

Psychiatrist: Trained in the diagnosis and treatment of mental and emotional disorders.

Pulmonary specialist: An expert in lung disorders, including emphysema, chronic bronchitis, tuberculosis, and work-related lung problems.

Radiologist: Specializes in making diagnoses and devising treatment plans involving the use of various forms of radiation.

Rheumatologist: Trained in the diagnosis and treatment of various types of arthritis and other related bone and joint diseases.

Surgeons: Along with general surgeons, there are now subspecialists in surgery. The *general* surgeon may perform a wide variety of operative procedures, working within the chest on the heart or lungs, in the stomach and intestines, on the gallbladder, appendix, and hernias, or on the arms and legs. *Thoracic* surgeons work within the chest, on the heart, lungs, and esophagus, and on the great blood vessels leading to and from the heart. *Vascular* surgeons operate on the veins and arteries.

Urologist: Treats the urinary systems of both men and women and the reproductive organs of men.

About the Author

Lawrence Galton, perhaps the nation's most respected writer and editor of medical and health books for the layman, is a former visiting professor at Purdue University. He is a columnist for *Family Circle*, executive editor of two professional publications, *Integrative Psychiatry* and *Political Psychology*, and his articles frequently appear in *The New York Times Magazine, Parade, Reader's Digest*, and other national publications. He is the author of more than two dozen other books, including the *Adult Physical Fitness Manual for the President's Council on Physical Fitness*, and has served as a consultant to the U.S. Public Health Service.